The African Adventurers

PETER CAPSTICK VIDEOS

Capstick/Botswana Safari
Capstick/Hunting the African Lion
Capstick/Hunting the Cape Buffalo
Capstick/Hunting the White Rhino
Capstick/Hunting the African Elephant

Peter Capstick's *books* are available from St. Martin's Press.

His *videos* may be obtained by writing to:

Sportsmen on Film
5038 North Parkway Calabasas
Calabasas, CA 91302

BY THE SAME AUTHOR

Death in the Long Grass
Death in the Silent Places
Death in the Dark Continent
Safari: The Last Adventure
Peter Capstick's Africa: A Return to the Long Grass
The Last Ivory Hunter: The Saga of Wally Johnson
Maneaters
Last Horizons: Hunting, Fishing, and Shooting on Five Continents
Death in a Lonely Land: More Hunting, Fishing, and Shooting on Five Continents
Sands of Silence: On Safari in Namibia

THE PETER CAPSTICK LIBRARY

Peter Capstick, Series Editor

The Man-Eaters of Tsavo Lt. Col. J. H. Patterson, D.S.O.
Hunting the Elephant in Africa Capt. C. H. Stigand
African Hunter Baron Bror von Blixen-Finecke
The Book of the Lion Sir Alfred E. Pease
Big Game Hunting in North-Eastern Rhodesia Owen Letcher
Memories of an African Hunter Denis D. Lyell
African Game Trails Theodore Roosevelt
African Adventure Denis D. Lyell
Big Game Hunting in Central Africa William Buckley
Kill: or Be Killed Major W. Robert Foran
After Big Game in Central Africa Edouard Foà
Big Game Hunting and Collecting in East Africa, 1903–1926 Kálmán Kittenberger
The Recollections of William Finaughty: Elephant Hunter 1864–1875 William Finaughty
Lion-Hunting in Somali-land Captain C. J. Melliss

The African Adventurers

~~~~~~~~~~~~~~~~~~~~

*A Return
to the
Silent Places*

**PETER HATHAWAY
CAPSTICK**

ST. MARTIN'S PRESS NEW YORK

Production Editor: David Stanford Burr

Design by Judith C. Christensen

Library of Congress Cataloging-in-Publication Data

Capstick, Peter Hathaway.
  The African adventurers : a return to the silent places / Peter Hathaway Capstick.
      p. cm.
    Includes index.
    ISBN 0-312-07622-3
    1. Big game hunting—Africa. 2. Hunters—Africa—Biography.
    3. Adventure and adventurers—Africa. I. Title.
    SK251.C267 1992
    799.2'6'0960922—dc20
    [B]   92-3450
                                                                        CIP

To the Kyriazis family—George, Edna-Mae, Stephen, and Natalie—with appreciation of their warm friendship over many years

Contents

Acknowledgments

The author wishes to express his gratitude and thanks to the people who, through their hard work, understanding, and enthusiasm, made this project possible:

First, to Fifi, my wife, who was invaluable in checking the manuscript with her usual raven's eye. Behind every male writer there is a good woman telling him that he is wrong.

Michael Sagalyn, senior editor, Ed Stackler, assistant editor, and Eric Wybenga, editorial assistant, all of St. Martin's Press. Thank you both for your cooperation, suggestions, and favors.

My agent, Richard Curtis, of Richard Curtis Associates of New York City. I so much appreciate your creative ideas and help.

Donald G. Broadley, Ph.D., of the Bulawayo Museum in Zimbabwe, who was so helpful in matters Ionidean.

Paul Mills of Clarke's Book Shop in Long Street of Cape Town, South Africa. Many thanks for your usual help in the matter of materials for the book and arrangements for the reproduction of photographs.

Foreword

I have always thought of writing as the art of alchemy: the turning of ink into gold. But there are many ways to get paid other than in cash.

To spend eight months awakening each morning to the sounds of African doves, bush coucals with their gurgling, tippling cries, and the smell of *brunsfelsia* and jasmine is part of my life in Africa, but there is a real anticipation with each dawn for this writer to get back into the company of his new cronies, the heroes of this work.

Imagine spending days on end in the company of Fred Selous, hunting lions, exploring unknown country, prowling the wastes of the Kalahari thirstland or the lushness of the untouched Chobe River. For weeks I caught black and green mambas with the eccentric "Iodine" Ionides and hunted man-eating leopards at his shabby side. I was the first—if you discount Johnny Boyes—to enter the forbidden Kikuyu country of the infant British East Africa and shared with him the excitement of savage tribes and many battles and ambushes. My time with Jim Sutherland was a dream, taking 150-pound-per-side bull elephants any time I cared to flip a page. Writing is generally hard work, but this one was as relaxing as the writing of *Death in the Silent Places* was back in 1979.

The Bible says—or at least as I remember from my very early days from a sermon in Boonton, New Jersey—that there were giants in those days. Well, there are giants in my library, too.

This is not really a history book or a collection of potted biographies of great men and great times. It really is escape reading; perhaps you will be able to escape by reading it as I did while writing it.

Of course, to my knowledge not a word is historically incorrect, every detail and date recorded are to the best of my research and ability. At least I hope you will not suggest that Capstick is back at his tripewriter. . . .

—Peter Hathaway Capstick
August 28, 1991
Waterkloof, South Africa

Part One

Frederick
Courteney
Selous

It was not just cold, it was *cold.*

The giraffe hunt was almost a distant memory, the faces of Dorehill and Mandy almost blurs; that of Sadlier, who had taken the extra horses, a blank.

The nineteen-year-old imagined the path to be parallel to the road. Upon seeing some twenty giraffes, the party had split, the youngster was on one side and the two older men on the other. The newcomer and his friend and partner, Dorehill, had already grown tired of the lean African game; the prospect of a giraffe in fine condition, oozing fat that crackled and spit in the fire, was almost too much. Yet the young man was alone. He had fired three shots and had had an answer at a distance off to his right. But although he had fired twice more, the bushveld of King Khama's country was as silent as a good child. Fighting hard, he swallowed the panic in his already dry throat and settled down for the icy night, the ancient sands of Gondwanaland spreading their chill through his buttocks.

He had ridden a long way, so far that the sun had already set, thin and anemic, a washed-out reddish disc in the west. Where was the road? he thought. It should have been here before this. That the road was only faint wagon tracks bothered him not a lot; his friends should have taken a similar line. They would be just ahead. Sure they would. . . .

There was no night wind, the killing wind, as he settled down. It was a creep-

3

ing cold, a cold that oozed like water into his limbs and ignored him as he pulled the thin shirt around him. It was so cold that he decided to make tracks toward where the road had to be. Shivering, he resaddled his horse and moved wraithlike into the brassy moonlight.

It was perhaps three hours before he called a halt. He *had* to have a fire. He had heard of chattering teeth but he didn't really believe it before this. Yet, he was new to the country of Khama, and as fast as he would break open the huge paper cartridges for his four-bore, ignite the powder with his percussion caps, the fire was snuffed out by the dew-dampened grass. Suddenly he was out of ammunition, the greasy dark gunpowder spread into the torn fragments of his shirttail gone. Frustrated but still sure that he would hit the road, he cut some damp grass with his clasp knife and lay down for the night. Using his felt hat for a pillow, he slipped down to his icy bed, the saddle over his chest. Still, the cold attacked, sliding inexorably from his numb feet to his bare head. Soon, his shivering became uncontrollable and he was forced to sprint back and forth to a nearby tree to keep his chilled blood flowing. So much for tropical Africa, he thought. The lonely, lunatic calls of spotted hyenas—perhaps on their way to drink?—haunted his shudders until finally the sun advertised that it would be along shortly and, with it, some warmth.

It was the end of the first day.

There is no color in the winter bushveld, only the flitting and chirping of fire finches and waxbills; and only these where there is water. There were no birds. There was no water, either.

He pulled the saddle over the exhausted hunting pony and freed and tied-off reins, noting how the belly of the horse had shrunk as he tightened the cinch. The horse would only plod along at a slow walk, its thirst and hunger obvious. Yet, it was a good horse for which the young man had traded for the equivalent of seventy-five British pounds. Considering that a first-class ticket by steamer to England from South Africa cost less than half that, it was a most valuable horse indeed, having survived the horse sickness or horse distemper. Yet, without water it was nothing, not so much as the creaking of leather that it produced as it walked.

He still had the smooth-bore, the huge four-gauge, but it was useless without its ammunition, which had been wasted trying to make the fire. His trousers, bush-torn and tattered, were as futile against the night cold as was his hat. If only he had brought his coat with him from the wagon when they had first seen the giraffes in the wonderful heat of day. If only . . .

A tree loomed ahead as the sun began to slide silently upward and the young man decided to climb it. Perhaps in this land of few landmarks there might be just one? The winter bush was uniformly gray, but there was a scraggly line of furred hills in the distance, a single *koppie,* as the Afrikaners call it, a huge mound of rocks in front of the bearded shadow of the hills. Was it familiar? The young man didn't know. Three gemsbuck, the giant oryx antelope of southern Africa, passed very close, as if knowing that there was no ammunition left.

The man continued, his sun-blond hair now matted and streaked with precious sweat. He knew the Southern Cross and its brilliance in Khama's skies and decided to follow it, but he had convinced himself that he had already crossed the road of wagon tracks in the dim light of early morning. His horse, nearly dead with thirst, hunger, and exhaustion, reluctantly spun about when the man decided to retrace his tracks. After all, he was *positive.* It was a very expensive conviction in early Africa.

The miles melted by in a grayness of bush. At last, there was a small *koppie,* home to hyrax, leopards, and cobras. The man climbed it and looked into the distance. He climbed it, arguing with himself all the time if the road lay ahead or behind. But the mocking winter gray of the bush met his every glance until he turned around. There was a thin, tenuous tendril of smoke. He thought it too central a spire to be a grass fire and he thought that it was kindled by some Masarwa—half-breed black Bushmen—who would be able to guide him to Pelatsi, his goal.

He turned his horse around and made for the fire, but when he arrived at the point where he thought the smoke should be, there was nothing. He concluded that the road was now behind him and swung his horse around once more. As the sun was at its highest, he decided that he was again wrong. There was no road and he would die, dried to leather if the hyenas didn't get him. They probably would.

At this point, the blond young man realized that he had never reached the road and he thought that he might have passed it during the low light of dawn or night. His spirits buoyed by his realization, he thought how good a cup of tea might taste when he reached his wagons at shortly after sundown. Yet, his thoughts sank with the copper and cerise of the sun as it bedded down for another night. So did the young man, now as parched and hungry as his bedraggled horse.

The second night was spent on the icy earth, under the gaze of a full moon that tinted the colorless bush into gilded foliage. As the young man thought, there was no food, water, fire, or blanket, and he was right. Leaving his own problems, he turned to those of his horse. Rather than tie all seventy-five British pounds worth of him to a tree, he decided to hobble him with *riempies*—rawhide thongs—in the hope that the horse could crop enough of the pale, shriveled winter grass to carry its master when dawn came up, frozen and chill. Perhaps, the young man thought, the horse might even wind water.

It was even colder than the night before, a Kalahari blackness that would freeze even the tea kettle if he were back in camp. When dawn reluctantly bled over the eastern sky, the man found that he could not even rise, so wooden had his legs become through the long night. After some minutes, he was able to restore circulation by frenzied rubbing and went in search of the horse. It wasn't there. Gone. Disappeared.

After a few hundred yards, the young man realized that he had not the strength to follow the hard, scuffed spoor on the dry earth. Now, he had nothing, neither fire nor blanket, neither loaded gun nor even horse. He was as completely alone as he would ever be and, he knew, he was close to death.

He knew he could not carry the saddle and hung it in the crotch of a tree above the reach of hyenas, who would love the leather as much as his own hide if they caught him. Yet, he shouldered the empty smooth-bore duck gun rather than leave it behind. To leave it would have been a sort of surrender that he was not prepared to make, at least not yet.

He walked as fast as he could go, a mechanical, drag-stepped shuffle, all of that day toward another long row of hills that he prayed might be the Bamangwato Range. Thirst corroded his mouth and tongue, making swallowing almost impossible. But, then, there was no saliva left to swallow in any case. He knew that hunger had reached its long, cold hand far past his belly and was now gnawing on his ever-weaker muscles. When the moon was an hour high for the third night he reached the edge of the mysterious hills. Praying that cool, wind-washed fields of native corn would meet his gaze, he almost foundered. More bush and no sign of water or food. Blinking back tears of desperation, he wandered his bloodshot blue eyes over more rocky, low hills and, with a strangled cry of horror, fell to a ragged sitting position. With no promise of water or food he knew that his best ally was rest. Far away, a jackal mocked him.

The young man slipped behind a boulder and thought for a few moments of his fate. Bamangwato—the small native settlement—was not there. Realistically, he knew that he was almost surely doomed to die of hunger and thirst in a place that might not even be known to God, let alone to any rescue party. Yet, he thought further and summoned his remarkable powers of recuperation. It would be too much, he thought, to die like this, like a rat in a hole. He was still thinking about this when he fell into an exhausted sleep, warmer tonight due to the slight elevation and freedom from the shrouds of cold that haunted the low valleys like a lonely wraith.

When he awoke, it was near dawn of the fourth day without food or water. He hated the cold, but he also knew that if he had to contend with heat at night he would be dead by now. Already his terrible hunger pangs had ceased—he knew this was a very bad sign—but his thirst was a living, dry, strangling noose that ran from his swollen lips down past his protruding tongue into his raw throat. As the taunting varicose veins of dawn stretched ahead, and he glanced across the wilderness of broken rock and bush, he noticed a smallish *koppie* that somehow looked familiar. It looked curiously like one that he knew to be near the Shakani *vleis* or dried marshlands. In fact, several other features seemed familiar, including a low line of stone hills and a few more *koppies*. There were a few Bushmen tending goats there, he recalled, if it was the same place. In his desperation, the young man convinced himself that they were the same features of his memory, although when looking at them he never dreamed that their further identification would mean his life.

But they were far away, gleaming in a purplish hue in the distance. Staggering and limping, he made his way down from his evening eyrie and finally made the plain while the sun was still relatively low. As he reached the plain and started forward, he knew that he could not survive another night without water or food. He was completely exhausted, but also saw that the bush was so dense that he would be forced to climb trees now and then to keep his bearings. Although he knew that he must rest, he also knew that delay meant death and when he stopped, each two or three minutes drove him onward with what might well be futile hope. For some reason he noticed a cock and hen ostrich on his tortured march. So run the minds of the delirious. . . .

The sun was making its last, fatal move below the horizon

when the man saw two Bushmen at some distance, coppery and shimmering in the late sun. A garbled scream caught their attention and they hastened over to the man, one taking the four-bore gun and the other helping the youngster to camp. There were three huts that denoted the scarcity of what was then the rarest animal of the desert areas: man. Collapsing into a rather dignified heap, the young man thought he was saved and that fountains of precious water would be his for the asking. Wrong. An old Bushman, fondling a section of giraffe intestine full of water spoke in Setswana: "Buy the water."

The young man was stunned. He knew that the spring at the *vlei* was only two hundred steps away, but he was caved in. While he battled with his irritation and his lack of trade goods, a child came in with a big calabash full of goat's milk.

"Reka marsi," the young man croaked. "I'll buy the milk."

He pulled out his large folding knife to trade and was rewarded with not only the milk but the water as well.

The only problem that the young man had from then on was with the language. He spoke no Bushman dialect at all and but little Setswana—the general language of Khama's land of Tswana people—but was finally able to make arrangements (although he would have to walk all the way himself) to reach Pelatsi, where the wagons were. That night no one ever had a more restful sleep at the side of a large fire and with a small chunk of duiker antelope rumbling around his stomach, making that organ remember what it was meant for.

When he arrived at Pelatsi after an absence of five nights and four days he was almost considered a modern Lazarus. A huge feed was prepared for him and he drank enough water to pry amazement from his companions, hardened bush hands. He was saved.

The next day he found that his friends had not deserted him but had hired six men, four Bechuana *Kafirs* (a regretfully still-used term originally used by the Arabs to designate a nonbeliever in The Prophet and which became later pejorative) and two Masarwa Bushmen to track the young man. That the six shunned their duty after a few miles and declared to a man that the youngster had galloped to Bamangwato was obviously not so. The trackers had been supplied with meat and no doubt sat against some trees and ate it with no further thought of their charge. I hope it went hard with them. Incidentally, the horse made it to Bamangwato alive through what must have been serried ranks of hyenas and lions. Despite his value, the young man took a price of ten pounds in case the horse should return, which he thought unlikely. This was money that transferred ownership of the animal based upon speculation at a fraction of the regular price. If the horse did not come home, the buyer was out the price. In any case, although the animal *did* come back, he was badly injured by his rawhide hobbles, which reduced the horse's value.

The young man was almost well again, his ordeal a memory, and he could laugh at a story that one of his bush pals told. The great American frontiersman, Daniel Boone, was once asked if he had ever been lost in the wild territories of America. Dan'l thought for a few moments and said: "Nope. Ain't never bin lost. But there was a time in Kaintuck when I was powerful confused for five days."

The young man was Frederick Courteney Selous, probably the most shining example of English manhood that the Victorian Empire could field in the Britain of those days.

Selous was the *beau ideal* of the "playing fields of Rugby." In fact, he was not the only hero of Africa who went to the school; several, including Ionides, also attended. My treatment of Selous should be explained in the context of my own efforts.

I really don't care about his miscegenational love life or his intrigues when he led the "Pioneer Column" into what is now Zimbabwe or his friction with Cecil John Rhodes in doing so. I am a *hunting* writer and hardly fit to handle the nuances of sex, personality, or performance that are apparently most important to British writers. Thus, please excuse me if I do not get into the intrigue of Selous's life. I can recommend two excellent books on his life if this sort of thing appeals to you. Try the older book by his close friend, John G. Millais, *The Life of Frederick Courtenay* [sic] *Selous, D.S.O.* or a much newer and well-researched work entitled *The Mighty Nimrod* by British author Stephen Taylor. Taylor writes very well and cannot be blamed if he had not had exposure to early hunting terms such as Baldwin's use of "lions, tigers and wolves" in his classic book *African Hunting and Adventure*. Taylor says correctly that the last two species don't exist in Africa. Well, not in English, they don't. But they—or their translations—do in the early language of the interior, which was far more Dutch or Afrikaans than English. The leopard was called the *tijger* (tiger) and "wolves" covered a plethora of doglike carnivora such as Cape hunting dogs and, sometimes in early works, jackals and other critters that went *whooop* or *yawwwrl* in the night. Hell, the early Flemish peasants who became the Afrikaners even called the wildebeest a "wild cow."

Why Millais chose to substitute an "a" instead of the correct "e" in Selous's middle name is one of the great questions of Africana collecting. Just put it down to error, I suppose. If anybody meant well by his biography, it was Millais, Selous's old friend.

I recall a remonstration that was common when I was, several hundred years ago, in the army. Recruits were somewhat fuzzy about the difference between "gun" and "rifle." Only for a while. They used the M-1 Garand in my day, and any recruit who became confused about the relativity (a gun being smooth-bored and a rifle with rifling) was required under threat of a stroke of lightning from God to hold their Garands at a right angle to their bodies and repeat fifty times: "This is my rifle, this is my gun"—pointing to their lizard—this is for fightin', this is for fun."

I am only interested in Selous's rifle. . . .

*   *   *

It is pronounced "Sel-*oo*," and a hell of a Victorian he was. He came from a good family and had the best of education, although he and University never met. He went to Rugby, which is about as elite as you can get, but didn't go to college in the American sense: he was in Africa at age nineteen. That pleases me; I was never able to get past freshman mathematics although I tried four times. I went eight semesters to the University of Virginia but could never pass it. Never even close, even though it was the same course. Since I deal in such esoterica as mathematical internal, external, and terminal ballistics with no problems, you'd think I would have learned by rote. Nope. That I never got more than a "C" in English is obvious. No sense of humor, those professors. They certainly professed doom for me. . . .

Seeing as how we might as well call him Fred, as his family did, he arrived in Africa on September 4th, 1871, at what was then Algoa Bay and now Port Elizabeth in South Africa. He had 400 British pounds in his pocket, which was a mighty amount of wherewithal at that date. It was $2000, and very lucky was the laborer who earned $10 a month. Fred Selous had trained for this moment all his life, even sleeping on the bare wood floor of his shared room at Rugby as well as raiding innumerable birds' nests for his egg collection while he was growing up. Probably nobody arrived with the will that he did to make a great career of the "Far Interior," as it had been called by such luminaries as William Cornwallis Harris (one of the earliest hunter/adventurers who went north from South Africa some forty years before Selous).

Fred started trying to make his independent fortune on the diamond mines in Kimberly. But he also realized that the farther north he went, the easier it would be to break off and head directly for the Far Interior. That he had 300 pounds of luggage consigned to a transport rider (a huge amount for personal luggage in those days even for a stay of years) showed his greenness. The young man journeyed for two months to Kimberly, arriving on October 28th. Fred had some "small" shooting on the route. He killed a male bushbuck, a springbuck, a klipspringer, and eight rheboks. He was most proud that he had carried them all to the wagons on his own shoulders. He was five-foot-nine, at his greatest height and all muscle, although he didn't know what to be in shape meant until he started hunting elephant.

Selous learned about Africa early, the day he arrived at Kimberly. A "small double breech-loading rifle by Reilly" was stolen without a trace from his wagon. He now had a double ten-bore by Vaughan, "a very inferior weapon as it threw its bullets across one another, and a little double gun that shot well with both shot and bullet." Might it have been one of the very early Fosbury Patents of rifle and ball guns?

Whatever, Selous rode over to Pneil, a gold town, and there met one Arthur Laing, then going on to the gold and diamond field by cart. Although completely broke, Laing charmed Selous into writing the following in later years: "A passionate devotion to the flowing bowl had dragged him down step by step, till he did not own so much as the shoes he stood in. He was, however, in his sober moments, which, when within ten miles of canteen, were both short and infrequent, an intelligent and a well-informed man."

This not being a biography, suffice it to say that Selous and his partner made it to Kimberly and beyond, and Kuruman, which was more or less the jumping-off place for the Interior. Since he had first left by ox wagon, Selous had formed a friendship and a partnership with "a young man about my age named Dorehill, a son of General Dorehill, with whom I had contracted a great friendship on board ship." Dorehill was sharing digs and a tent with Sadlier, whom Selous proposed to come along into the Interior, and Sadlier accepted.

Selous and his young partners had not very much money for tea, coffee, mealie meal (corn meal), sugar, or salt, but decided to try anyway. A few beads completed their outfit. Selous had paid 145 pounds for their wagon, 6 pounds 10

13

shillings each for at least twelve head of oxen, and 11 pounds apiece for some horses. He was no longer a rich immigrant.

Sadlier had been in the American Civil War and knew something of how things went on *trek*. Probably his first test was occasioned by a terrible turn of events when Dorehill leaned over Selous's shoulder as Selous was reloading ammunition and about a pound of black powder was free. Of course, thanks to one of Murphy's antecedents, a spark got into the powder, which went up with a *whoof!*, and burned both Selous's face and that of Dorehill until they were almost skinless. Sadlier mixed a solution of salt and oil that was "guaranteed" to prevent scarification. Though it was something less than painless, Selous remained without marks of the black powder even though he took weeks to recover.

In the meantime, Selous had been forced to buy two muzzle-loading duck guns, smooth-bores that would take a four-ounce ball. God Almighty, they kicked something fierce when given a load of a *handful* of black powder, well over twelve drams when loaded. This is substantially more than triple the magnum load of a twelve-gauge in modern times, and three times the resistance of the ball to shoulder, which translates into "kick." But *does* it! I've tried a four-bore.

Selous, in later years, said that he was "heartily sorry that I ever had anything to do with them." Their kick made a "ferocious" sound like a love word. Several times Selous was smashed out of the saddle by recoil and many times more was knocked over by raw kick. He said that his reputation as a hunter was not due to fine shooting and perhaps these early four-bores by Hollis of Birmingham had something to do with it. They destroyed his nerves and he never shot really well again. That he was a great hunter was due to his ability at getting in close where he could not miss.

A fortunately atypical circumstance arose when he was hunting elephant some time later. He was using the Hollis four-bores. Incidentally, the definition of "bore" is the num-

ber of pure lead balls that equated the diameter of the gun.
A four-bore or gauge (the same) meant that it would take a
quarter-pound, four ounces of round lead, about .91 caliber—a lot more trouble than the quarter-pounder that you
buy at a fast-food chain.

Selous was hunting with his gunbearer, Balamoya, and another retainer, Nuta, when he had a failure of his cap, meaning that the gun would not go off. He "snapped" ignition of
his first shot when one of the Hollises did not fire. Selous was
following a bull elephant when he was handed the second
gun. He put a ball straight into the bull's chest and brought
the bull to his knees, but he was up again and ran past Selous
at thirty yards: "Taking a good sight for the middle of his
shoulder, I pulled the trigger." He didn't know that the gunbearer had reloaded it *again* with a four-ounce ball and another twelve drams of powder!

*This time the gun went off—it was a four-bore elephant gun,
loaded twice over, and the powder thrown in each time by a
Kafir with his hands—and I went off too! I was lifted, from the
ground, and turning round in the air, fell with my face in the
sand, whilst the gun was carried yards away over my shoulder.
At first I was almost stunned from the shock, and I soon found
that I could not lift my right arm. Besides this, I was covered
with blood, which spurted from a deep wound under the right
cheek-bone, caused by the stock of the gun as it flew upwards
from the violence of the recoil. The stock itself—though it had
been bound, as are all elephants guns, with the inside skin of an
elephant's ear* [it works, I tried it] *put on green, which when
dry holds it as firmly as iron—was shattered to pieces, and the
only wonder was that the barrel did not burst. Whether the two
bullets hit the elephant or not I cannot say. But I think they
must have done so, for he only went a few yards after I fired,
and then stood still, raising his trunk every now and then, and
dashing water tinged with blood over his chest. I went cautiously
up to forty yards or so of him, and sat down. Though I could not
hold my arm out, I could raise my forearm, so as to get hold of
the trigger; but the shock had so told on me, that I found that I*

could not keep the sight within a yard or so of the right place. The elephant remained perfectly still; so I got Nuta to work my arm about gently, in order to restore its power, and hoped that in the meantime the Kafir, whose shouting had originally brought the elephant to me, would be able to go up and fetch W[ood]. No doubt if I had shouted he would have come at once, for he could have not been very far off; but had I done so, the elephant might either have charged, or else continued his flight, neither of which alternatives did I desire. After a short time, seeing no chance of aid arriving, and my nerves having got a little steadier, I took my favorite gun from Nuta, and, resting my elbow on my knee, took a quiet pot shot. I was, however, still very unsteady in this position, but I do not think the bullet could have struck very far from the right place. The elephant on receiving the shot made a rush forwards, crashing through the bushes at a quick walk, so that we had to run at a quick trot to keep him in sight. He now seemed very vicious, for, hearing a dry branch snap, he turned and ran toward us, and then stood with his ears up to try and get our wind.

Selous was many things, but an author who was especially subdued or terrified by paragraphs was not one of his weak points.

Selous, in his first visit to the Far Interior, was one of the early hunters to reach the *kraal* of the Matabele despot, Lobengula. The Matabele people held sway in the north, but they had also been an immense power in the relative south until the Afrikaners drove them from the Vaal River north to mostly the area of today's Zimbabwe, not even Rhodesia at the time of their move. They had been founded as a fighting tribe by one Mzilikazi, an *impi* (or regimental) leader under the famous Shaka Zulu, the black conqueror of southern Africa. Mzilikazi—all spellings of his name are phonetic—was esentially a bad-ass. He grabbed a good amount of cattle, in which tribal wealth was then and even now reckoned, and refused to pay his tribute to Shaka. The translation of *Matabele* has some astonishing presumptions, but it is generally conceded that it meant "refugees" or "runaways." Makes sense to me.

Lobengula called his capital Gubulawayo, the "place of killing," and it was not badly named. Even to sneeze in the presence of the king meant instant death by having one's brains bashed out with knobkerries—the fierce fighting clubs of the Matabele. He was a true ruler, his word being law. Yet for all of the folderol he was a pretty nice guy, at least to Selous. But Fred was hardly the first to enter Mzilikazi's country.

There was Mr. G. A. "Elephant" Phillips and a host of other men, mostly Afrikaans names, some of whom were famous despite the fact that their owners were usually illiterate. Perhaps Selous's early book, *A Hunter's Wanderings in Africa* (Richard Bentley & Son, London, 1881) painted them too pale. Besides Phillips in the *kraal* were a Mr. Kisch, late auditor-general of the Transvaal, Sadlier, Jan Viljoen, and several others.

When Phillips translated at his meeting with Lobengula, Selous was badly underestimated. Lobengula was a little under six feet, according to Selous—a corpulent chocolate majesty dressed in a greasy shirt and a dirty pair of white men's trousers. Yet there was no question that he was regal.

Lobengula, son of Mzilikazi, asked Selous's interpreter, Phillips, whose wagons were before him. Phillips explained that they belonged to the young Selous. Lobengula asked why he was at the *kraal* and what Selous intended to do.

"I have come to hunt elephants," said the fuzzy-bearded Englishman. Lobengula burst out laughing.

"Was it not steenbucks that you came to hunt? Why, you're only a boy."

Selous answered that although he was only a boy, this was his purpose. Lobengula, without answering, rose and left followed by fifty retainers who called out his praise names, Black Elephant, Prince of Princes, Calf of the Black Cow, and such. Selous noted the low doors of the Zulu/Matabele huts—made low so that an enemy could only enter by crawl-ing, thus reducing his fighting effectiveness—and Loben-gula's difficulty in crawling in because of his bulk. Well, Selous thought, at least the king has not said no.

Two days of indecision racked Selous until he was able to see the king again. Phillips again interpreted: "I ask leave to hunt elephants in your country," said the Englishman.

"Have you ever seen an elephant?" asked Lobengula.

"No," answered Selous through Phillips.

"Oh, they will soon drive you out of the country, but you may go and see what you can do."

Selous grabbed the initiative and, as Lobengula had rele-gated elephant hunting to certain parts of his realm, asked the potentate where he might hunt.

"Oh, you may go wherever you like; you are only a boy." Selous's early trip was made.

Selous had always been fascinated by the statement of Dr. Livingstone, when the great man had himself been mauled by a lion, that the claw and teeth wounds had not hurt until after the mauling. One of the great characters of Selous's early ac-quaintance was the then-old Petrus Jacobus, who Selous reck-oned to be the oldest and most experienced elephant and lion hunter of all. Jacobus was even then recuperating from a se-vere difference of opinion with a lion about eight days before. Selous had learned quite a bit of the Dutch-based Afrikaans language and was able to speak to the old man.

This meeting was with many other Afrikaans hunters on the River Sebakwe, north of Gubulawayo. Selous, who had barely driven off a night-intruding lion not long before, asked Jacobus how he had come to be mauled.

Petrus Jacobus had been on the Umnyati River, some dis-tance to the north, with only his daughter-in-law. I know the area pretty well, having hunted there myself in 1971. Jacobus was resting in the shade of one of his wagons when the young woman saw what she thought was a wart hog coming down to water. Jacobus grabbed his rifle with the comment

18

that the pig was a lion and that it was stalking the horses. Petrus Jacobus took off after it with three dogs.

Jacobus tried a running shot at the lion with his muzzle-loader but missed, yet the dogs had bayed the lion. Jacobus approached with a small black boy. The lion, on the side of a hill, immediately broke through the ring of dogs and charged straight at Jacobus. Still a distance away, he fired his only shot and missed. Reaching the old man, the big cat slammed into him and bit him terribly in the left thigh and then in the left arm and hand. Fortunately, the three dogs were all this time doing their own chewing at the lion's tail end and eventually drew him off. Selous says that Jacobus was terribly mangled and thought that the lion "had done for him."

Always believing in home remedies as they had little access to drugstores, the Afrikaners were great fans of herbal medicine. In the case of Jacobus, this entailed bathing the wounds in a mixture of fresh milk and castor oil. Well, it worked and Jacobus recovered to tell Selous, many years later, that his wounds sometimes gave him great pain, especially in wet weather.

Some forty miles due south of the Sebakwe lie the first *kraals* of the Mashuna (now known as Mashona or Shona) people and Selous had a high opinion of them from the start. They were the fragmented clans who won the Rhodesian bush war against the whites and many of the Matabele in the 1980s. Curiously, as my good friend Brian Marsh, the novelist and writer, points out, it was Selous who later gave the name to the Shonas of "Maswina." As Brian notes, the name has a very interesting origin, although it is now considered beneath Shona dignity to use such a derogatory name for themselves.

This interesting footnote to history was a product of 1890, when Selous was both building roads for the Pioneer Column that invaded what would become Southern Rhodesia and making treaties with certain Portuguese East African tribes such as the Manica, who were settled about where Wally Johnson lived and hunted ivory (see *The Last Ivory Hunter*, St. Martin's Press, New York, 1988).

An old informant of Brian told the tale that when Selous was using Shonas to build roads, the labor was always hungry. When an antelope was shot by Selous, the road builders would gut it and run sections of intestines through their fingers to clean them before throwing the ropelike intestinal lengths on the fire to cook.

Selous asked his interpreter—he could speak no Shona dialect at the time—what it was called in Shona when the men cleaned out pieces of offal between thumb and forefinger as they did.

"Ku-svina," the interpreter said, using the verb form.

"Then they shall be known as Masvina [those who strip entrails] from now on," pronounced Selous, using the plural Ma- form. This became "Maswina" as the whites could not properly pronounce the word in Shona and each time Selous would kill an antelope he would call upon the Masvina to eat it. In fact, the word became a general term for the many fragmented tribes and clans of the Shona who shared a similar language. As Brian says, the people became known in those days as the Maswina and their language as Chiswina, the tongue of the Maswina. Interesting stuff, history.

Fred Selous is generally considered to be one of the finest hunters produced by Western civilization. Curiously, he did not agree with such a pronouncement, declaring that the fact he hunted a lot did not necessarily make him a great hunter. But on his first trip to Mashunaland, as Selous called it, he did spend some time with a man who was Selous's own idea of the greatest hunter. He was a diminutive, alcoholic ex-jockey from Grahamstown in South Africa, a Hottentot named Cigar.

Cigar was himself well worthy of inclusion on the list of great African hunters. He shot a six-bore gun, which was in itself quite remarkable for a man so slight that he had once been a jockey. He originally got to the Far Interior driving a wagon for a Henry McGillewe some years before Selous met him and was even employed on "halves"—just like the grub-stake of the itinerant prospector, getting a horse, gun, ammo, and food in exchange for half of the ivory, or other species such as rhino, that he shot—by none other than the scalliwag and great elephant hunter William Finaughty. (See the Peter Capstick Library of classic reprints of African hunting.) Selous had originally been slated to join the company of the Boer hunter Jan Viljoen but he sliced his foot badly and was unable to leave with the group on time. Sadlier went with Viljoen's party with the promise that Selous would be picked up later when his foot had healed. This hope proved in vain and it being an ill wind that blows nobody any good, Selous was blown to Cigar.

Selous thought the world of the wizened little hunter and declared that he had never seen his equal on foot after elephants, which was really saying something as Selous hunted with some of the great names of the Interior. At first, as Cigar says himself, he was scared green of elephants, which shows that he was no idiot. Gradually, he got over his nervousness and his natural fine marksmanship against game won out. He became one of the aces of the ivory world.

Cigar took Selous under his wing and tried either to teach him or kill him. The Boers lived roughly, even their families subsisting in pole-and-dagga huts during the hunting season, but with the luxury of coffee, sugar, and tobacco. The "native" hunters had none of these frills and Selous lived the same way. Hunting was on foot, through necessity, in tsetse country. They had their guns, limited ammunition—twenty shots—blankets, some mealie meal, and water. Selous had run out of tea (he was an inveterate tea drinker all his life and nearly a teetotaler) as well as sugar but Cigar allowed himself no such luxuries.

When Selous and Cigar left the wagons, they were eight—two men also hunting who carried their own gear as well as three porters lugging fresh meat and incidentals and one teenager of Selous, what the Zulus used to call an *indibi* boy, who humped his blankets and spare ammunition. Selous carried one of the old Hollises himself. Very possibly, he was the first Englishman—at least with a Rugby education—who had assaulted the bush with so little. He was to get so much from the experience.

As he said, "This was hardly doing the thing *en grand seigneur, I* was young and enthusiastic in those days, and trudged along under the now intense heat with a light heart."

You know, to really appreciate the hunting Selous had with Cigar, you really must read *A Hunter's Wanderings in Africa.* Space, short of a hunting biography, does not permit going into each kill that Selous, Cigar, and his followers made. Yet from this crucible was formed a great personality who could run for hours on spoor and usually kill when his run stopped.

Selous had jumped off from a place called Jomani, and when he returned with Cigar, his pals Mandy and Dorehill had arrived. Mandy had been hunting with a George Wood, the same who shared many close ones with Selous. I would leave this part of Selous's history but for a macabre incident that would warm the heart of any exploratory small boy. . . .

There was—as Selous calls him—a "bastard" man named Lucas who had a Hottentot employee. I think that he means a "Baster" man, whose community now lives in Namibia and whose name implies no illegitimacy. The Hottentot had, however, lost his cool and executed one black servant for not serving water quickly enough. I presume he was very thirsty, as he killed the boy quite dead by blowing out his brains. Most efficient. However, that same night—to use Selous's words—Lucas caught and bound the young murderer and brought him into the encampment.

> All the Kafirs at once assembled and demanded his life in
> expiation of that of their comrade, and upon Lucas giving him
> up, at once knocked his brains out with knobkerries. I did not
> know anything about it until the execution was over. From what
> Lucas told me there was little doubt that the ruffian deserved his

*fate, but I was glad I did not see him killed. His body was
dragged just over a little ridge not three hundred yards from the
wagons. In the night hyenas came and laughed and howled
around the corpse for hours, but never touched it. The second
night the same thing happened, but on the third they ate him up.
Now, as these hyenas were beasts belonging to an uninhabited
country, they were unused to human remains, and had not, I
think, lost their instinctive dread of the smell of man; for in the
Matabele country, where the bodies of people killed for
witchcraft are always "given to the hyenas," a corpse is
invariably dragged off even from the very gates of a kraal before
the first night is many hours old.*

Trust Selous to be the naturalist interested even in hyenas
eating bodies.

Following his time in the bush with Cigar, during which he
had killed his first elephant, Fred came away with almost 450
pounds of ivory that he had shot himself and another 1200
pounds that he had accumulated by trade. His net was about
300 British pounds, a mighty nice living for anybody in the
1870s, and a very fine return on his original (or his father's)
investment of 400 pounds. But his great triumph came when
he saw Lobengula at Gubulawayo again: "When I told the
king that his elephants had not driven me out of the country,
but that, on the contrary, I had killed several, he said laugh-
ingly, 'Why, you are a man; when are you going to take a
wife?'—and upon my telling him that if he would give me
one I would take her at once, he said. 'Oh! You must *combeesa*
[sic] [court one] yourself; there are lots of them.'"

Selous decided to stay in the Matabele country while his
friends such as Dorehill figured on going to the diamond dig-
gings, probably for a bit of recreation and trading. Selous
reckoned on remaining behind to do the next dry season
hunting elephant with his new pal, George Wood.

Wood was known as a hard, smooth article, which Selous
endorsed when he confirmed him to be "a very cool and cou-
rageous man, one whose pulse beat as calmly when face to

face with a wounded elephant and snarling lion, as it did when quietly eating his breakfast." He had hunted for many years with Henry Hartley, William Finaughty, Gifford, Leask, and Biles, all retired since things had gone the tsetse fly's way. They were all horsemen, hunting from the saddle. It took a different breed of man to hunt elephant on foot. Selous was one of the new ones. . . .

Wood, according to Selous, arrived from the gold and diamond fields somewhat shop-worn. He stopped at Hope Fountain (taken from the Afrikaans *fontein* meaning "spring") and was nursed by Mrs. Thompson, the wife of the local missionary, for quite some time. His problem was not at all rare—malaria, called just "fever" in those days. In fact, he had to be lifted out of his wagon and carried to the house, so bad were his symptoms. Yet, he recovered, which was fairly unusual in that place and time.

Wood was strictly H. Rider Haggard material. He was raised in the north of England, Yorkshire, and had an excellent education but, like yours truly, he was an African at heart. Wood was a white chameleon, fitting in with the most elaborate African ceremonies. He astonished the young Selous with his fluency in Sindebele and his demeanor at the beer drinks and meals. He was, to all practicalities, a white Ndebele.

Selous spent the best part of two years with George Wood, although they hunted separately. The Matabele, when there was no brewing facility available—brewing was usually done by the women—used "pot" or, if you want to be formal, cannabis, to revive their spirits. Certainly, they were revived. . . .

Selous had now been in Africa for about three years and had transmuted his original stake from 400 pounds into almost 2000, a pretty fair return, although he had earned it in blood and sweat.

When he returned to Tati, a small village full of lazing dogs, hot wind, and the smell of dung in bright sunshine, he got his mail for the first time and, unknown to history, decided to go back to England, where he stayed, avoiding the biographer's pen from May of 1875 until February of 1876. Family problems? We just don't know.

Fred was a pretty good son and, when there had been no contact at all for these three years, he was thought at home to be dead. There is no surviving mail whatever to his mother, Ann Selous, for all this time. Personally, I suspect that it had been lost somewhere in the Interior before it reached the mail ship. It was not like Fred Selous not to write for three years. When he arrived home, the fatted calf was killed and he was a hero both to his family and his friends. Whether he had not written or his correspondence was lost remains to be seen, but he promised his mother that he would write regularly, especially if he was off into "the blue" and would not be in touch for some time.

Selous was largely educated in public school (why it is called public school when it is private has always eluded me, despite some serious research), at Rugby, by a headmaster named James Wilson, who took over in 1869 from a man named Temple, himself an institution. Wilson always overlooked major transgressions such as Selous's having a gun, although Selous thought he was much more clever than he was. Wilson knew all about it and other such infringements. There was a supper in Fred's honor, the "Old Boy" come home. That it was an extraordinary success was to the great surprise of Selous himself, who thought that he had no particular talent in public speaking. History was to prove him wrong.

Fred made his second landing at Algoa Bay on the ides of March, 1876. Perhaps, like Caesar, he should have taken note. . . .

Selous had decided to go to the Zambesi River and put most of his early profits into the endeavor. He had an immense amount of baggage—three tons—and it was so much that another ship rather than his transport to South Africa had to take it. The ship was about six weeks late and Selous had to wait for its arrival. To put it mildly, he was royally irked, and it took him another four months to get to the Matabele country. Also, the freight rates by wagon were up about fifty percent, which did not please him either. Of course, most of his 6000 pounds of baggage were trade goods with which he planned to buy ivory.

After a rather extended giraffe hunt, he got mixed up with a wounded lion—the wound being caused by Selous the afternoon before the showdown.

At this point, Fred and his partner, Dorehill, had joined up with two other English sportsmen/hunters, William Grandy and Lewis Horner, capital chaps, what? Yet, Fred was alone when he stuck a ball—ten-bore—into a large male lion and finally lost it after hours of tracking through the wait-a-bit thorn near Tati. Yet, despite some showers, the spoor and the blood were still sufficiently visible to enable the lion to be tracked. As the hunting party drew near to give the lion his quietus, it roared in a hollow vortex that rattled the bushveld. Selous was likely scared—or stupid not to be—but he walked in on the spot where the grunting roars were emanating from. It charged.

It rushed, as lions usually do, in a low, khaki streak rather than bounding like those who have not been charged by lions would have you believe. Let Fred tell it:

> As it was, however, I was peering about into the bush to try and catch sight of him, holding my rifle advanced in front of me, and on full cock, when I became aware that he was coming at me through the bush. The next instant out he burst. I was so close that I had not even time to take a sight, but, stepping a pace backwards, got the rifle to my shoulder, and, when his head was close upon the muzzle, pulled the trigger, and jumped to one side. The lion fell almost at my very feet, certainly not six feet from the muzzle of the rifle. Grandy and Horner, who had a good view of the charge, say that he just dropped in his tracks when I fired, which I could not see for the smoke [of his black

26

powder rifle]. *One thing, however, I had time to notice, and
that was he did not come at me in bounds,* [this was Selous's
first wounded lion] *but with a rush along the ground.
Perhaps it was his broken shoulder that hindered him from
springing, but for all that he came at a very great rate, and
with his mouth open. Seeing him on the ground, I thought I
must have shattered his skull and killed him, when, as we were
advancing toward him, he stood up again.* [Oh, my . . .]
*Dorehill at once fired with a Martini-Henry rifle and shot him
through the thigh. On this he fell down again, and, rolling over
on to his side, lay gasping. We now went up to him, but as he
still continued to open his mouth, Horner gave him a shot in the
head. . . . He was an average sized-lion, his pegged-out skin*
[rather than between the pegs] *measuring 10 ft. 3 in. from
nose to tip of tail, sleek, and in find condition, and his teeth long
and perfect.*

Selous had shot him above the right eye, which he believed
caused enough brain damage to kill the lion. Both his English
pals had fired at the lion but, with the exception of the thigh
shot, had missed as there were no bullet marks. Take it from
me, an angry lion in a hurry can be a tough target.

Selous's initial problems on his return to Africa after his
English trip seemed to portend how his life would change
for the worse. It was during the prolonged stay at Tati that
George Westbeech would enter his life as well as those of
Dorehill, Grandy, and Horner.

Westbeech was practically as much of a fixture of Mashonaland as was Lobengula. He was really sort of an African Davy
Crockett who had known and been a pal of Lobengula since
before he became king and was also a good friend of Sepopa,
the ferocious king of the Barotses. Westbeech was almost
larger than life. He had come to the Matabele dominions almost fifteen years before, a well-educated man turned about as
native as a white could get. He was almost malaria-proof, a
strange brand of British Levantine who typified the energetic
trader. He had traded with Sepopa since 1871 some 20,000 to
30,000 pounds of ivory at favorable rates as he stocked better

trade goods—especially guns and powder—than did his competitors. But as there was considerable tribal warfare when Selous met him in 1876, ivory poundage was drastically down.

Because of these firearms in the hands of the tribes, Selous found out from Westbeech that Matabeleland was almost "shot out" of elephant, and he elected to head down to Kimberly from Tati on a round-trip journey that took five months. Among the incidents of his trip were the killing and eating of his horse by a lion that got away wounded and a fall from another horse that cracked the tibia, bone serum actually leaking from his leg. Typical of Selous, the injury is only mentioned in a brief footnote.

It was April of 1877, the beginning of the winter dry season, when Selous again arrived at Tati and found out what had happened to the hunting party Westbeech had organized to the Zambesi. Fred had decided against going—instead heading down to Kimberly—because of the severe risk of malaria during the wet season. Just as well that he did: Grandy had died of it just when he seemed to have the fever beaten and both Dorehill and Horner also contracted bad bouts. Selous left for the Zambesi, having gambled all his earlier profits on outfitting a party that included an Englishman, Mr. Kingsley, a young colonist reputed to be a fine shot and rider, a Mr. Miller, and five Africans. All his companions were shooting for Selous on "halves" and a disaster was the result. The total score of the trip was the taking of three small elephants by Miller and a gross profit of two pounds! The party hunted separately to cover more ground and Selous never so much as saw an elephant.

Thirst, hunger, fever, and lions were not the only adversaries that nearly cost Selous his life. There were also Cape buffalo. One of his closest shaves took place on the Nata River, near the modern border of present-day Botswana and Zimbabwe, in May 1874.

Fred was hunting for the pot early on the morning of the 20th when, an hour after sunrise, he hit the spoor of two huge old buffalo bulls. Riding hard along the tracks in the sandy, dry riverbed, he finally caught up with them. This small mutual admiration society consisted of what the Bamangwato call *kwatales,* almost hairless with age and tremendous in body. Fred thought that they looked nearly like rhinos.

Reaching a relatively open patch of bush, Fred reined up, sliding from the saddle with his four-bore in hand. At thirty yards, he looked down the barrel of the duck gun and squeezed the trigger. There was the sharp metallic click of the hammer striking the bare nipple of the muzzle loader. Somehow, the percussion cap must have been brushed away by branches.

Remounting, Selous stuck on another cap and took up the chase as the two bulls cantered away with their strange rocking-horse gait. One buffalo had fallen behind the other and Fred decided to concentrate on him. The bull crossed a small, dry gully and turned to face Selous, his bosses looking like oak burls and his worn horns gleaming wickedly in the early sun. He had been chivvied around enough, Selous knew, and he would likely charge. Not dismounting this time, he hoisted the gun and fired. Once more there was the hollow click. Again the percussion cap had fallen off. The buffalo spun around and ran off. Fred put on a third cap and held it on the nipple with his thumb.

After several minutes of chase, Selous got back into range just as the bull disappeared into a patch of mopane scrub. Suddenly the bull stopped short, whirled, and came back out looking for trouble. It found it. It saw the horse and came straight ahead, its nose pushed forward and bass grunts echoing the slam of its dinner-plate hooves against the dry ground. Selous would never forget it:

> *There was no time to be lost, as I was not more than forty yards from him; so, reining in with a jerk and turning my horse at the same instant broadside on, I raised my gun, intending to put a ball, if possible, just between his neck and shoulder, which,*

*could I have done so, would either have knocked him down, or
at any rate made him swerve, but my horse, instead of standing
steady as he had always done before, now commenced walking
forward, though he did not appear to take any notice of the
buffalo. There was no time to put my hand down and give
another wrench on the bridle (which I had let fall on the horse's
neck), and for the life of me I could not get a sight with the horse
in motion. A charging buffalo does not take many seconds to
cover forty yards, and in another instant his outstretched nose
was within six feet of me, so, lowering the gun from my shoulder,
I pulled it right off in his face, at the same time digging the
spurs deep into my horse's sides. But it was too late, for even as
he sprang forward the old bull caught him full in the flank,
pitching him, with me on his back, into the air like a dog. The
recoil of the heavily-charged elephant-gun with which I was
unluckily shooting, twisted it clean out of my hands, so that we
all, horse, gun and man, fell in different directions. My horse
gained its feet and galloped away immediately, but even with a
momentary glance, I saw that the poor brute's entrails were
protruding in a dreadful manner. The buffalo, on tossing the
horse, had stopped dead, and now stood with his head lowered
within a few feet of me. I had fallen in a sitting position and
facing my unpleasant-looking adversary. I could see no wound
on him, so must have missed, though I can scarcely understand
how, as he was very close when I fired.*

*However, I had not much time for speculation, for the old
brute, after glaring at me for a few seconds with his sinister-
looking blood-shot eyes, finally made up his mind, and, with a
grunt, rushed at me. I threw my body out flat along the ground
to one side, and just avoided the upward thrust of his horn,
receiving, however, a severe blow on the left shoulder with the
round part of it; nearly dislocating my right arm with the force
with which my elbow was driven against the ground; and
receiving also a kick on the instep from one of his feet. Luckily
for me, he did not turn again, as he most certainly would have
done had he been wounded, but galloped clean away.*

*The first thing to be done was to look after my horse, and at
about 150 yards from where he had been tossed, I found him.
The buffalo had struck him full in the left thigh; it was an awful*

*wound, and as the poor beast was evidently in the last extremity,
I hastily loaded my gun and put him out of his misery. My
Kafirs coming up just then, I started with them, eager for
vengeance, in pursuit of the buffalo, but was compelled finally to
abandon the chase, leaving my poor horse unavenged.*

By 1877, Fred Selous had succeeded in forging his circle of
friends from the hunters of the Interior. Although still in his
middle twenties, Fred had earned the respect of his peers not
only for his bush skills but because of his reputation of fair
dealing and not being a gossip. That October, in the company of a soldier of fortune named L. M. Owen, a man who
had fought in one of the "Kaffer Wars" against the Xhosa
people of South Africa, Selous finalized his plans to make a
foray north of the Zambesi into the Mashukulumbwe (Baila)
country where he had heard that elephants were behind every bush. Fred had met Owen on the banks of the Chobe
River in today's Botswana and perhaps made a too-quick
character judgment of the man. He later wrote, "Unfortunately we did not hit it off very well together," and in his soft
way, "as much through my fault, no doubt, as his, owing to
what I may call incompatibility of temper." This is a classic
of understatement even for Selous!

The Mashukulumbwe area of northern Zambia and parts
of the then–Belgian Congo were cannibal territory and the
people fierce warriors. If you have read my earlier book,
Death in the Silent Places, you will recognize this area as the
same one in which P. J. Pretorius was ambushed and nearly
killed and eaten in 1904.

As soon as Fred and Owen crossed the Zambesi, they realized that the relative order of the Matabele had given way to
that of the Portuguese and black slavers. As the thoroughly
horrible trek continued through the country, Christmas came
and went, leaving both Selous and Owen very sick and starving, their not having found elephants. Little time went by
before they realized that far from making a successful hunting trip of the venture, they would be lucky to return the 700

31

miles to the nearest mission station at Inyati alive. They had reached a *kraal* that was under the chieftainship of a man named Sitanda, a sable rascal if ever there was one. This place was some three weeks' walk north of the Kafue River in what became Zambia, and the first day after their arrival, Owen came down with severe malaria and Selous the same on the third day. Sitanda refused to grant them porters and even their own headman was sick. By January 8th, Owen was "very bad; he had lost all power in his limbs." Selous had been sleeping badly, but the next day he foolishly went lechwe hunting in the marches and got fever himself. There was nothing but Warburg's fever tincture—in which Selous had great faith—but no quinine or even decent food or water. On January 15th, Selous noted that he felt somewhat better but Sitanda had refused to sell them food or to help them get porters. Obviously, the old man thought the whites would die and he would get their kit.

They also had little help from a Portuguese slave trader whom they had met earlier and who had come up to Sitanda's *kraal*. The man would not give them any calico barterwear to buy food, and Selous was forced to sell the man a fine elephant gun, half a bag of powder, and fifty bullets for the ridiculous price of twenty-four feet of shoddy cloth (called "Mericani" in those times as it was made in America). On the 23rd, the Portuguese came by with a slave for sale and since, as Selous noted, it was of vital importance to get carriers, he bought the eighteen-year-old whose teeth were filed to cannibal points. He cost Fred 320 loaded cartridges and he made it clear to the young man through an interpreter that he was not wanted as a slave but could either go free on reaching the Zambesi or continue working for wages. Despite the fact that Fred had had another bout of fever during the night, they began their return trip on the 24th of January, only making a few miles a day in their condition. On the 29th, the slave escaped, taking with him a valuable breech-loading elephant gun and all of Fred's Martini-Henry cartridges. The elephant gun was later recovered by tracking the slave's spoor.

By the 10th of February, reduced to two-and-a-half pieces of the calico, it was obvious that unless Selous—who was feeling better—went on ahead to try to make Inyati and the missionary station there, the whole party would starve to death. It was decided to leave Owen with two servants and two whole pieces of calico, which should enable him to buy enough food to hold out for a while as Selous went for help as far as a Portuguese place run by one Mendonça, who sent two men with some food for Owen. The sick man reached the small Portuguese island on March 5th. Fred's health ranged from very poor to recovering but there was no way that Owen could walk on. Selous managed to trade with Medonça and got seven pieces of calico with which he hired eight men to carry Owen on a litter from a point on the south bank of the Zambesi. Owen was carried from April 6th until the 17th despite much grumbling from his Banyai carriers. Fred reckoned on at least three weeks walking until he reached Nyati, but on May 3rd, he was told at a small Matabele outpost that Nyati only lay twenty miles away! The next day he staggered into the station practically into the arms of the Reverend W. Sykes.

Within two more days a relief column was sent to rescue Owen and in a few weeks was back with him and Selous's servant, Franz. It took Selous, who was in better health than Owen, two months and three weeks to recover his health and condition. He was alive but much chastened. Selous would never be the same again.

Selous was broke and despondent, almost all of his profit and his family grubstake gone. He considered new ways of making a living, but a rare bit of good news finally came his way in August of 1878 when he was visiting Lobengula at Gubulawayo. It was an interesting little intrigue that the Matabele king worked at, but he realized that Selous had become an important figure in the circle of Interior hunters and that they would make better friends than enemies. Lobengula amazed him by granting permission to hunt ivory in Mashonaland itself. Carte blanche to hunt the area had also been given to his friends Clarkson, Cross, and Wood. Selous left Gubulawayo and caught his friends, who had left in June—near the Umfuli River—in September. He traveled with a partner of Clarkson named Goulden.

A couple of days before Selous and Goulden arrived, there had been a macabre incident with a Zulu—appointed by Lobengula to head Wood's Matabele retainers—that involved an overdose of elephant. The man, Quabeet, had been running after a wounded elephant when he was charged from some cover by a *budi* or tuskless bull. The elephant caught him and was heard screaming as a bull will when it gets lucky. The parts of the body were recovered three days later. Clarkson told Selous what had happened when the body was discovered: "He had been torn in three pieces; the chest, with head and arms attached, which had been wrenched from the trunk just below the breast-bone, lying in one place, one leg and thigh that had been torn off at the pelvis in another, and the remainder in a third. The right arm had been broken in two places and the hand crushed; one of the thighs was also broken, but otherwise the fragments had not been trampled on." As if there were a need. . . .

Some days later, Selous almost joined Quabeet in happier hunting grounds. . . .

Selous had never hunted elephant on horseback before, all his experience having been on foot in tsetse fly country where a horse would not survive the *nagana*. He had been warned never to dismount with elephant because of the speed of the charge but to take his shot from the saddle. When quite a large herd was met, they were chased in a circle by the horsemen to tire them, but Fred found that he could not get a bead from the quarterdeck of a nervous horse.

Selous had killed four elephants, but had remounted for

the last shots. The final tusker, a bull, almost caught him as his horse was so bushed, but he managed to pull away from it before his horse collapsed. Had it not been seriously wounded, Fred was sure it would have caught him. But the elephants were also exhausted and, due to the fidgeting of his horse, Selous hadn't opened fire as early as had his companions; he had thirteen cartridges left. He thought that he would be able to kill three or four more tuskers with these—Fred reckoned himself only a fair shot as his shooting nerves had been ruined by his early experiences with the horrendous kick of the four-bores—and decided that he would have done so except that he almost became part of the day's bag himself.

For his next victim he chose a nearby large cow (cows have finer-grain ivory than bulls although much less weight) and slammed a round in behind her shoulder. Hurt, she left the herd and began to wander away by herself. As Selous cantered up behind her to give her a finishing shot, she swapped ends and faced the hunter, ears spread like gray billboards and her head raised. Fred's horse now being completely whipped, he stood well enough for Selous to deliver another between the neck and shoulder—also his favorite shot on buffalo—and he believed this stopped her from charging. At least for a moment it did.

Fred had just extracted his empty cartridge as the elephant took a few steps backward. He was about to chamber a new cartridge when he saw that she was about to charge over the mere thirty yards that separated them. He grabbed the bridle and turned the horse's head away just as she began her rush. Instinctively, Selous dug in the spurs but the pony was so exhausted that he could only crank out a slow walk, which became a moderate canter far too late. The infuriated elephant had caught them.

There were two ear-splitting screams above the man's head and he just had time to think that he had made his last mistake with dangerous game. Both the horse and the man were smashed to the ground. The first thing he became aware of was the permeating barnyard stench of elephant. The same second, he realized that he was still uninjured but for the initial shock and that he might have a chance to live.

Selous was pressed into the ground by an inexorable weight and saw the cow's two hind legs like gray pillars a few feet away. He knew that he was under the elephant's chest and that the cow had already sunk her tusks into the hard ground trying to gore him. With a tremendous effort, he wrenched himself into a lying position supported by his hands, in much the same posture as that of the classic sculpture, *The Dying Gaul.* Fred managed to drag himself from under the forelegs, made it to his feet, and ran toward the elephant's rear. She had lost him; or perhaps she had forgotten where she had put him.

But Selous was clever enough not to try a flat-out sprint to safety and ran slowly, watching the cow over his shoulder as the elephant realized that he was not under her tusks. She turned first to one side, then to the other looking for him, but never quite reversed ends. Each time she would whirl, Fred would run obliquely away, keeping the cow's rear straight toward him. Finally, he made the shelter of a small bush as the female, enraged, kept looking for him.

He was sure his horse was dead and his rifle had been knocked from his hand by the impact. As the elephant moved off, Fred saw Cross's gunbearer and ran over to him. He fished some cartridges from his pants pocket and looped them in his belt. As the cow had now moved some 200 yards away, just over a little rise, the two men chanced recovering the rifle and seeing what had happened to the horse. Oddly, except for a bad wound in the rump, which poured blood down his leg, the horse was safe and survived. The native came back with the rifle, but the action was full of sand, having been open for reloading as the cow charged. Using the man's spear blade, Fred took the lever out and managed to clean it. The cow was standing still fifty yards off when Selous—making sure it was the same one—killed her with a shoulder shot and a final bullet in the back of the head. Perhaps he finally took a deep breath of relief. Not many men see another dawn after being under a wounded elephant.

The party of hunters killed twenty-two elephants that day; no big tuskers but all a very respectable weight totaling about 700 pounds of ivory. As fate would have it, the cow that Selous killed last wasn't the one that had savaged him and his horse after all. It was a similar cow that had been wounded above the eye by Cross. Selous's cow was the only one wounded and lost, it being impossible to sort out her tracks from the jumble of the herd.

Selous's final trip after ivory, to the Chobe and Botletlie (Boteti) rivers of King Khama's Country—Botswana—was the final blow to his luck. It was now 1879 and Fred had gambled what was left of his capital on this trip, taking more than a hundred blacks and hoping to be joined by three pals from South Africa's Transvaal, Clarkson, French, and Collison. By the time the trip was over, two of his three friends would be dead and Fred completely disillusioned about elephant hunting as a vocation.

The three friends started to join Selous, leaving from the diamond fields of the south, but Matthew Clarkson—I wonder if it was the same Clarkson who gave his name to the wildebeest of the Luangwa Valley of Zambia?—never even came close. He was struck by lightning near Klerksdorp in the Transvaal and thoroughly killed. Selous, who got the story from Collison who was inside the wagon next to the one where Clarkson was killed, advises that the bolt struck him squarely on the head, even putting a neat hole in his hat. The lightning strike then passed out through his side, above the hip, and ran down the iron rung of the wagon and into the earth. Collison was stunned and the horses broke loose in panic, not to be found until the next day.

The death of French, a few months later, was more involved and probably could have been prevented if an attack of pig-headedness had not come over the man. The episode started when, against Fred's advice, French decided to follow a wounded elephant in the late afternoon. He took two natives with him, including a Bamangwato lad that Selous knew well to have a fine sense of direction and who knew the area. When darkness fell, Selous fired a total of four signal shots when French had not yet returned to camp. Earlier, French had himself fired two closely spaced shots, and then a single shot was heard near to a place where the grass had been set on fire, a couple of hours' walk from the wagons and in the direction of the Chobe River, an area that I have hunted many times close to the then-village of Linyanti, near Lake Liambezi.

Fred walked fifteen miles that night, all the way to the burning grass, but could find no sign of French or his men. Sure that French had struck for the river—he commented that he would do so if "bushed"—Selous returned, but the next morning, September 26th, took a tracking party out.

There was very little spoor but on their return in the afternoon, Selous found a dead giraffe and it had one of French's eight-bore bullets in its paunch. This probably accounted for the two quick shots heard. When French hadn't returned by the 29th, Fred sent a letter to a place called Mamele's advising French, who, it was presumed, had gone to the river, that he would be met in two days at Sasinkoro's town. Fred also sent French's light rifle and blankets. On October 1st, Selous was feeling the first effects of a bout of malaria and was sitting near the wagons when he saw "Boy," the gunbearer at the head of a line of blacks from Mamele's. The first words out of the man's mouth were that French was dead.

The gunbearer told Selous that much of his reasoning had been right. French had shot the giraffe, but instead of making camp, he tried by walking all night to get back to the wagons. "Boy" told his master that the direction was wrong but French told him that it was none of his business. Yes,

French had set the grass on fire and even decided to sleep there, but later, like the fool he was, he changed his mind. The rest of the night and the next day were deadly confusion as French insisted on wandering around the bush to the extent that he even disoriented his guides, although "Boy" insisted that he could find the river if only French would stop trying to make for camp. That afternoon, French began to cough up blood and called a halt. Late that night, after more fruitless miles, his internal bleeding became worse and he finally told "Boy" to light some stems of grass so that he could write on his rifle forestock. He was dying. Shortly afterward, he was dead.

French's death is usually attributed to thirst or sunstroke, but it doesn't sound to me as if that was what he died of. True, they were out of water, but not for that long. However, as Selous points out, October on the Chobe is murderous for heat and thirst and mentions that three natives hunting with another friend of his died within twenty-four hours under similar circumstances. I will agree that the Chobe can be as hot as a tamale that time of year.

When Selous received the rifle, he deciphered: "I cannot go any farther; when I die peace with all."

French's body was never found under the small pile of branches that the two blacks heaped over it to keep off vultures and hyenas. According to the men, he had died the night of September 27th and it was not until October 2nd that Selous got the word. The spoor was too old to backtrack and both the gunbearer and the water carrier, Makuba, were too confused to find it. Africa strikes again. . . .

Selous blamed himself, although he was not responsible for French's stupidity. Yet, the news almost killed him. His malaria became worse and he was so weak that he had to be carried on a litter. As Fred said, his troubles were very nearly over.

When he joined up with Collison and another friend, a German named Sell, he found both of them severely ill with fever. The journey home was a cold clam sandwich of a nightmare of thirst and dying oxen. Selous made it to the diamond fields and to Klerksdorp, but that was not until March 1880 and he was still too sick to hunt.

Selous made one more trip to the Interior, but it was not the one he had originally planned. He had hoped to make one more great trek to Lake Tanganyika that would take two years to complete, but he was denied in his application for a permit for 300 pounds of powder for himself and 100 pounds for Collison. He also requested permission to have 500 Martini-Henry cartridges. Possibly for personal reasons, perhaps for political ones, Sir Owen Lanyon, Administrator of the Transvaal (Selous always seemed to have bad luck with people named Owen), refused him rather curtly in a note from his secretary: "The Administrator has received instructions not to grant permits for any arms or ammunition whatsoever." Considering that Lanyon had okayed 100 pounds of powder for the 1879 season, Selous was angry and disappointed.

But a different type of trip, which would typify those of the rest of his life, came up. He made a deal with the Irish whiskey heir, James Jameson, to hunt up to the Umnyati River, which I also know well, and the Mashona Plateau. Jameson would foot the cost of the expedition and Selous would act as guide, mentor, professional hunter, and organizer. Happily, Fred and James hit it off splendidly and had a very good hunt together for a mixed bag. Further, Selous was able to fill in a few blank spots on the map of the day as well as to correct errors. Ten years later the seeds of this trip would earn him the Gold Medal of the Royal Geographic Society in London.

But Selous not only scored on future claims to fame in geographic circles; he was the first to hear that Cecil John Rhodes's brother, Herbert, had been killed in a bush fire the year before in Mashonaland and on his next trip to England he stopped off to inform Cecil of the news. The Selous-

Rhodes relationship would become one of the most important liaisons in southern Africa in later years.

As Selous became more aware that ivory hunting had had it commercially, the more he became determined to return to England to write a book of his adventures and to chuck hunting altogether. He thought he might become a farmer in South Africa later, possibly ranching ostriches as his friend Mandy had done, with great financial success. Yet, although not a great student, Selous had always been selectively bookish. Fred admitted that the 1863 book by William Charles Baldwin, *African Hunting from Natal to the Zambesi,* was responsible for his going to Africa in the first place. Baldwin may have consisted of a large beard wearing a small man, but he was a hell-for-leather action storyteller.

Selous arrived home in England in early April of 1881, just in time to hear of the drubbing the British had gotten at Majuba Hill, the crucial battle of the First War of Independence—as the Afrikaners called it—or the First Boer War, as it is better known.

Selous had his journals to work from and he wrote quickly. The first edition of *A Hunter's Wanderings in Africa* came out before year's end, a thousand copies strong. In a year, they were sold out and have become prime Africana in not only the first, but subsequent two of five editions. But seemingly there was no money in books and Selous wondered if this might be his publisher's fault. In fact, the first year he lost money as he personally financed the seventy-three pounds necessary to have the book illustrated by his sister, J. Smit, and E. Whymper, and he only took in sixty-one pounds in royalties!

When the smoke cleared after some six months of staying in England with his family, Selous was still in financial trouble and was reduced to roughly the same 400 pounds that had been his family's grubstake. Fidgety with "civilized" life, he yearned to get back to Africa but he was not sure what he should do. Happily, the British Natural History Museum in the form of Albert Gunther came to his rescue with the idea that Selous should collect large fauna for the new department. For the next six or so years, Fred supplied both the British and the South African museums with specimens, although at the time he returned to the Cape in November of 1881 he was still bent on ostrich farming. Practically as his ship docked, he heard that the man who had agreed to finance him in ostrich farming had killed himself after some ill-advised speculation in the diamond fields. Furthermore, the man died broke. While Selous had been away in England, the ostrich market for skins and feathers had collapsed, but maybe it was just as well for Fred. His friends advised him that in six months he would be bored stiffer than a plank with farming and would want to head back to the Interior. Well, thought Selous, at least I have the orders from the British Museum as well as a hefty potential deal with a London dealer in natural history specimens. Coupled with the orders of the South African Museum, Fred decided that he could make a living by collecting animals and immediately headed north even though he had to borrow a considerable sum of money from Thomas Leask, an old friend, in Klerksdorp. Fred took the loan out mostly in goods, including a wide wagon and oxen as well as enough food for a year's expedition. Perhaps the ten years spent elephant hunting were not wasted after all. He would at least be doing the things he loved best in the place where he loved them. In any case, he was past thirty now and it was high time he found something in his life a bit more stable than elephant hunting.

Things went smoothly enough with Lobengula and the Matabele until December of 1883 but then there was a very severe misunderstanding regarding hippopotamuses, which Lobengula had placed on his protected list because his people believed that killing them would cause a severe drought, especially if their bones were not thrown back into the river. This seems picturesque enough a belief today—stranger things are still believed here in Africa—but it was not so in

1883. The Nguni people of the Zulus, Matabele, Angoni, and Shangaan, all related, had some strange ideas of Englishmen themselves. One Zulu told artist, writer, and hunter John G. Millais, Selous's first biographer, that white men came from the bottom of the sea ten days east of Delagoa Bay where they lived entirely underwater with salt waves splashing over them. Another was certain that they came to get *biltong*—dried meat—and took it home to buy wives with it. Another opined that the Englishmen came to his country just to get dry as it was always raining in England. Perhaps that fellow wasn't so far off the mark. During the First Matabele Rebellion, when Cecil John Rhodes had taken over the country with the help of Selous, it is recorded that the Matabele attempted to spear those British artillery shells that were duds, as the tribe was firmly convinced that each shell contained an armed white soldier. So, "sea-cows," or hippos causing droughts, made as much sense as anything else. Whatever the case, the incident known as the "Sea-Cow Row" drove the first major wedge between Selous and Lobengula.

Possibly the Matabele were in a rather poor mood due to the failure of a major raid against the Batawana tribe of western Botswana, but when Selous came through Gubulawayo at the end of the 1883 hunting season, he immediately knew something was up. Lobengula had been told of the slaughter caused by a trader named McMenemy, who had a storehouse crammed with raw *sjamboks*, the terrible hippo or rhino hide whips of South Africa. As Selous came up to the king's house, McMenemy was leaving under a tirade from Lobengula to the effect that he had sinned and he would pay for it. Discussing the matter with him, Selous mentioned that his driver, John Slaipstein, had killed a hippo for food for his men but Lobengula brushed it off saying that there was no case against Fred. But a devious *induna* called Makwaikwi had probably been harboring a jealous grudge against Selous for years and now he struck. He influenced the king to have all the white men tried by a court of *indunas* with the king to give judgment. Selous was blamed as John's boss for killing hippos and fined 60 pounds; ten cattle by the king's reckoning. McMenemy was fined 300 pounds. Fred was furious at what he considered royal perfidy and his relationship with the king as well as the Matabele in general started to decline. Selous had been becoming disillusioned with the bloodshed of lesser tribes caused by the Matabele in their raids, particularly irked by the murder of a man he liked and admired, a native called Lo-Magondi. When the Matabele wiped out to a child an encampment of Mashonas, he was further upset and began to lose his respect for the tribe.

Selous was so upset by the hippo affair that he decided not to hunt in Matabeleland the following season but to the west in King Khama's country. Ultimately he had to stop by at Gubulawayo—now being called Bulawayo—for some business but did move west to the Mababe (Mobabe) Depression.

Selous had had the usual run of luck that the bushveld offered: in 1883 he fell from his horse and smashed his collarbone; he rode into a game-pit chasing kudu in 1886. The fall broke his horse's back and so badly injured the tendons of one of Selous's legs that he was unable to walk for three weeks. But perhaps the most interesting and painful of his injuries was suffered in October of 1880 when he turned his head while chasing a bull eland and as he turned it back, he got a sharp stick in the eye at full force. Despite the terrible pain and temporary loss of sight in the eye, he killed the eland! As he got to camp he became concussed and although the wound to the side of the eye opened and closed several times, he eventually regained his sight even though the tear duct was destroyed. This in itself is not terribly interesting but what is is that eight months later, while walking down Bond Street in London with the famous taxidermist Rowland Ward, Selous began to sneeze. Ward asked him if he had a cold. After a few more sneezes, Fred felt something slide into the back of his mouth. He spat it into his cupped hand. It was a thick chunk of hardwood, three-quarters of an inch long! It had originally been rammed through Selous's facial bone and had been in his head all that time until it worked its way into one of the sinuses and then down to his mouth!

Although he had not actually seen any Mashukulumbwe on his terrible trip with Owen in 1877–78, you would think he had had enough of the northern country. Yet Fred was not one to be defeated in his plans, as he was when he was denied powder by the Transvaal Administrator in 1880. He decided to go alone despite the obvious risks of such a trip. He left Bamangwato in April of 1888 with two wagons, five "salted" horses—ones that had had distemper and survived—and sixteen donkeys. In May, he reached George Westbeech at Pandamatenga; Westbeech advised him against the trip as the northern areas were badly unsettled politically, especially that of the Barotse, and that he should rather take advantage of an invitation from a Mr. Arnot to whom Selous had given a lift some time before. Fred knew that Westbeech would not give him a bum steer and thus decided to head to the Garangazi area, crossing the Zambesi at Wankie Town. With him there was Daniel, a Hottentot mule skinner; Paul, a Natal Zulu; Charley, an interpreter who had been trained among Westbeech's elephant hunters, and two of Khama's men. All of these had the latest breech-loading rifles and knew how to use them. Selous hired other men at Pandamatenga, the plan being to leave the wagons at Wankie and to proceed by donkey train along his old route of eleven years before. No sooner had they crossed the Zambesi than the usual troubles began with Daniel dying of malaria in only four days. Then, the men hired at Pandamatenga all deserted, probably because they had realized that where they were going wasn't too healthy in terms of bullet lead.

Selous hired some Batonga men to replace his depleted entourage and almost came to grief when a Batonga chief arrived with a small army demanding gifts. Selous saved the situation but got some idea of how difficult the Batonga could be: they had seen no white hunters or traders since

David Livingstone came through thirty-five years before, but several Jesuit missionaries had either died or been maltreated in addition to David Thomas and a Portuguese trader having been murdered close to the Zambezi. Selous was very much aware that if he proceeded as far as the Kafue River junction, he would probably be wiped out so he decided to head due north to the Mashukulumbwe despite their bad reputation. After all, there were reputed to be elephants farther north than he had gotten on his first trip.

The next day, Selous and his party reached Monzi, a Batonga chief who lived on a high plateau said to be filthy with game, and so it was. Fred gave Monzi a zebra and an eland he had shot and the chief gave him two guides to take him to the Kafue, but Selous knew better than to cross it. At the second village he struck, he found himself among the ill-reputed and naked Mashukulumbwe, where he was met with a mixed crowd of the cannibals and Barotse, armed and surly. They had come to buy ammunition and powder, they said, but Selous was wary of their attitude, refusing to sell probably because he thought that the stuff would be used against himself. He was probably right as their spokesman told Selous that, "You will live two days more, but on the third day your head will lie in a different place from your body." Hospitable chaps, what?

Selous ignored them and went on the same day, telling his guides to head east to the Mashukulumbwe villages with the intent of camping in the open veld. Paul and Charley, both of whom had experience with natives north of the Zambesi, agreed that camping in the open was the best policy, but Selous allowed himself to be dissuaded and duped into the "jaws of death" by the guides, who insisted that water was only to be found near the villages and they would be forced to camp there. Yet, all went fairly well through a couple of villages until he reached the village of Minenga, the chief of the district. Minenga absolutely insisted on Selous camping next to the village and would not take no for an answer. Although he knew he was in a bad spot, Fred decided to brave it out and started making a camp and a stockade of flimsy cornstalks and poles to secure the donkeys.

There was a lull and Selous wondered if perhaps he had exaggerated his fears. Weapons—mostly fiercely barbed light javelins—were put away and the Mashukulumbwe even had a dance with the Batonga men. When the women came down to eat with Selous's men, even he gave a sigh of relief as the presence of women usually meant that there would be no violence. Maybe Selous had misjudged the cannibals. Yup, maybe . . .

When night fell, Fred decided that he had wronged the "savages." He had already gone to bed when an invitation—interpreted by Charley—came from Minenga to come and drink beer. Selous turned him down with thanks. Later, Selous thanked his stars that he did not go as without a doubt he would have been murdered.

Everything went fine the next day; Selous hunted and was later engulfed by virtual herds of natives in camp. However, they left at sundown. Selous went to bed, where his brain whirled with plans until at about nine o'clock he noticed the figure of a man coming around the edge of the donkey herd and passing on tiptoe along a line of smoking, smouldering fires. He recognized him as one of the guides Monzi had provided. The man knelt down and shook Paul by the leg, urgently whispering to the Zulu in an excited hiss. What the hell was going on? Paul said to Charley, "Tell our master the news; wake him up."

Selous answered in anxious tones, "What is it, Charley? I am awake."

"The man says, sir, that all the women have left the village and he thinks something is wrong." Oh yes. Something was wrong!

Fred shared the guide's opinion and put on his shoes and coat as well as his cartridge belt, which only had four rounds in it. As he was dressing in a quiet frenzy, Selous ordered that all the fires be put out and doused with sand. An absolute African black engulfed the little camp, only the sounds of insects punctuating the night. Then they stopped.

Selous held a whispered conference with Charley and Paul, who were sitting on their blankets with their rifles in their hands. Fred proposed a reconnaissance of the village to eavesdrop and perhaps find out what was going on. But, first, he had better restock his cartridge belt, he thought, and reached for his ammo bag. As he did so, three shots went off almost in his face and several more gave their flaming muzzle blasts around the little camp. Selous realized that the muzzles were actually in the circle of the camp and that the Mashuku-lumbwe must have wriggled up to the perimeter and shoved their barrels between the cornstalks of the *scherm* they had built. Somehow, even though the first three shots were obviously meant for Paul, Charley, and Selous, nobody was hit so far. Selous snatched for his rifle beside him as Charley and Paul jumped up and ducked past him. "Into the grass!" Selous yelled in Afrikaans as a sleet of the javelins thudded and pattered through the large leather bags that held his baggage.

"I can fairly say that I retained my presence of mind perfectly at this juncture," Selous recalled. His rifle was unloaded as it always was to prevent accidents in camp. As he slipped a cartridge in, he ran backward across the furrowed ground that separated his camp from the long grass, but the Mashu-kulumbwe were already a milling mass among his own men. Three times Selous drew a quick bead with his express sights as one of his own men came between the muzzle and the enemy. He was within thirty feet of the murky grass, his back to it, when with a fierce yell another detachment of the cannibals charged out of it to cut off retreat. At this point, Fred caught his heel and fell backward as two men rushing out of the grass actually fell over him, one over his body the other tripping on his legs. Fred regained his feet in a second and bulled his way across the few yards into the cover. He had made it into the grass, which covered him like a dark blanket. It was every man for himself.

In the black miasma of the grass, Fred sat listening. Cautiously, he stood up and heard the Mashukulumbwe looting the camp, but it was too dark to get a shot at any of them; each time a fire would blaze up it was extinguished with sand. He was starting to realize his position: there was no point in firing at the enemy. He had only four shots between him and a terrible death and being eaten.

> But I now thought no more of firing at them. I had had time to realize the full horror of my position. A solitary Englishman, alone in Central Africa, in the middle of a hostile country, without blankets or anything else but what he stood in and a rifle with four cartridges. . . . Could I only have found Paul or Charley or even one of my own Kafirs, I thought my chance of getting back to Pandamatenga would be much increased for I should then have an interpreter, I myself knowing but little of the languages spoken north of the Zambesi. . . .

Fred began to ease through the grass, whistling softly—very softly—to see if any of his men had taken the same refuge from the attack and might be lying doggo. But there was no one. Reasoning that if there had been any survivors they wouldn't stick around near Minenga's village, he thought this was good advice for himself. He decided to head for Monzi's, where he had been well received because of the meat he had given the chief. As he began his terrible journey, he saw that the Mashukulmbwe had now built up the fires and were dividing his property by their eerie, flickering light. First, Selous made his cautious way to the Magoi-ee River ford, but he was lucky to spot a group of warriors obviously meant to intercept him. Slipping downstream, he eased into the crocodile-swarming water and swam to the other side.

Selous also had a knife and a few matches as well as his watch, but he also had some 300 miles to cover through hostile country where the enemy knew he would likely travel.

Alone, perhaps even previously friendly natives might murder him for his gun and shoes.

Fred walked all night until he came to another river. This he crossed by walking on rocks, which left no tracks. He spent all day watching the ford and heard voices on the far side of the small stream. He almost gave a shout, thinking the voices belonged to his own men, but fortunately resisted. Instead, he slipped the safety off his rifle. Soon, he saw the tall, waving conical headdresses that were exclusively Mashukulumbwe and eased down. He couldn't understand how the two warriors didn't see him, so close across the water were they, but, after discussing his boot tracks in the sand, they went away. Selous was ready to kill them both instantly had they seen him as they would have spread the alarm over the countryside.

When the warriors were safely gone, Fred realized how hungry he was and thought he was far enough away from the village to shoot. Happily, a wildebeest wandered by and he was able to kill it with one shot.

He had a good feed and set off again at sunset with a supply of meat, heading south by the Southern Cross. He traveled all night, lay up the following day, and at dusk the next evening he started on his way again. After a hard hoofing, he reached the last Mashukulumbwe village, only about two hours from Monzi's, and decided that as it was far from Minenga's he would risk stopping at it. It was well after midnight and Selous was half-dead of cold when he arrived to find a boy sleeping by the fire near a half-dozen huts. Selous woke him and asked for water and understood the boy when he said there was none. The talking must have disturbed the inhabitants of one of the nearby huts as a man appeared and, as he was unarmed, Fred told him his story. The white man spoke in Sindebele and the native in Satonga so the conversation was something less than satisfactory. Yet, when Fred told him that he was thirsty, the man went to his hut and brought Selous a calabash of water. He had just finished the water

when he heard whispering going on in a hut next door and
saw a man emerge, scuttle off into the darkness, and return
with a muzzle-loader. Shortly after, there was the ominous
sound of the gas-pipe being loaded and tamped with the
ramrod. But Selous was so comforted on the icy night by the
fire that he decided he would spend an hour or two by the
fire and warm up. Unfortunately, he fell asleep. . . .

Selous didn't know how long he was asleep, but he awoke
with a start when he sensed someone near him and leaped
to his feet. There were two men of the village, but they were
unarmed. Selous understood that they were asking him how
he came to be back and he told them of the treachery at
Minenga's village. Sitting back down, he told his story—again
in Sindebele—and could not tell how well he was understood.
As he explained, he gradually kept turning his body toward
the men until his rifle lay almost behind him. He heard a
faint sound behind him and before he could grab the rifle it
was snatched by a third man who immediately disappeared
into the darkness beyond the fire's light. Before he could say
anything, a stunned Selous glanced at the hut where he had
heard the musket being loaded and sure as hell there was
another man aiming a gun at him from less than ten yards
away! Instantly, Fred leaped into the darkness, grabbing a
chunk of wildebeest meat as he went. He made the long grass
near the camp and was not followed. His would-be killer
never got off his shot or perhaps the musket misfired.

Selous knew only too well that his chances of getting back
across the Zambesi without his rifle were now ten percent of
what they had been. An unarmed white man hardly stood a
chance. Still, he had no choice but to head for Monzi's village,
walking as fast as he could to keep out the cold. He could no
longer kill food and knew he was as good as naked prey for
any warrior who might wish to spear him to death.

At the first smear of false dawn he reached Monzi's and sat
by a fire until the village was awake, not risking a spear
thrown in fear. Monzi and his men—thank heaven he had

one that could speak a bit of Sindebele and Selous was able to tell his story—were friendly, much to Fred's relief. But old Monzi was quite upset when Selous got to the part about his rifle being stolen at the next village and told the white that he must leave the village immediately as he would be followed and killed. Monzi stuffed Selous's pockets with peanuts and hustled him off with three of his men, who told him in no uncertain terms not to trust the Batongas, who would murder him if they had the chance. After a mile, Fred was on his own again.

Soon after the three had left him, Selous hid in some bush, lit a small fire, and roasted some meat and peanuts. Then a thought hit him as he stared at some hills about ten miles away. Somewhere in those hills lay the village of a friend of Westbeech, a Barotse named, depending upon the language he was addressed in, Sikabenga. Although Selous took many chances asking directions of intervening Batonga villagers, he finally made it to Sikabenga's and then, after days of intrigue with the Barotse, down to the banks of the Zambesi. There he met, to their collective joy, Charley, Paul, and some of his other men. There had been twelve killed and six wounded out of his party of twenty-five. His men greeted him with wonder, kissing his hands and patting his chest. By a miracle both Paul and Charley had made it out of the camp unwounded, and Charley said that he was at one time close to Selous and even heard the shot that killed the wildebeest but was unable to find him. Paul had lost Selous's double ten-gauge Rigby rifle while crossing the river and had nearly drowned. A month later, having replaced some of the things he had lost, Selous was again hunting across the Zambesi!

That Selous finally turned against the tyranny of Lobengula is as much African political history as is his association with John Cecil Rhodes, who prevented the Portuguese from annexing what became Southern Rhodesia. Selous led the first pioneer column of the Charter Company personally, and as they neared their destination, he received from the British South Africa Company a check in the amount of 3858 pounds and 10 shillings, enough money to solve his financial problems. He worked for two years, 1891 and 1892, in Mashonaland making treaties, surveying and such, and in 1892 he returned home to England. In 1893 he published *Travel and Adventure in Southeast Africa,* which contained not only a riveting account of his many adventures since the publication of his first book, but also glowing descriptions of the many potentialities of Mashonaland and Manicaland. He returned to Rhodesia in 1893 and assisted in the suppression of the first Matabele insurrection. When he went back to England that year, he thought it was for good and married Marie Catherine Gladys Maddy, who became his widow. However, he returned to Rhodesia in 1895 with his wife to manage an estate and was just in time to serve in the Second Matabele War, during which his homestead was burned by the rebels. In 1896 Selous wrote *Sunshine and Storm in Rhodesia,* a chronicle of his experiences as well as a recounting of the causes for the two Matabele wars and the resources of Charterland.

From this time onward—probably because he both loved the outdoor life and could now afford it—he devoted most of his time to big-game hunting, but now as a passion rather than as a profession. In 1894–95 he visited Asia Minor, and in 1897 and 1898 he made two visits to the Rocky Mountains. He was in Newfoundland three times, in 1900, 1901, and 1905. In 1904 and 1906, he was shooting in the Yukon. In later years he again turned to his beloved Africa, spending time in British East Africa and the Nile regions. But throughout his career, Selous was much more than merely a successful hunter. He once said that he wasn't really a hunter but a naturalist. Wherever he went he took the deepest interest in the habits and personalities of all the animals he encountered. His keen observation, immense patience, and a retentive memory combined to make him a field naturalist of exceptional excellence. These qualities, along with his decades of experience, raised him to the position of acknowledged doyen of the whole tribe of modern hunters. He was a close friend of Teddy Roosevelt and came out to Kenya Colony on the same ship as Teddy and Kermit. But despite popular belief that Selous was Roosevelt's white hunter, they did not hunt together. Fred was also a guest at the White House.

One of Fred's best books is his *African Nature Notes and Reminiscences* (1908), in which he summarizes much of his incredible knowledge of African game as well as such diverse fauna as butterflies. Perhaps *The Times* (London) of January 8th, 1917, sums him and his writing up best: "All his books are written in a spirit of transparent honesty and in a simple and direct style, reflecting the character of the author, whose straightforwardness, integrity, hospitality, and kindness of heart were as well known to hosts of friends as the qualities which made him so successful a hunter."

That's not a bad thing to have one of the world's most respected newspapers say about one. . . .

Selous and Gladys had two children, Freddy and Harold. Freddy became a fighter pilot when he entered the army at seventeen and was killed when the wings of his plane simply folded up in flight as he was diving at 15,000 feet on a German plane, exactly a year after his father's death. Harold must have been sort of a black sheep, as even Selous's friend and first biographer, Johnny Millais, after heaping praise on Freddy, said only that Harold was educated at Radley College and that he was expected to take a commission soon, in October of 1918. My good friend, Brian Marsh, adds credence to this idea when he recounts that a family friend who was with Selous when he was killed ran across Harold Sherborne Selous in Nyasaland in the 1920s. The friend, G. P. Fuller, contacted Harold, who was in the local administration, going some miles out of his way to do so. When they arrived, they found that Harold could care less about the last day of his father's life, his death, and funeral. Harold offered Fuller and his wife tea but they refused and left.

54

But I get ahead of myself. . . .

When World War I broke out, Fred immediately volunteered for front-line duty in France. But despite a medical certificate that showed the sixty-three-year-old was in wonderful health and the fact that he could speak French, quite a bit of German, and could make himself understood by the Belgians with his Afrikaans, he was turned down personally after his case had gotten as far as Lord Kitchener, who was then the British Secretary of State for War. Steaming with rage, he could do nothing else but join the Surry Special Constabulary. He might have spent the war there had it not been for the battle of Tanga, an East African action in which the German Lt. Col. Paul von Lettow-Vorbeck with his *Schutztruppe* whipped almost ten times his strength in empire troops who tried an amphibious assault. It was a massacre. To date, East Africa had been very much a side show compared to Belgium or France but Tanga thoroughly scared the British. The British were also slaughtered at Moshi. To crown things, the retreating, beaten force of Tanga actually had to talk the customs officials at Mombasa out of charging them duty on their equipment!

A personal friend of Selous was a Col. Daniel "Jerry" Driscoll, who had fought in both Burma and later in the Second Boer War, where he had raised his own irregulars, called Driscoll's Scouts. With war looming, he wrote Selous a week before hostilities opened on August 4th, 1914, proposing that he form a "Legion of Frontiersmen," the 25th Battalion of Royal Fusiliers, to fight in German East Africa (Tanganyika later, then Tanzania). In fact, Selous had his physical exam to join this outfit first, but the authorities, wrapped up in the war in Europe, looked askance at such a ragtag group fighting in Africa, and Driscoll's proposal was turned down. But after Tanga, he was advised that perhaps he didn't have such a bad idea after all. The Legion of Frontiersmen, better known as "the Old and the Bold," came into existence.

A stranger or more colorful battalion couldn't be imagined.

Naturally it attracted dozens of professional hunters and other Afrophiles, but it was also composed of the zaniest group ever to put on uniforms. In fact, many men, tired of waiting as the war got on, had joined other units but deserted their regular army posts to join when Driscoll was given permission to form the 25th. One of their sergeants was also a well-known writer on things African, C. T. Stoneham, an Englishman:

> *They were the oddest crew; from music-hall comedians to border gunmen, with some university professors thrown in. There were Moroccan bandits and Chinese generals, all British, but imbued with the exotic customs of their adopted lands. In common, they had knowledge of the remote parts of the Empire, and the will to fight. But their discipline was deplorable and to the last they considered themselves guerillas rather than regular troops.*
>
> *The Legion had been founded by Roger Pocock as a sort of brotherhood of adventurers and its members were drawn from all the social classes. We had two ex-Members of Parliament, cowboys, prize-fighters, ex-regular officers, a one-time submarine commander—all in my company alone. Distributed elsewhere were painters, singers, acrobats, comedians, and, I should imagine, burglars. We could put on a concert composed entirely of well-known stage professionals and hold a boxing tournament in which famous glove-fighters contended. Professional composers wrote our marching songs, idols of the footlights sang them. Quite a number of them were deserters from other regiments, for whom the police sought desultorily, having other, more important, things to engage their attention.*
>
> *While we trained there was much speculation as to where this special corps would be employed. It was thought the Near East would be our venue; we might be landed in Egypt to fight the Turks. The presence among our officers of such men F. C. Selous, Cherry Kearton* [African wildlife photographer], *and George Outram* [early professional hunter], *all experienced big game hunters, might have suggested Africa, but we never thought of that. It was natural to find hunters and explorers in the Legion regiment* [sic], *we had them from China*

and the Rockies, with a few tiger-shooting sahibs of the old
school in addition.

Other sources list as Fusiliers: a Honduran general, a Buckingham Palace footman, some French Foreign Legion troops, an opera singer, and a lighthouse keeper. Quite a crew, indeed!

Selous was commissioned lieutenant and was company commander of Company A.

The Frontiersmen were sent to Mombasa in May of 1915 where they were reviewed by General Tighe. One of those present was Captain Richard Meinertzhagen, himself a great hunter and naturalist. Although Selous stood to strict attention, Meinertzhagen was delighted to see him and the two of them got off into a long discussion of the validity of the Nakuru subspecies of hartebeest and the nesting habits of Icelandic ducks. Tighe indignantly cut them off after a while, suggesting that he and Meinertzhagen were present to inspect a battalion and not to hear the debate of a natural history society.

There being little point in refighting in print the history of the East African Campaign of World War I, just let me say that the Fusiliers suffered terribly and had very few victories against the wily will-o'-the-wisp, Lt. Col. (later Major General) Paul von Lettow-Vorbeck and his black *Schutztruppe*. In fact, when the war was over and lost, von Lettow was the only German to have a parade in his honor in Berlin. But the biggest cause of fatalities, especially on the British side, which was mostly white, was disease, primarily malaria and dysentery, which killed three times as many men as were taken by the enemy. The Fusiliers arrived in Africa with 1100 men and had been whittled down to 700 in six months, at the start of 1916. Of the 700, Selous opined that no more than 400 were up to a twenty-mile march with full pack. By the first anniversary of the Old and the Bold, only 450 men of the 25th were still left for combat. Selous was quite proud that he was one of them and that his excellent constitution had withstood disease.

After the ferocious Battle of Bukoba, Selous was promoted captain and Driscoll was very proud of him. He even received Teddy Roosevelt's congratulation in a letter for a "first-class little fight."

Selous wrote to Johnny Millais (the only friend he corresponded with on a first-name basis) on May 2nd, 1916, that from May 4th of the year before until February 6th of 1916 he had never taken a day's rest or leave and was never a single day off duty or away from his company. From the last date, he had to lie up for a week because of an infected attack of "jiggers," a type of flea that lays its eggs under a victim's toenails in a small sac. I have had jiggers several times and assure you that they are a matter best left to one's black gunbearer or camp staff. They are marvelous in their microsurgery, removing the sac full of eggs without rupturing it. They use a long, sharp thorn or a steel needle. But Selous wasn't so lucky and the inflammation spread all the way to his groin glands.

Fred was also suffering from a most unromantic malady, hemorrhoids, which he had been able to keep in check for a while with ointment, but it finally got the best of him. On the first anniversary of the 25th's landing at Mombasa, he wrote again to Johnny that he had seen a doctor and that he was advised not to take any long marches. In June, he was invalided home by a medical board for an operation that was completely successful and spent twelve days in the hospital and then home for a short rest. In August, he went to Africa again with a draft of 400 men, going by way of Cape Town, Mombasa, the Uganda Railroad, to the Usambara Valley; then to Tanga where he was stuck with his men for almost eight weeks, until December 2nd. Writing to Abel Chapman, another friend and hunter-writer, Selous says: "With the latest drafts our batallion has had 1400 men out here. All we have left of them are 149 at Kijabe (but these must mostly be unfit for further hard service) and 394 here, of which latter number 101 are sick. Two have died in hospital this week. Of the two fine Rhodesian regiments, it is said that only 68 are fit. The North Lancs Regt. has wasted to nothing in spite of many drafts. . . ."

Although it seemed mostly twilight for the British in East Africa, there was one bright ray of sun for Selous: he was awarded the Distinguished Service Order for "conspicuous gallantry, resourcefulness and endurance." The British D.S.O. is no small gong to have on your uniform breast.

Selous was adored by his men. Often he gave lectures of reminiscing his elephant hunting days and, as by far the oldest man in the 25th Royal Fusiliers, he must have seemed a father figure to some. Their subsequent comments would have made him blush in life: "He was my hero as a boy and remains so now. He was the easiest of all men to cheat, but no one ever dared to do it. Anything mean or sordid literally shrivelled up in his presence." And, "Everybody liked and admired him."

It was during a British push that began on New Year's Day, 1917, that Selous was killed. The *Schutztruppe* were fighting a vicious rear-guard action and on January 3rd had made three bayonet charges and fought hand-to-hand. Although more numerous, they were nearly as exhausted as the British at this point. Near Beho-Beho, German East Africa, Selous and his men were ordered to cut off the German retreat on a bush road. However, they were late and the Germans had already started to pull out. Selous and his men attacked them and he was shot through the head and killed. Or, better said, he was *finally* shot in the head and killed as there may be a case that he was first shot in the right arm or side and fought on for as much as half an hour. His old friend, Denis D. Lyell, a famous writer and hunter in his own right (see the Peter Capstick Library), some time later wrote a piece for *The Field,* a sporting British newspaper magazine, quoting a soldier who had been actually in the fight in which Selous died.

We were on a crest line at the time with the Germans in front
and on both flanks. We were subjected to heavy enfilade fire, and
could not locate the enemy properly owing to the wooded nature

of their positions. At this stage Selous went forward down the slope about 15 yards, and was just raising his glasses in order to see (more particularly) where certain snipers were when he received his first wound in the side. He was half-turning towards us when he was shot through the side of the head. He died instantly.

This is interpreted by me to mean that he was shot "bang-bang," first through the right side and then through the head. There is another story, among others, that also has merit—that of a Corporal R. Davis, who was actually commended for helping the stricken Selous. Davis says in his report to the *Times:*

He was not killed instantly, as I fought over him for fully ten minutes. He was shot in the head but this wound was not the cause of his death; this wound was caused by a splinter some half an hour previous and when Captain Selous was asked if he was wounded he stated that it was nothing very much and insisted on going on. He went over the ridges at Beho-Beho and was kneeling near a small tree and was seen after the action had been in progress for about 15 minutes to drop his rifle. I immediately went over to him and stayed with him for fully ten minutes before he received his fatal wound, and then I carried or dragged him to the rear of a small hill and there he died. His boy [batman], Ramizani, who had been with him some considerable years, cried when he saw Captain Selous dead, and stood upright on top of the ridge in face of terrible German machine-gun fire and brought out [from] a tree the black sniper who wounded Captain Selous.

I think that any who may have been legitimate snipers during their military careers would agree with me that, in fact, the term "sniper" is flattering the enemy. Accurately aimed fire does not necessarily come from "snipers," and I would be very surprised if there were any formal snipers in that campaign.

Captain R. M. Haines of the South African forces was told by those who were at the action at Beho-Beho that Selous was first hit in the right arm and that it was broken and bandaged, but that Selous stayed with the company. "A little later he was hit again in the mouth and was killed instantly and apparently painlessly."

General Jan Smuts, who later became Prime Minister of the Union of South Africa and who was the leading general for much of the campaign, told John Millais, "Heavy firing on both sides then commenced, and Selous at once deployed his company, attacked the Germans, who greatly outnumbered him, and drove them back into the bush. It was at this moment that Selous was struck dead by a shot in the head."

Colonel Driscoll, commander of the 25th, wrote of Selous's death, "Captain Selous, the great hunter, was one of the hardest men in battalion, in spite of his sixty-five years. He was shot dead while leading his company through the bush against an enemy four times their strength. Lieutenant Dutch, another very gallant man, took his place and received a mortal wound immediately afterwards."

Whatever the actual technicalities of the action, Frederick Courteney Selous, D.S.O., was dead. Perhaps Millais put it best when he wrote of his friend, "Thus died Frederick Selous of the Great Heart, a splendid Englishman, who in spite of age and love of life, gave up all pleasant things to follow the iron path of duty."

Selous was buried with four of the six who were killed at Beho-Beho and his funeral was one of the most impressive of the campaign. Even von Lettow-Vorbeck later wrote that Selous was "well known among the Germans on account of his charming manner and exciting stories." Some years later, the other bodies were exhumed but Selous's grave was capped with cement and a tablet giving his name and the date he was killed attached. The grave is in modern-day Tanzania, in one of the world's largest game reserves. It is called the Selous Game Reserve.

During his lifetime, Fred gave many specimens to the British Museum (Natural History) as well as keeping what he called his own museum. Shortly after his death, his widow, Gladys, gave the entire contents of Selous's "museum" for the British people to enjoy at the Natural History Museum. The sole memorial that was dedicated to Selous was presented by subscribers and unveiled at the Natural History Museum on June 10th, 1920. It is the work of W. R. Colton, Royal Academy, and consists of a fine bust in bronze in a granite setting with a plaque below depicting some of the better-known species of African big game. The stone is a block of syenite from the Bon Accord quarry, presented by the government of the then-Union of South Africa. I have seen it many times while visiting the world's largest known pair of elephant tusks in the cellar of this museum.

Selous's name also was chosen as the name of Rhodesia's special forces unit, the "Selous Scouts," during the bush war that only came to an end when Robert Mugabe came to power in 1980. It is fitting that the elite were named for the elite.

Part Two

C. J. P.
Ionides

The stars were like diamond chips against black velvet as the young man stole closer to the big hut. He paused as a Scops owl chirped to the setting moon, carefully picking his way along the bare earth studded with dry corn husks and patches of moon-yellow grass. His sandals, cut from the tread of an old automobile tire, padded softly against the bare path as he slipped closer through the sleeping village; ever closer to death.

She was the old man's youngest wife, not very bright for her fourteen years, but her pointed breasts jiggled interestingly, he thought, when she carried a pot of beer on her head. The man listened to a distant yap of jackals and the hilarity of hyenas somewhere over the dark bush. And she was pretty, he decided. That she spent most of her time living foolish dreams, chasing mental butterflies, mattered to the man not at all. She was already married to the *Mzee,* the old man who now was at least a march away into the bush of Tanganyika, where "one wanders in the wilderness." But the young man decided that she was worth all the trouble he was going to. She certainly knew how to, well; she was a natural talent, enthusiastic and skilled for her short years. He knew that it would be an interesting night as he saw her in a shade of moon shadow and slipped to her side. Oh, yes, it would be a very fine night. It would be so fine that he had forgotten the spirit of the *mundumgu,* the witch doctor, that lurked in the dark, killing and eating people. He did not see the greenish yellow dilated eyes that followed his every move, but they saw him as he took the girl's hand and led her from her husband's hut to a wall-less, grass-roofed shed. Once there, she giggled and took over.

The eyes saw everything from twenty yards away and the lion stifled a small sound in his throat as he lay quietly in a fringe of dead grass and branches off the path. A small night breeze rippled his amber mane and shimmered the reflected starlight on his tawny hide. He relaxed. He knew he had plenty of time.

When the moans had reached a quiet crescendo, the lion slithered forward on his belly toward the shed. A few feet from his victim he sank his whitish claws into the red earth for his final rush. It was easy. . . .

The man was not dead when the lion pulled him off the woman, its teeth sunk into the muscles of his back. He clung to grass on the floor and even grabbed a support pole as the lion dragged him off. But his struggles were wasted against the irresistible strength of the big cat. The lion pulled him into some light cover and started to eat him. That the man was not dead and his screams slashed the night meant nothing to the lion. Not a hut door opened and soon only the screeches of the young wife, lightly clawed herself, were to be heard against the luminous sky. When her husband returned, he found he had a great reputation as a wizard who kept lions as slaves. For what other reason would a lion choose to destroy his youngest wife's lover? Yes, the old husband had new respect and decided to say nothing of his vengeance.

It was dawn when the drum call of two shorts and a long throb was heard in the white man's camp. "Iodine" Ionides knew what the drum was saying: *ngula mtwe,* a man is eaten. In a few moments the fifth-generation Englishman of Greek descent left his ranger's camp with a tracker and a gunbearer named Hemedi Ngoe. As his quick strides covered several miles of the ground to the source of the drum, Ionides was met by the game scout of the area, who had already found fresh lion spoor. The scout immediately led Ionides to the drummer who was almost paralytic with fear. It was believed as gospel that the "slave" lion had no patience with people who told Ionides—the game ranger—what he did and where he did it. Ionides was delighted to find a man more afraid than himself as the lion spoor was almost smoking, the big cat walking a short way in front of Ionides.

Some dusty distance went by through the native compounds until Ionides realized that the lion was only a little bit ahead of him and his man. It was then that the bird arrived, a "honey guide".

The honey guide is half of one of the strangest symbioses in nature, the other half being sometimes man, sometimes a honey badger, that super tough, little, testicle-attacking badger also known as the "ratel." The nine species of the honey guide form temporary alliances with either man or badger, trading knowledge of a beehive for some of the spoils, usually the bee grubs. If a very good supply of these grubs is not left for the honey guide, it is legend and quite possibly fact that the honey guide will lead its next client to other than a beehive: perhaps a snake or a lion. Vindictive little bastard, isn't he?

Whatever the truth—and it is believed that a honey guide capable of guiding a person is also capable of *mis*guiding a person—the bird in Ionides's case was definitely playing both ends against the middle. As Ionides says, there is definite proof of this activity—but not of the bird's motive, no matter how obvious it may seem.

Ionides says that the hot spoor of the man-eater led through fairly open country and the bird spent about half its time with him and the other half with the lion. Fairly spooky stuff, what? "It would fly to us twittering insistently, then go over to the man-eater: it was fairly open country and we could follow the passage of our quarry by the birds [sic] suddenly getting up from bushes as it passed under. We came upon several places where the lion had tried to lie down for a rest, but had got up and moved on because of the racket this infernal bird was making. This performance went on for quite a long time, till the lion suddenly bolted away, probably in an attempt to shake off the pest."

At length, or perhaps with darkness, the honey guide gave up, but "Iodine" Ionides was not an easy man to discourage. Over the next four days, the white man clung to the lion's tracks but kept losing him. On the fifth day, word came that the lion had killed a pig in a nearby village—this probably made Ionides wonder if the lion was the same animal, as man-eaters usually do not kill anything but men. Yet, checking the spoor with his trackers, Ionides definitely determined that this was the same lion. A man had heard the pig squealing in the cover, and Ionides immediately followed on his hands and knees behind his tracker. But he was quick to recognize that there was no need for a tracker now. He made the man get behind him; by the spoor the lion was only a few yards ahead. Ionides even saw the bushes moving as the lion decamped. He had seen the white man. The half-eaten carcass of the pig drew flies in a steady whining drone, especially where it was still wet with the lion's saliva.

Iodine followed the lion tracks until he saw where the cat had stopped on his own spoor to see if he had been followed. Of course, he had. Ionides called the hunt off to the narrow-eyed disbelief of his men. The "Greek" went back to camp for breakfast.

Ionides lolled away the morning reading a book until he had lunch. He waited until it was a searing, scorching temperature at two o'clock and then snapped the book shut. Hemedi looked up at him.

"Now we will hunt that mother-seducer. We will get him while he is having his afternoon sleep." Ionides checked his .470 Nitro Express and clicked it shut with the finality of a fine safe. Somehow, I feel that he used a term other than "mother-seducer."

Iodine found that the lion had taken a circular path around the village and for two hours followed the tracks. A couple of times the Greek found where the lion had lain down and then gotten up from his still-warm impression. Ionides knew that he had only missed the lion by a couple of seconds. The lion had moved. In my opinion—and I wasn't there but have hunted man-eaters before—the lion had moved as the angle of shade had shifted as the sun moved. Ionides kept on his hands and knees, following the fresh tracks through the impossibly heavy brush.

As Ionides and his gun-bearer, Hemedi Ngoe, crawled along the lion's spoor, Hemedi suddenly froze to ebony as he saw something ahead. Iodine, somehow sensing that Hemedi had stopped, eased his gaze back. Yup. The Tanganyikan had seen something. Certainly his fixed eyes were on the lion, but where was the cat?

The Greek now smelled the lion through his thin nostrils, a smell that nothing else smelled like. Wet, musty cat . . .

It was only a couple of yards away, a white blaze of lion fur that shone through a gap in the bush. It was so thick that Ionides could not even bring the rifle to his shoulder but had to bring his shoulder to his rifle. He squirmed the Nitro into place and, his index trigger finger being infected, used his middle finger to fire a 500-grain slug into the lion. In the cover, the bellow of the rifle was so loud that Iodine was almost stunned. The lion smashed bush and grass for a few yards and then there was almost no sound. Frozen into stone, Ionides waited with his second barrel. There was no need. There were a few groans and a blood-wet roar. The man-eater was dead.

This particular man-eater changed Iodine's tactics with lions forever. He killed several of these cats with the cheek-by-lion's-jowl approach of hunting at midday, the most sporting if not the most popular method of lion hunting in southern Africa today; having done it I will assure you of that!

Lions are as poor sleepers as large dogs, usually having

nightmares with the frequency that most pooches run in their dreams. Iodine would take up a spoor with the greatest care, following on hands and knees and stopping every few minutes to listen for snores. He recalls the time when he hunted a man-eater that had eaten a fat woman as his last victim. She apparently gave the lion bad dreams or perhaps it was the fault of the wart hog upon which the lion had snacked for dessert. When Ionides caught up with the big male man-eater, the lion was having nightmares at midday, groaning and moaning as Iodine crept up to him. As the Anglo-Greek says, "He never knew what hit him."

Somewhat socially and racially unreconstructed, "Iodine" Ionides was nothing less than an eccentric as well as a character of the first order. By his thinking, that a man-eater took a few tribesmen was to be expected, but when a female man-eater ate his bathtub one night, it became an open declaration of war! As he said, this was a fairly young lioness that had managed to swing a young and impressionable male into her game plan, although she was the prime mover in what so far had netted three human victims. He noticed that she had become bolder with each killing and finally noted that, "She had the makings of becoming a real menace," which seems fair evaluation of a lioness that has already killed three people and eaten them!

That Ionides knew what he was doing was shown by the fact that he used "roaring sticks," cut branch direction-finders that spelled out the nocturnal movements of lions each time they roared during the night. When it was light enough to hunt, the last stick positioned by his staff would indicate the distance, by its length, as well as the direction of the roars. But when Ionides arrived at the scene of the last human killing, it was too late to hunt. Relying on his men and the roaring sticks, Bwana Ionides settled down in his small tent for a good night's "kip."

By his own admission, Iodine slept unusually securely that night as he normally barely dozed in man-eater country. Staying near the village, he had made sure that all his men were sleeping in huts but the sound of snoring natives invariably made him sleep far enough away so that his slumber would not be disturbed by assorted "sawmills."

When he awoke early next morning to have "a slash," as the British would put it, he saw lion spoor all around his tent. At this moment his personal servant came up and asked where Ionides's canvas ground sheet might be. It acted as his bathtub, a shallow depression being scraped out of the earth and the hollow filled with warm water for the Greek's bath. Usually the canvas sheet was kept rolled like a blanket at the base of Ionides's bed. There were lion tracks exactly there.

What had happened during the night was that the lioness had actually entered Iodine's tent, grabbed the canvas roll thinking it was the man, and run off into the night with it. It was found fifty yards away, literally in ribbons. Apparently the lioness was as upset with her "catch" as Ionides was when he found out what had happened. Suppressing the cold chill he got on finding the lady lion's tracks next to his bed, he told his men that the lioness would sure as hell pay for the ground sheet.

The fresh tracks led down a murky dry water course, but the spooring was pretty easy in the red earth. In less than the best part of an hour, Ionides put a 500-grain .470 slug into a pale patch of lion skin, the only part that he could see about twenty yards away. The lioness gave a helluva roar and instantly charged the sound of the shot. Ionides had two barrels going for him, but the cover was so thick that he could not see to fire. He knew he must wait until he was positive of the second shot being fatal. His life depended on it.

The lioness happened to hit a strong creeper across her chest and paused in her charge for a minisecond to bite through it. It was all Ionides needed. His final shot killed her at *nine feet.* The Greek noted that his first shot had been through the lioness' stomach, or "her lunch," as he put it. Had the female not taken the canvas sheet as a surrogate, that "lunch" would have been Ionides's body.

The Greek notes that this lioness was in terrible shape, little more than baggy skin and angular bones. He mentions that this was in the Kilwa district of Tanganyika where lions had little to eat but people. Ionides says that in the same district he hunted a pride of six lions over a period of two weeks in which he killed the four adults and let the two young members go as they were able to hunt for themselves. In my opinion, should I dare to question the great Greek, that may have been a mistake as they were already accustomed to eating human flesh. But I am satisfied that Ionides had his own reasons. He also says that he understood why the pride had turned to people for food as the four adults of this pride had not eaten in *two weeks* to the certain knowledge of Ionides, who stayed on their tracks the whole time of the hunt.

One of the worst frights of Ionides's life came from a female member of this particular pride when he had bad ammunition. I know how he felt. I was in the middle of a lion charge from a huge male (he places number twenty-seven of all lions killed in Africa and registered with Rowland Ward) when my good friend and professional hunter, Gordon Cundill, had three misfires and a dud with his .500 Nitro Express double rifle. We were repelling the boarder at this time, which was a very poor choice of the chronology to start developing misfires or duds. (Please see Peter Capstick's Africa: *A Return to the Long Grass*, St. Martin's Press, New York, 1987, if you want the whole story. You also get a large strip of my skin as a souvenir. There is a slight extra charge for the epidermis. . . .)

Ionides had wounded this particular female and saw that it had taken invisible refuge behind a piece of cow crap, although it could have done as well with a supine dime. Amazing how lions disappear and hide behind the most unlikely of natural features such as small clumps of grass and chunks of bad breath.

Ionides had already wounded this lioness, which likely didn't help her outlook in the first place. With one loaded barrel left, he ran after the lioness into scrub cover. At ten yards she came out of cover and Ionides put the wide rear sight with the mated front sight on the center of her chest and squeezed.

Nothing happened except the most depressing sound in dangerous game hunting: a *click*! Ionides was somewhat disconcerted as he'd thought he had an easy time coming of finishing her off. He switched barrels, ejecting the case of his first long brass round, and inserted the second. As Ionides says: another *click*. Oh, my! *Big* problems! About 400 pounds worth. . . .

Ionides put his hand behind him for more ammo, but the cool lead-and-nickel lengths of brass were not forthcoming. Oh, yes, thought Ionides. It's not the usual fellow. It's a fresh game scout recruit that has taken the place of the regular gunbearer—both Ionides's usual men being gone from his service on sick leave, probably for malaria.

Ionides watched the tail. I agree that it is the most reliable sensor of a lion's intentions. He had two volatile situations: the lioness and the substitute gunbearer, the latter rolling his eyes and sheeting sweat, but he was bright enough not to move.

"Don't run," Ionides told the gunbearer. He knew that a moving target would bring an instant charge. Ionides told the man that he was going to go to the rear and that the African was to follow his moves. To break and run would bring a charge.

Ionides's retreat reminded me of a situation I had had with a lioness with cubs about twenty-one years ago along the banks of the Luangwa River in Zambia But the lioness was not wounded in my case.

Ionides's substitute gunbearer had not panicked, showing that he was a brave man. The hunter took a step back, the lioness took one forward. She was the mirror reflection of the man. When he went back one pace, she came forward one pace. The Greek stopped and the lioness stopped. This went on for several lifetimes as Ionides tried to get out of a potentially fatal situation. He was wondering if he had really hit her hard with his first barrel when he saw her stagger. She broke off the eyeball-to-eyeball stuff and disappeared behind a piece of shrubbery. Ionides and his substitute gunbearer got the hell out of there!

A few minutes later, when Ionides was able to rearm himself, he returned and quickly shot the female. But he remembered the day always, even after the time near the end of his life when he had his legs cut off. . . .

Ionides liked lions, which may be a bit of a revelation given his business as a game ranger. As he said, if they were reasonably fed they would be good neighbors. Nobody could find fault in their man-eating considering that they had to choose between starving to death or eating man. I agree.

Ionides mentions several cases in which man-eaters were "playful," even to the extent of fooling with baskets and cooking pots while the people of the village were hunkering in their huts beside themselves with terror. However, there our opinions diverge: I never considered man-eaters "playful." Death is death. I could never afford to consider the circumstances.

"Playfulness" often means death, as Ionides himself pointed out with the example of a man bitten in the stomach all in, of course, the name of good fun. A white man was sleeping in a dry water course in Tanganyika with several others when a lion came by and took his stomach and half his intestines. It was all good sport, of course, unless you were the man eviscerated, hmm? Odd chap, the Greek. Ionides had seen lions try to eat melons and a sack of corn; in fact, he doesn't mention his own bath sheet. Yet, the humor is left to the lions and Ionides, who didn't think it so funny that night when the lioness mistook his canvas sheet for himself. Oh, no. That was different.

Ionides personally killed over forty lions during his tenure in the Tanganyika Game Department, more than half of

which were man-eaters and the remainder either about to become people-conscious or cattle killers.

Brian Nicholson, Ionides's assistant in 1950—he went on
to make a wonderful reputation on his own—was only twenty
when he started to learn that man-eaters were girded with
spooks and superstition as far as Africans were concerned.
Almost all man-eaters were considered to be the spirits of
people who had returned in lion form to take revenge against
their enemies for wrongs done in their lifetimes. The man-
eater, of course, hugely resented such things as game rangers
and that any tribesman would rat on him. One experience of
Nicholson would make anybody think. . . .

Brian was near the Selous Game Reserve, sleeping in his
tent, which had the walls rolled up and the door open against
the heat. Two lions walked within two feet of where he was
sleeping, probably in a warm pool of sweat. I am sure that it
became cold sweat pretty quickly when Nicholson discovered
the tracks at dawn. Perhaps Nicholson's mosquito net saved
him; I think so. The gauzy structures suspended over safari
beds kept out a lot more than mosquitos. I personally think
that most predators such as hyenas, lions, and leopards think
that such an unlikely film of gauze is part of a trap and stay
away except for casual sniffs. At least, this was the case that
night near the Selous Game Reserve.

I might point out that whereas a mosquito net is usually
proof against careful man-eaters, it does not always work. Peter Hankin, my old boss in the Luangwa Valley of Zambia,
was killed and partially eaten in 1972 even though he used a
mosquito net.

But one never knows. When I was doing a safari with Daryll Dandridge, a well-known Botswana professional, a lion
walked between us through a small professional hunters'
tent, passing, by his spoor, not a full six inches from each of
us in what became "Splash" Camp, which Daryll and I built
on the edges of the Okavango Swamps in 1970. We did not
use mosquito nets that night, either.

But Nicholson's experience was enough to make the casual person a believer in the "revengful soul" idea. Two lions came through his camp that night in 1950, and actually walked twice within two feet of Brian's body, recumbent under a mosquito net. What developed almost seemed as if the lions were looking for a certain person who had been chosen, hexed.

When the lions finished wandering around Nicholsons's tent, they then went to a bunch of porters who were sleeping in the open, walked in as if they were invited to a gourmet dinner but couldn't decide on the main course. They stepped between, across, and over the sleeping men and finally decided that none of the sleepers met their culinary demands.

Finally, the pair of lions decided upon inspecting a grass hut in which slept two black men. But the weird thing was that the female, who was the more active, decided that the door, which was open, constituted a trap! She merely went a few feet from the open door and proceeded to tear a large hole in the walls of the grass hut. When she was finished with the small excavation, she stepped into the hut and on a man, whose screams awoke the whole group. He must have gotten a terrible fright when he, by reflex, threw his arms around the lioness' neck, which brought a horrible growl!

But it was not the first man's night to die. It was that of the second man, actually searched for by the lion, and that became a solid brick in the wall of native theory of revenge by man-eater.

Brian Nicholson was by this time well awake and listening to determine what had happened. In the yellow lance of his flashlight he saw that the man-eaters dashed by with the corpse, so hungry that they settled down to eat the body within a few yards of camp. Nicholson killed them both with two shots. Pretty good shot, Nicholson.

But what makes a lion choose one victim over another? Is one fatter? No. It is possible that one smells better, but there is some question about this. One can see how the natives on whom this depredation happens think that such matters as a man-eater's choice are predetermined. Of course, they're not.

Unless, of course, they are. . . .

I have written before of George Rushby and his years of following up the Njombe man-eaters who killed and ate more than 2500 people during World War II, and the fact that the man-eating only stopped when a powerful witch doctor was propitiated. Ionides had a similar case as a game ranger in more or less the same area of Tanganyika.

Of course, in the wilderness it's often hard to separate crap from fact. Yes, I think so, too, but when you have lived for many years where were-lions and devil-lions are thought to be fact, perhaps the relatively thin veneer of civilization somewhat peels away. . . . Tell me it isn't so.

Man-eating lions seem to have a choice of people to which they will go to extraordinary lengths to take. A particularly bad lion that Ionides had to sort out was originally thought to be an "angel lion," which killed wart hogs and bush pigs that ate crops, but never touched humans. Until it got too old to hunt its normal prey, that is; until it turned man-eater, it was a boon to the village and its agriculture. It was called *simba malaika*, the angel lion, until it turned into *simba ibilisi*, or devil lion. Ionides was called in to hunt him over several months, after he had killed more than ninety people in his 2500–square-mile territory.

He was no dope, the devil lion, and he quickly realized that if pigs were too quick for him in his dotage, humans were not. That he managed to kill ninety persons before he himself was killed proved that he was right. Ah, but the heavenly lion turned devil had been educated by Ionides's inept game scouts, who had muffed their chances and taught the male to be cautious.

Ionides says with some reticence that a wizard was finally paid off, the man believed by the locals to be the lion's master. Of course, Ionides didn't see a tiny bit of connection, but it happened that a couple of days after the money was paid, a nineteen-year-old native kid shot a lion with a muzzle-loader and the killings stopped.

Of course, it was just coincidence. I mean, it was, wasn't it?

Iodine was possibly the only person I knew that used "solid" non-expanding bullets for lion. Come to think of it, "Karamojo" Bell did also, and claimed that they were excellent. I have always carried solids as compared to soft-pointed expanding bullets, but I never used them in preference against lion or leopard. But maybe Iodine had a point.

He made his decision when having to kill a man-eater under somewhat unusual circumstances. It was a fine trophy-quality male that had killed a seventeen-year-old girl near a hut and Ionides had been called by drum to take care of the situation. This was a well-known man-eater but, for reasons best known to him, Ionides had sent one of his best scouts to handle things.

The scout settled down in the hut and waited for the man-eater to return. Time went by and the moon rose, but all he could hear was the shrill of insects and the *churrr* of insomniac partridges. It was not cold but he got a shiver each time he looked at the corpse, older than his oldest wife.

It was quite late and the scout still thought he was the only hunter until the hut shook under the heavy blow of a lion hitting it trying to get under the eaves to take him. Jesus Jenny, but he was nearly hooked by the huge paw when the hut collapsed and he was buried under roofing and poles with the lion! Happily, the cat was unable to reach him, but the man spent the remainder of the night beneath hundreds of pounds of poles, thatch, and the heavy mud used by the natives to hold the entire hut together.

Ionides spends a good part of the next portion of his text explaining the special and horrible tension that was the hunter's as he followed up the lion. He had managed to wound it and had just stuck a soft point into it as it disappeared from near where the game scout had been waiting for it. Ionides also tells the short tale of an Afrikaner he knew who decided that cartridges were too expensive to spend an "insurance" shot. The idiot walked up to the body of a lioness he had shot and tried to pull it out of a bush by its tail. As Ionides says, "The lioness was not dead and he went to hospital for the next six weeks." At that he was very lucky.

The Greek returned to the lion and was tiptoeing on the spoor when the bushes parted and the male came rocketing at him, a blur of teeth and mane. Ionides preferred—as I do—to either sit or kneel, as the most reliable shot is in the chest as the head or brain shot cannot be counted on in felines. Take a look at a lion's skull and you will see why: the brain cavity is almost the shape of an ancient greek Hoplite's helmet, the sides tapering away from the front.

Ionides was using a .470 Nitro Express and the first shot, a soft-point at a close range, was later found to glance off the cheek bone and to proceed into the chest where it did no obvious harm. In fact, the man-eater continued his charge with no sign whatever of being hit.

The lion jinked at a sapling later measured as being eight yards from Ionides and swung around it, only to fall on his nose, presumably from the first shot. Instantly, however, he was on his feet again and coming as Iodine fired his second and last shot. This one told and the lion was only a couple of paces from the Greek's feet. Never again did he use soft-points for lion.

I think Ionides is correct as he could have only used, at that date, the soft-point expanding bullet by Kynoch of Britain (Imperial Chemical Industries), and I have had such a soft-point go to shreds even upon such light-bodied stuff as a male leopard wounded by a client. Since such bullets as the Dead Tough by A-SQUARE have come along, though, I feel completely safe using that load for lions and leopards, especially in the .470 CAPSTICK, if that is not too self-serving.

I cannot shift from the particulars of Ionides, which are fascinating in themselves, before I have done with lion maneaters. It's too interesting. I almost said "fun." . . .

79

A good pal of Ionides, Bill Harvey—from whom this story comes—was a game ranger handling the Masai (often Maasai in recent writings) area in Tanganyika, a northern section.

Ionides brings this story into his narrative by mentioning that man-eaters often go at angles or circles and end up actually following the men who are hunting them. Usually, Ionides notes, this is not so much the man-eater's plan but that the danger lies when the hunter gives up the hunt and lets his guard down.

Bill Harvey had been following the worst man-eater in many decades in Masailand, a big male that naturally got many accolades as a special lion of witchcraft and magic. As usual, it was a "spook" lion. Of course, that's so much trash, I mean, that's crap, hmm?

Harvey was hunting this lion with four other men, tribesmen who were gunbearers and guides, late one afternoon when his tracker announced that a complete circle had been done, the man-eater's tracks over their own! It was half-past five in the gathering, black soup of equatorial instant dark, when Bill decided that retrospect was the best of man-eater hunting and turned back toward home.

Ranger Bill Harvey and his flock were still more than a half-hour from camp in a native village by seven, when it was as black as my credit rating. If you had nothing better to do you could always put your hand in front of your face and come to the conclusion that it was, indeed, dark. Anyway, make it an hour to camp as the party couldn't move as fast in the blackness as they had on the way out when the sun was streaming and they were following the man-eater and not the other way around.

When it is dark in equatorial Africa, it is *really* dark, especially on this night, which had no moon or stars and only featured impossible clouds overhead. The five men plodded on, first the local guide, then the man carrying Harvey's shotgun—as Ionides points out, Harvey was also an ornithologist and had originated a collection of the birds of Tanganyika—followed by Harvey, a local game scout, and finally, a gunbearer with Bill's heavy rifle.

At a short distance from the village, the men started down a steep gully and were almost at the bottom when there was a thump, a sound of struggle, and a shot!

Harvey yelled, "What is it?" The game scout answered that the tracker, the number-two man, had been taken by the lion and obviously killed as there was no screaming from him. Bill Harvey grabbed the shotgun that the man had dropped—it *had* to have been loaded with slugs or buckshot—and began to run up the slope that they had come down. At the lip, he caught a dim outline of what seemed to him to be a lion. He was right. Harvey fired and the cat scampered away. When Bill got to the spot there was only the dead and torn body of the black man.

The game ranger and his men were trying—in Swahili—to figure out what to do with the dead man when their problem was solved for them: the lion came back and grabbed it from under their noses. The man-eater got completely away and killed at will for several weeks. The eventual end of this episode is worth recording in that inexact form known as Africana. However, I believe that it is completely true:

The lion was doing pretty well in the people-eating department as of several weeks after the Harvey encounter. However, a couple of game scouts decided to fight fire with same and grabbed the wizard or head spook supposedly responsible for the lion as his owner or manager. They beat the living hornbills out of him until he agreed to call off his "familiar." My, but he chanted incantations, swore oaths and all that was necessary to call off the man-eating lion. Of course, we know that such shenanigans have no effect, or do we?

The lion at this point had lost all his natural fear of humans and was doing very nicely, thanks so much, as a man-eater. It no longer even bothered to drag its victims into cover but ate them in the open. Success, after all, is its own reward.

You must understand that the black game scouts were only native recruits and thought that the magic that affected the villagers was valid; in fact, who can really say that it wasn't?

After the ceremony that declared the man-eater sponsorless, the game scouts were able to raise more or less that same kind of group who decided to burn down Dr. Frankenstein's castle. The lion was, according to Harvey's description to Ionides, on a small hill in—of all things—a piece of rather open bush. The game scouts went out to slay their dragon secure in the knowledge that the lion was flat out of magic. The game scouts, however, had a few enthusiastic fans with them, tribesmen with spears, *pangas*, brush hooks, and whatever they could find. On seeing this lot, the lion rose to its feet, charged, and killed a man in the crowd. It presumably ate him, too, before decamping.

A lone game scout later killed the lion, but it was too late for the wizard who controlled the big cat. As a man was taken from the crowd, the wizard, possibly blushing furiously, was adjudged not able to control "his" lion and in shame hanged himself.

We have already met Hemedi Ngoe, Ionides's gunbearer, in terms of man-eaters, dabbling in a career not noted for its security. He was a favorite of Ionides, but, as the Greek noted, Hemedi was a womanizer of the most devout kind. Although he already had eight wives, which indicated a death wish if nothing else does, Hemedi fell in love again at a village called Tundura with a local beauty whose charms, rather obvious in native dress, could not be ignored by a connoisseur.

Despite Ionides's ire at being asked by Hemedi for leave to take his ninth bride back to headquarters at Liwale, permission was given and Hemedi told that when he had settled his new wife he was to join Ionides wherever he was. The next thing Ionides knew Hemedi had been killed and eaten by a lion, the same one that Iodine was hunting! The story Iodine was told went this way:

Hemedi and his new wife were traveling to Liwale, but the trip taking several days, they stayed at a very small village on their route. Hemedi Ngoe had already noticed that there were lion pugs mixed with his own footprints, but it was hard to say how old they were. Hemedi ignored the tracks and settled down to spend a night in the village.

Due to the lion's depredations, the gunbearer was warned of the danger, but he scoffed at it. He, of all people, should have known better. While all the villagers slept in a large communal hut, Hemedi insisted on sleeping with his new wife on a string bed—a surprisingly comfortable affair—on the verandah of the main hut. Curiously, nothing happened that night.

When Hemedi awoke, he felt a bit feverish from malaria and he decided to spend another night in the village, again on the verandah.

A few hours before midnight, the sound of a "thud" was heard by the communal hut inhabitants. At their yells of query, the new wife said simply and sleepily that Hemedi must have gone to take a whiz. She had not heard any *thud*. But the villagers knew better. They took torches and inspected the area. There was fresh blood gleaming like grape jelly on the lashings of the bed and no sign of Hemedi.

The villagers grabbed the new wife and hustled her inside the big hut, lashing the door shut despite her protestations. As Ionides says, it was well that they did as the man-eater was only fifteen yards away, watching them and possibly licking his chops. In the morning, only the well-chewed head of Hemedi Ngoe was found.

Hemedi was soon revenged, although it was of little help to him. The lion was shot eating part of an elephant that had been shot on crop control. Very much against Ionides's experience, the cat was not old, starving, and mangy but prime and obviously well fed as it had taken forty-five *known* victims, which probably meant at least sixty or so actual kills. Africans are terrible bookkeepers.

*   *   *

There is little doubt that Iodine Ionides was one of the great-est—if somewhat tragic—characters in East Africa. I certainly am not a psychologist, but it seems that his early years gave him the chip that he always carried on his shoulder, or per-haps shoulders. Obviously a very sensitive and bright young-ster, he learned the hard way that his "foreign-sounding" name would always keep him at arm's-length from his British peers at school; and he attended the best. The son of a suc-cessful surgeon, Ionides went to Rugby, where he was se-verely beaten or "birched" as a matter of course as he had an unbending personality and, after a couple of "crammers," Sandhurst, which is the British equivalent of the American West Point. Although he was a fifth-generation Briton, he was always thought of as a "sinister foreigner" and was—at least on principle—thrown out of Rugby for having "a sawn-off shotgun, two pistols, ammunition, six rabbit nets, a cosh [blackjack], a knuckle-duster, a tobacco pouch and a pipe." I can only suggest that this was hardly a reason for the Rugby authorities to become upset. If they wanted a genuine thrill of horror, they should have checked *my* room as a boarding schoolboy!

Ionides came away from Rugby possibly worse—but at least more realistic in his outlook—than when he went in. But he was a boy and young man of very tough stuff men-tally. Rugby taught him "the realities of life" and never to expect justice as a natural or automatic right. When he left Rugby, Ionides was disillusioned and probably right to be. There is very little justice in this world; only the law, which is a poor substitute.

A decision, expanded upon over a decade and a half, prob-ably was the guiding light in Ionides's life. He was only four years old, but the experience never left him.

He was chasing a red admiral butterfly in his best clothes when his nurse screamed at him to stop before he went over a wall where the butterfly had flown. The nurse possibly dictated the turn of his life when she screeched that he was not to follow the butterfly. "You can't have it both ways," the nurse said, and Ionides took her words to heart. Then and there he decided to live for himself and damn everybody else. He never married because he realized that he would be very unlikely to find a woman who would live in the self-imposed exile that he planned for himself. In fact, it would seem that his adult life was a continuance of his school existence when he turned—understandably from my point of view—to pleasing himself and nobody else. He was always irritated and angry when he was deemed a "dirty little brute" for the simple reason that he dissected mice he had trapped and preserved their skins. At the idea that he was a "foreigner," he stiffened his back despite the frequent whippings and was determined to show just how foreign and savage he could be—which was plenty!

Ionides was a natural poacher, possibly for the simple reason that such activities were against the law; also he enjoyed them. While at Sandhurst at Aldershot, he supplied illicit pheasants to a whorehouse, and to assorted patrons and customers thereof.

Ionides continued his most contrary frame of mind most of his life, certainly during his stay in India as a subaltern—second lieutenant—of the Second Battalion of the 24th Regiment of Foot, South Wales Borderers, stationed at Jhansi, Central India. The 24th was the same outfit that was slaughtered at Isandhlwana and defended Rorke's Drift in the Zulu war of 1879. It was school all over again. He was once more a "foreigner," even going out of his way to kill a wild boar with a rifle—rather than spear it—to earn the ire of his commanding officer, a most pukka type. I rather think Ionides did this on purpose.

As time went on, Ionides developed the reputation of being a misogynist, and perhaps he was, having come to look at marriage as a trap that would separate him from his usual pursuits. He was never willing to make the sacrifices obvious in wedlock. No woman, at least in his opinion, could stand the sort of life that he had envisioned for himself, but then, perhaps he was considering the wrong women. . . .

To this point, I have neglected to mention the reason for Ionides joining the army and going to India and, hopefully, Africa. In a word, it was hunting.

After several years in India, both poaching the game of rajas and legitimately hunting, Ionides managed a transfer to the King's African Rifles, following a three-month safari in India during the rains and a few weeks home in England. This was in 1925. Ionides was, having been born in Hove, England, on January 17, 1901, too young for the First World War and too old for the Second. On his first safari, he took an elephant, two lion, three Cape buffalo, and three rhino. After the safari, he became bored with India and transferred to Africa, arriving at Dar es Salaam in Tanganyika in December 1925. The sinister foreigner had made it.

Constantine John Philip Ionides (originally, in 1817, Ixplixis, which was Anglicized to Ionides) spent two years in the KAR and really didn't think too much of his fellow officers. They were a motley lot—according to Ionides—who backbit constantly and were difficult, having no sense of "regiment," what? But it was a very personal misunderstanding with a major's wife that led to Ionides's leaving the British Army for good.

There was a rule in the King's African Rifles that no junior officer would be given leave until he had passed an easy Ki-Swahili test. Ionides, anxious to learn the trade language, went to the adjutant and asked him why the new officers and men were not taught the language if the KAR insisted on a knowledge of it.

The adjutant reckoned it was a grand idea and, as his "better half" wanted to learn it, too, decided that classes would be held in his own home. Ionides immediately objected as he felt that some pretty personal words would have to be learned, vocabulary quite inappropriate for a British adjutant's wife. Alas, poor Ionides was again the goat as the wife took it personally and prevailed on her husband to complain to the commanding officer about it. The complaint showed up in mufti on Ionides's fitness report for 1927.

The fitness report was a disaster and Ionides was deemed to be "below average" in the area of "Zeal and Energy," and under "Remarks" by the second-in-command he was further smeared by the suggestion that he was far more interested in hunting than in the army. This certainly makes good sense to me! Of course, as Ionides says himself, it was true. The criticism, however, stifled any hope of promotion he might have had. Ionides left the army and in later years thanked the adjutant's wife more than she would ever know. The KAR had certainly proved him to be an individualist and not a "team player." Bless him.

The fitness report was, however, adjusted by the commanding officer, but overcompensation made Ionides sound like a Girl Scout. Ionides was particularly relieved that he was not believed "to love his men." God, he thought. What trash! Even worse, he did not, the original report intimated, think that the horse was the most important animal since man. He didn't like pig sticking and abhored horses. Seeing his career obviously washed up, Ionides resigned from the army, which must have been with mutual relief. He decided to follow his great love and become a professional hunter. Of course, his poaching background had not deserted him. . . .

The late twenties in East Africa were wild in more ways than one and Ionides certainly made his contribution. One thing I have always liked about the man was his sense of the outrageous, as illustrated by some of the tales told by him in his only book, *Hunter's Story* (Allen, London, 1965; first published in America in 1966 as *Mambas and Maneaters*, Holt, Rinehart and Winston, New York). A favorite is the short tale of Dynamite Dan Eldridge, a gentleman rather long on liquid refreshments but short of funds. Dynamite Dan developed a substantial thirst one day in Dar es Salaam and stopped off at a small bar run by a Syrian woman called Ma Hyder. Credit was as short as Dynamite Dan's pockets were deep; Dan, alas, was a troublemaker.

The bar was elbow to shank with dusty, paying customers when Dan played his ace. Reaching into his shirt, he dragged out a dull brown stick of gelignite explosive and a box of Lucifer matches. As Dan scratched one of the matches into sulphurous flame, he announced to the customers that gelignite, if they were unaware, was a most powerful explosive. As he touched the flame to the base of the explosive, Ma Hyer's place was emptied in a hurry. In a few seconds, Dynamite Dan had swilled all the drinks left on the bar, burped demurely, stuffed the gelignite and matches back into his shirt, and wandered away. He had neglected to tell the customers that gelignite needed a detonator to blow up; fire had no effect. As Dan might have said, "Nobody asked."

As Ionides points out, even a place as wooly as teenage Tanganyika could be a bit tame for some of the really wild citizens who had to cross the Ruvuma River to Portuguese East Africa—now Mozambique—to raise a little hell. How wild was it? Well, take this tale:

A pal of Ionides was accustomed to showing off by shooting bottles off his native servant's head until one day he fired a touch low and killed the black with a bullet through the brain. In due course, he appeared before a Portuguese magistrate who had a reputation of being very hard on Britishers from across the border. The judge made quite a speech saying that British hunters had always been a problem in Portuguese East and it was high time an example was made to show that the Portuguese would not brook such behavior. The man was fined 450 escudos, which was the equivalent of $22.50 in American funds! Wow! Talk about life being cheap—this was a proper fire sale!

Most of the men who were professional ivory hunters were, at least at some time in their careers, poachers. Yet, poachers in the 1920s or as far back as the turn of the century weren't the same as poachers we know today, gangs of ex- or current soldiers armed with heavy equipment and automatic weapons. Oh, yes, the old boys were poachers, but they were so only in terms of cutting foreign or domestic governments out of their slice of ivory profits—not in pursuing some species of elephant into endangerment. Bear in mind that the first year that Ionides hunted ivory professionally (or poached most of his ivory professionally), almost 3000 elephants had to be killed in Tanganyika alone to protect native crops. Mind you, I do not condone poaching of *any* kind, but it seems that there was at least a slight difference in the circumstances seventy years ago and now. It was a hard way to earn a living and most, like Ionides, eventually gave it up and either joined various game departments or went back to Blighty. But there were some happenings that are amusing in retrospect. . . .

Ionides, at the height of his ivory activities, used a ploy somewhat different from most poachers for hunting in the then–Belgian Congo. Iodine went openly to Congo, tried to take out a license for two elephants at Makata, in Manyema Province, but found that the *permis* was held up for weeks. Ionides did not realize that everything in Congo was done on the *baksheesh* or bribery system. Still is from what I hear. . . .

He found out at a local bar, speaking with old-timers, that the man who needed to have his hand gilded was the chief clerk of the issuing office, who simply put various papers before his superior and had them signed without a second glance. Ionides did this deed and *violà*, his *permis* was ready!

Ionides quickly learned that the secret of success was to have a ready source for disposing of the ivory. He used an Irishman named Baggott, an ex-South African and not the sort to take home to mother. Further, one needed to make a deal with the local chiefs, who were permitted to kill any elephants that tended to develop an appetite for their crops. The result of this skullduggery was to give a commission of fifteen percent to the chiefs, who had an ivory export exemption. Ionides could shoot ivory on their lands, which they would claim as theirs and, until the chiefs became greedy, it was a fine arrangement.

Ionides—much to my personal surprise—was in the habit of burning dead elephants rather than giving them to the locals for meat. The idea was to register one set of tusks only and burn other elephantine corpses rather than to make them available to the locals. There was nothing secret about twelve tons of dead elephant, and some interesting things happened to Ionides. . . .

I think the story of the two elephants that fell in the middle of a village cultivation plot to be classic, especially as one of the bulls shot by Ionides had tusk weights of 107 and 109 pounds.

Ionides was having a snooze in one of the village huts when he heard a commotion caused by the arrival of the Belgian *administrateur,* the equivalent of the British district commissioner. The *administrateur* was stiff with police and porters. The honcho asked how Ionides's luck had gone. Nope, none at all, said Ionides, about a hundred yards from the two dead elephants. A woman then rounded a corner of the huts behind the Belgian's back, almost worn out with her load of elephant meat. "No," said Ionides again to the *administrateur.* "No luck at all." Ionides's gunbearer shooed her away.

The official next wanted to speak with the chief of the village. Ionides knew that the man was up to his armpits in elephant blood and meat. He sent immediate word what was happening and a few minutes later the chief appeared covered with red dirt to mask the bloodstains. Butter wouldn't melt in his mouth. The Belgian thought that unusual efforts were being spent on the crops.

Because women kept showing up with huge portions of meat the next day, Ionides went out and shot two Cape buffalo on his "pot" license to mask what was happening.

Ionides says that some time later he tried to bribe the *administrateur* but found that the man was trying to gain a higher title through honest labor. Through reciprocity that I do not understand, the Belgian made a "gift" of a camp bed or "stretcher" to Ionides, and then asked for it back. Ionides later heard that the *administrateur* had been in a liquor-induced quarrel with some Africans at Kilombo, a rail stop. During the altercation, the Belgian had realized that his perfidy with the camp bed had become common knowledge. Ionides, always a step or two ahead of the powers that were, was sure the *administrateur* would seek revenge for this blot on his reputation. The hunter sent quick word around to keep an eye open for plainclothes police, who eventually did show up.

Ionides got a message from one of his "tame" villages that two men had shown up who could be nothing but undercover police. Ionides sent back the message to the village: "fix them," meaning to bribe them. The "detectives" cost only six shillings each, a little over an American dollar. Ah, for the days before inflation!

The worst time that Ionides had was due to a native chief named Ungu Lukenya, into whose territory a badly wounded elephant wandered a few hundred yards and fell dead, having been shot on the friendly turf of a chief called Lukali Lunga. Ionides and his men rushed to take out the tusks but had no time to cremate the carcass. That the dead elephant had tusks that weighed 114 and 112 pounds may have had something to do with the following hassle.

After a few weeks, the chief, Ungu Lukenya, sent a message asking Ionides where the chief's half of the ivory was, this head man being among those not bribed by Ionides. The usual deal was that the chief of an area got one tusk and the hunter the other if the local ruler had not been bribed first. Half of the ivory was due Lukenya or he would bring the matter up before the *administrateur*.

Ionides went immediately to the friendly chief, Lukali Lunga. He told Lunga that he had received pay for Ionides's activities and, therefore, they were partners in crime. He told

Lunga about Lukenya's threats and promised him that if he himself went to jail, Lunga would have the next cell. Ionides told Lunga to take his young warriors and remove the bones across tribal boundary lines so that no trace remained. This Lunga did.

The case finally went to court but was dismissed for lack of evidence.

It was astonishingly hard work, elephant hunting, either legally or with one eye over one's shoulder. Ionides realized that anything under sixty pounds a side of ivory wasn't worth his trouble. Ivory hunting was a walking game and a deadly hard one. Ionides came to wear "plimsolls" when he was elephant hunting as he had had a pair of rawhide boots simply disintegrate under him. Plimsolls are a type of British tennis shoe that Ionides found so comfortable that he wore no other kind for the rest of his life, which made him look even odder than he was when he visited Britain in a snowstorm.

Ionides noted that the local natives in his area of the Belgian Congo—probably Mashukulumbwe—were ex-cannibals, or perhaps the "ex" part was not true. The original Belgian official who had caused such delays for Ionides until he bribed the head clerk was, in fact, eaten by insurrectionists. Ionides described him—with a macabre chuckle—as a red-headed chap who had created problems with his *permis de chasse*.

When Ionides was hunting ivory at the end of the twenties, he became just another victim of the worldwide depression. He got for legal ivory just six shillings a pound after the Belgian tax, not counting his safari expenses. In five months the price of elephant bicuspids had fallen by half. His total profit for five months of extremely hard work was 150 British pounds, about a pound a day for his labor in a very risky business.

As Ionides realized that there was no longer a reasonable profit to be earned in ivory, the McDougall and Ionides times began.

Ken McDougall was a professional white hunter who Iodine ran into in Dar es Salaam. Ionides said he was immediately attracted by McDougall's drunken manner and his horribly criminal face. Iodine could always judge people. . . .

As they met, Ken was fuming about certain relations with his *bint,* a local girl chosen to relieve some sexual tensions, which she did very well; nevertheless, her skill was not to the satisfaction of McDougall. However, as Ken had a very fine naturalist's knowledge of game, plants, and trees, Ionides decided to form an alliance with him in which they would start a professional hunting business as well as take the odd elephant as "found" ivory to be credited to the tribesmen.

The first decree of the new partnership was that all concerned go on the "water wagon," a promise that Ken kept for about eight hours. Well, the poor chap was probably thirsty.

To the astonishment of his partner, the deal went bad. McDougall chased ticket collectors with an automobile bung, beat up guides, and generally horrified Ionides who had hoped for a good arrangement. Yet, Ionides had forgotten that he had given McDougall full power-of-attorney on his bank account. By the time the dust started to settle, Ionides was out some 600 pounds to McDougall's thirst. *That* was a lot of money in those days.

Ionides went into hiding hunting elephants. It took him a long time before he was able to pay off McDougall's debt. I suppose that the partnership was never dissolved but Iodine and Ken McDougall split company forever.

Ionides carried on for a while as a professional hunter on his own until he had a nearly fatal run-in with a cow elephant. It was in February of 1932, after a classically bad safari with an American client, although I wonder if Ionides was the easiest person to get along with under field conditions. Iodine had a license for two elephants and had already taken one but had passed up several good tuskers, hoping to get something outstanding for his own collection in his house. In the Lushoto district of Tanganyika he started hunting with a gunbearer and tracker and a cook to watch over his camp, but he soon realized that he had better take any decent jumbo that came along as he was running perilously short of money.

Ionides and his men discovered two sets of tracks in the area: those of two bulls traveling together and those of a breeding herd of cows and calves. Naturally, Iodine went after the bulls.

Ionides and his two men had found a place next morning where the bull spoor was crossed by the trail of the cows, going to the hunters' left. Ionides was pleased to have the females out of the way as he could now hunt the bulls carefully through the dense forest where the men had gone without fear of cows and calves messing things up.

Later in the morning, Ionides heard a muzzle-loader shot, a clearly different sound than that made by a modern rifle. He had picked up a local guide that day and asked him if his people were poaching the cow elephants. The man answered that he didn't think so and the shot was probably at a waterbuck at the edge of the woods.

Ionides in those days only had a .500/.465 Nitro Express Purdey double rifle, plenty of gun to be sure, and when he heard elephants ahead he told his men to stop and went on by himself. Of course, when he saw there were two elephants he naturally assumed them to be the two bulls they were following. The jumbos were only six paces away, across a small opening in the bush. Both acted as if they had no sense of humor.

At first, Ionides still presumed that they were the bulls he had been following. Like that of most young hunters—Ionides was thirty-one—it was a very bad presumption. They were two god-awfully irate cows.

Even after looking at the tusks, Ionides had not realized through the brush that these were females and not bulls. He quickly ran across the front of the first female and tried to have a squint at the second's ivory. Out of the corner of his eye he saw that the first elephant, to his surprise, had started a determined charge!

Ionides didn't want to kill the jumbo as it had very small ivory and he didn't want it to count on his license. She was coming fairly slowly with her chin thrust out and her tusks near the ground like a cow catcher. The Greek decided to shoot her high in the frontal part of the head and try to knock her out with bullet impact. But it didn't work and the cow came on without a sign of being hit, her ears like great, gray sails and her trunk tucked up against her chest.

The cow was very close for the first shot and was nearly on Ionides by the time he was able to blaze off his remaining barrel into her face. He tried to side step into a bush but he snagged his foot and fell over a fallen branch. Knowing that he was almost a dead man, he fell on his face.

The Greek lay playing dead in a ferocious snarl of under-growth, hoping that the elephant would miss him. But he realized that his prayers were in vain as the cow stuck her tusks into the dry earth on either side of his head.

Ionides noted that what he had heard from others in similar situations was indeed so—he had no sense of fear and could think in a detached manner. As his brain whirred, he was aware of a terrible pressure between his shoulder blades and a scraping sensation as he was pulled along the ground. The hunter stayed absolutely motionless, still hoping that the elephant would think him dead. He realized he wasn't quite as smart as he thought he was when the cow began to kick him around between her hind and fore feet, probably trying to get him into a nice position for squashing. He passed out.

When he next awoke, Iodine was lying face down a few steps from where he was last. He could still hear the elephant above him, but the sound started to edge away. At last he dared to turn his head, finding that he thought his right eye had been lost. Happily, it was not and soon joined the left in a clear view of the area. The blood that had shut it turned out to be the elephant's and not his. Ionides then got up to run, but his bush shorts, nestled around his ankles from the mauling, tripped him. Fortunately, his faithful Africans were within a few yards and ran quickly to him.

As Ionides came back to camp, he realized that his .500/.465 was still on the field of combat and sent his men to fetch it, giving them a borrowed rifle for protection. They were gone a long time and even fired a shot, but the cow was dead from the Greek's bullet, which had passed through the head at a high angle and then ploughed into the neck and eventually caused the cow's death. There was also a muzzle-loader slug in the cow elephant, a very new wound that had probably made the cow so bad-tempered in the first place.

The white man felt for several days as if he had been beaten with staves, so sore was he from his battering by the elephant. After three days, he was able to rise and go to the closest village where he registered his tusks, a mere 16 and 17 pounds. But, as Ionides says, he vastly upped the average next trip when he took two bulls, one with 126 pounds in one tusk and a few less of ivory in his other and another that went 113 and 117 pounds. Iodine was really untouched by the encounter with the cow except for his left ear: he had had a client that had hurt him badly with muzzle blast and the murderous cow also seemed to have hurt his hearing. At any rate, Ionides spent the rest of his life more or less deaf in his left ear. I am also deaf to a large extent in that ear, but mine is from shooting large-caliber rifles and ordinary shotguns without proper protection from nerve deafness. Ionides says he lost most of his ability to hear higher-pitch sounds as well as a certain proportion of human speech. This is my problem, too, as it is that of many professional shooters, as I once was. Wear earplugs or muffs, as I assure you that this is a club you would not really appreciate joining. Of course, I must agree with Ionides that there are certain aspects of human conversation unworthy of hearing. . . .

Ionides spent nearly three years at professional safari hunting, until September of 1933, and he earned between 50 and

75 pounds per month, which will give some idea of the problem he was faced with when he had to repay the 600 pounds of McDougall's perfidy.

Ionides and his clients seemed not to be of the same mind and it was no wonder that he only spent three years in the business. At the time Ionides was hunting in Tanganyika, it cost the astonishing sum of forty pounds a day per client; today it is a thousand dollars per day and rising. I have no doubt that the time will come when we laugh at these figures as being pathetically low, a joke of inflation.

Ionides says that all the time he was hunting in Africa, he always aspired to be a game ranger. Well, this may be true, far be it from me to guess his inner thoughts. He claims that all his years in professional poaching were to gain enough experience to be able to make his way as a legitimate hunter. Again, I can't say nor would I like to. But, on the premise that it takes a thief to catch a thief, Ionides was hired as a professional assistant game ranger in Tanganyika on September 9, 1933. Perhaps Constantine was without guile after all: at the same time that he took the assistant game ranger job he was offered 150 pounds per month for three months by an Indian rajah to take him on safari. He refused in favor of a salary of 40 pounds per month from the Tanganyika game department.

Very possibly Ionides made the decision based upon a variety of options, not the least of which was that of his African staff. However, there was also the interference of his old commanding officer, Jock Minnery, as well as that of Monty Moore, VC, a winner of the famous Victoria Cross, the equivalent of the American Medal of Honor.

Philip Teare was the head of the game department and Ionides's superior. Ionides had signed on to work in a area well over a third of a million square miles and sporting a staff of 6 white game rangers and 120 scouts. Technically, he was an elephant control officer, and he was first assigned to destroy elephants that were ruining African *shambas* or farms.

Ionides hated the job, which may seem surprising for an ex-ivory poacher. The truth was that he soon found that his new occupation was simply boring.

In about 1934, Iodine came across his first genuine "rogue," quite a rare fellow for Africa compared to India, where there are a fair amount of males maldisposed to human beings.

Ionides believed that this rogue was created by some damned fool emptying the ten-round magazine of a .303-caliber British military rifle into its backside. That the man saved himself by climbing a tree that was too big even for the sixty-pound tusker was a piece of luck. The man was terrified for many hours, but escaped unhurt. This was not so for the next twenty-eight people whom the new rogue came across. Before Ionides began to hunt him, he had aquired a name—Lihogoya—and a hell of a reputation. His last two victims had been a woman and a baby whom he spitted on a single tusk.

Dispatched to the village of the latest victims, Ionides took up the spoor immediately through open country until he came to a patch of bush and was lucky to see the rogue waiting for him in ambush. Iodine had a blood-chilling few minutes of inspection of the bull; it was acting every way that an elephant usually does not. It was more hunting cat than an elephant, its walk a stalk and its trunk doing a continual Indian rope tick. Even its body language was sinister, different from an ordinary elephant's. It scared Iodine as no other had done.

The wind was swirling as it will in the bush and Lihogoya was stalking across Ionides's front—then the elephant caught a whiff of the Greek's scent. Instantly it rushed, not with trunk tucked in, head low, and ears somewhat laid back, as in a usual silent charge. The trunk, like a tortured python, was writhing high in the air and the animal charged to within five yards, all the time screaming like a ruptured locomotive.

It was too close for the classic brain shot, forcing Ionides to drive a .470 bullet through the roof of the mouth at halitosis distance. It did not take the brain but it was close enough to fuddle the elephant. A second point-blank shot in the heart finally toppled the rogue, now as dead as his victims.

As a game ranger and hunter, Ionides was fascinated yet horrified by man-eating leopards. Having hunted man-eating leopards myself, I can see why. They are the only animal that seems to kill for the sheer hell of it, often not eating their human prey. In fact, one leopard that completely terrorized the Tanganyikan village of Masaguru on the Ruvuma River in the late fifties, slaughtered twenty-six small women and children without ever taking a bite out of any of them! It just licked their blood.

When it comes to killing, the leopard is the champ, far exceeding even man-eating lions at their trade. A good-sized male weighs perhaps 120 pounds as opposed to 450 pounds for a lion. Being a smaller animal, it has to take smaller prey, a full-grown man being unusual fare, as I found in Zambia and Botswana. Yet a leopard can and often has raised far more hell and death, pound for pound, than any lion or tiger.

The man-eater of Masaguru was killed by Ionides's protégé, Brian Nicholson, when it deigned to feed on an elephant carcass. When it was killed, it was in wonderful shape, hardly the tooth-worn and mangy old cat that we are led to believe constitutes the usual man-eater.

When it comes to taking advantage of cover for his stalk, nothing is in the same league with a leopard. Its dappled coat of dark rosettes and honey-colored background look like a patch of African sunlight and he can seemingly hide behind a matchbox and remain unseen.

Leopards are survivors. They are the last game species to enter sites of the greatest urban sprawl. Where I live in Pretoria, South Africa, every year or two brings a brush with an urban leopard. It happened two years ago when a woman was embraced by a big male on her apartment doorstep! The leopard was killed after about an hour of pulling his disappearing act throughout a prominent suburb. The cat was executed by police with a service pistol and a 9mm Uzi submachine gun! The pelt was awarded to the officer who killed the cat, but this was shortly vetoed by a furious public who seemed to think that it was okay for a hungry leopard to be prowling among the townhouses and flats of the Capital City.

Perhaps rats are marginally more successful, but leopards are not far behind. If the inhabitants of Pretoria were ever to know how many of them lived in sewers and such, eating stray dogs, cats, fish, mushrooms, and garbage, the city would be a ghost town.

If you have any doubts of how camouflaged a leopard can be, note that a sharp-eyed tracker of Ionides once actually stepped on the body of one before it was recognized! That I have nearly done this myself underscores the fact that the leopard always has a huge edge in a tracking situation.

The leopard is the apogee of a game animal, given that it is not big in size. It is almost impossible to track because of its soft pads and lightness compared to a lion, and the only way that a safari client will obtain one is either by baiting—in itself a very fine art—or by a practice still in use in Botswana's Kalahari Desert, that of running down a leopard. This is done by locating a track, as fresh as possible, and using Bushmen in relays to follow the spoor while the professional hunter and clients follow in hunting vehicles. When the leopard has gone as far as it can, it will usually charge the vehicle or the Bushmen, if they have been a tiny bit sloppy in their tracking. It can be tough to tell how old a spoor is in that *gussu* sand of the Kalahari. Needless to say, many people have been terribly injured at this pastime on a hot Botswana afternoon. . . .

As Iodine found, there was only one way to bring a man-eating leopard to book, and that was to use traps—either gun traps or live traps. The trouble was that nobody could tell whether a successful set would take the right or wrong leopard—in which case the child-and-woman-eating would go on as before. Even if the traps were multiply successful, how would a game ranger know which was the guilty leopard? The only way to tell was if the killing stopped, which would take several weeks to ascertain.

As Iodine was to find, southern Tanganyika was the end-all-beat-all for man-eating leopards. Iodine's first frustration happened with the man-eater of Ruponda, in the Nachingwea district.

Probably the most important factor in the making of the Ruponda man-eater was the tragic "groundnuts" scheme, (read "peanuts") in which most of the large fauna of the area were killed off. Except for leopards, that is.

Certainly, the resident leopards felt a tightness in the belly as they were left when the large game cleared out or was shot. One, at least, took to the only reasonable meat available—human.

The story begins when the "scheme" was well underway and a pair of brothers were playing outside their hut in Ruponda in 1950. In a flash of dark lightning, one boy was grabbed by the skull and the leopard tried to pull him into a thicket. The older brother had the presence of mind to hang on to the boy's feet and held on until his parents appeared. The leopard released the child and slunk away.

That night a woman was awakened by a sound she couldn't place. The door to her hut stood wide open and she knew she had closed it before bed. The next thing she did was check on her baby. It was gone. The man-eater of Ruponda was in business.

The child the man-eater snatched must have been small indeed since only two days later it made its next kill. A mother had been teaching her child how to walk and went back to her hut for a moment. It was the toddler's last moment. He was gone. Score two. . . .

Iodine got the reports about seventy miles from Ruponda, and they were so scrambled that he did not know what was happening until he got there. When he arrived, he was sure. It was a leopard.

As Ionides reached Ruponda, another child was killed and while he was surveying the scene, another was taken some seven miles from the village. The only thing that Ionides could do was place a series of gun traps, three of which were prepared on obvious footpaths with a series of warnings for humans on the assumption that leopards can't read. Apparently, the local people couldn't either and the first victim was a woman who was properly shot in the arse.

Ionides was outraged and furious that the woman had interfered with his traps. But, his biggest problems were to come from the local district commissioner, a personage who has no parallel in American law. He was essentially a godhead who set and collected taxes on huts and generally saw to every facet of the business of the district. Game rangers fell under his jurisdiction.

Ionides thought that the D.C. took a "narrow and obstructive" view of what the game ranger was trying to effect, that being the man-eater's death. The D.C. had the traps removed. Immediately, two more children were taken by the man-eater. Iodine went to see the commissioner:

"These animals have always given trouble," pontificated the D.C. "I want them shot out. If necessary, bring twenty of your game scouts."

"Twenty?" asked Ionides astonished.

"We must have more firepower," said his nibs.

"Why?" asked Ionides. "Are we going to hunt in close columns of platoons?"

As Ionides would discover later, a child was taken even as they spoke. A week later Iodine was commanded to attend another meeting. It yielded the information that the D.C. would take matters up with his superior and ask him to relegate the leopard to the status of "vermin" in the district. Ionides was thunderstruck. He knew that the provincial commissioner would have no qualms about declaring the species as such since he was antiwildlife anyway. Ionides even states that the provincial commissioner, a few years past, had suggested that hippos be kept in check in Lake Malawi by means of depth charges and aerial machine-gunning! Ionides tried to explain that it would hardly solve the problem to have all leopards in the district declared vermin as the price of leopard skins was high and people would trap them all over the province and declare them to have been killed in this district. Tough luck. The leopard was declared vermin.

While all this was going on, Ionides had been building a series of traps that would use live bait and trap a leopard in its open half when a door came down. He used live chickens for bait and even went to the trouble of barring them off from the other half of the trap. Then, Ionides came up with his first major injection of Africa: the chickens were being stolen by the same people who were losing children at about one per week!

Five months had gone by and Ionides noted that sixteen children had been taken in Ruponda and three outlying villages. He also noted in cold ink that the average was four years old and that the eldest was a girl of nine and the youngest, six months.

Of course, Ionides was dealing with the same mentality that I encountered when I was hunting man-eaters. There was no cooperation, incredible as it may seem. After a child was taken, the tribesmen would close up their *kaias* for a couple of days and then leave them open as if nothing had happened. I saw the same thing with crocodiles—this extraordinary and frightening sense of fatalism that seemed to come over people who had seen with their own eyes a woman or child taken at the same place where they were bathing. Damned if I know. . . .

Finally, Ionides boiled over and went to a village where there had been five children killed over the past months—a village that did not even bother to bait its traps. Iodine was hardly a gentle fellow and favored the *kiboko* or *sjambok* whenever it was needed as he believed that the whip would bring results where other measures failed. This should be stated. It is fact, not racist emotion.

Iodine spoke with the headman and advised him that he had been warned many times about leaving his traps unbaited. "It seems that you suffer from a poor memory. Therefore I shall have to do something about a remedy for it," Ionides said. He cast a glance at his scout: "You have the *kiboko*?"

"It is a willing slave, waiting to serve, Bwana," the African said in KiSwahili.

"Very well, put him down on a sack and see if fifteen is sufficient medicine."

"Gladly, Bwana."

The *kiboko* worked and there were three leopards caught in the environs of Ruponda within a couple of days. Even so, a seventeenth child disappeared. Ionides could only presume that it had been eaten. By this time a wave of terror had cascaded over the whole district and even whites were holding shotguns while their children played in the yards.

Then, one late afternoon at about five, there was a great hullabaloo and Ionides took off following Hemedi Ngoe, who not long after would be the late Hemedi Ngoe. A leopard had killed a chicken and run into a field of beans with it. Immediately, Iodine and Hemedi followed it.

Ionides and Ngoe worked together with the knowledge of long experience. The Greek had gone but a few yards on his belly when he saw what he was sure was the leopard. He asked Hemedi with a cocked eyebrow and the African showed which way the leopard was lying. Ionides figured where its heart would be and fired his .470 (actually a diameter of .475). Nothing moved. The leopard was dead.

Ionides was certain that it was the child-killer, dead with the chicken still in its mouth. But Hemedi said that it was not, having a personal theory that there was a claw missing from the true killer's front paw. Hemedi was correct. Another child, number eighteen, was taken in a couple of days to Ionides's horror and despair.

The Greek waited all night over the body, which had not been eaten at all, an electric flashlight taped to his gun barrel, a poor practice as I have found that invariably the filament of the bulb is broken by the recoil of the gun, leaving the hunter in stygian darkness with a possibly wounded big cat.

The first golden thread of the African dawn had not yet blossomed into carmine when Ionides started back from number eighteen. He was intercepted by Hemedi Ngoe, who announced that a fifth leopard had been caught in a trap close by a village. It was a large male and was missing a front claw. Ngoe had been correct.

After a month, when all were certain that the man-eater of Ruponda was dead, the leopards were reestablished as a protected species, open only to game licenses. Possibly Ionides drew a few relieved breaths, but then he did not know what lay ahead.

Constantine Ionides was not a devotee of the principle or application of brotherly love when it came to his dealings with Africans. Much of his experience during World War II certainly bears this out. Ionides was always sorry that he was not old enough to fight in what he called "the Kaiser war" and his age again worked against him in the tiff with Hitler's boys. However, he volunteered and was disgusted to find that El Alamein was already over and that the Italian Army was somewhat disheveled by that time. But the Italians had managed to use a very cute ploy when they left Somaliland: they had armed the Somalis and it was Ionides's job with his 3rd Company of the 6th King's African Rifles to disarm what could only be called a substantial body of professional guerrilla fighters.

Ionides says: "I began with the gentler methods I had been

reluctantly forced to adopt in Tanganyika, where painful memories are long and my displeasure was still sufficient to cause some alarm. The kid glove made no impression at all on the Somalis."

I must here mention that Ionides had a frightening reputation that followed him throughout Africa. It seemed that anybody who angered "Father," as Ionides called himself in his self-styled patriarchal role to Africans, shortly died. It was quite uncanny, but Iodine ended up with the reputation of being a powerful sorcerer.

Probably the whole thing began when he once bearded four crop-raiding elephants and killed two with his .470. Within a couple of yards of the remaining two with no time to reload, Ionides just raised his empty rifle and screamed some exceptionally ferocious epithets at the pair. They swapped ends and disappeared. Of course, his African staff believed that the Greek had turned the elephants by powerful witchcraft. Soon after, Iodine's powers as a wizard got another boost.

As a game ranger in 1935, Ionides experienced many problems recruiting labor from the tribes, especially for porters. On one occasion he sent one of his men to get porterage from the son of a chief who drunkenly lost his temper and even pulled a knife on the scout. Losing his nerve, the chief's son ran into the bush as he knew that Ionides's wrath would be severe. It was. Ionides said to the people surrounding him that the son would be sorry, and soon. God would see to that. Piously, he turned to heaven and said in KiSwahili, "Patience brings blessing." Within a few days the chief's son was dead, killed from all signs by a leopard as he hid from Ionides in the *pori*.

A year or so later, Ionides again whipped up some seeming black magic against a poacher operating in the Liwale district of what is now Tanzania. The man and his cohorts had been shooting Cape buffalo with poisoned arrows from platforms over their crops. One of Ionides's scouts had caught them literally red-handed, and as there was little official support for game rangers in those days of poor communications and African vastness, Ionides had used the power of a paramount chief to set matters right. In any case, when he passed through the man's village—the African himself was a chief—he let it be known that he was monumentally displeased. He even refused to speak with the black but used one of his men to address him, a grave insult. The Africans heard all Ionides's comments well.

"One was heard to remark," wrote Ionides, "I don't know if we will ever survive this because the Bwana is very displeased." The man Ionides had used as spokesman then said that he didn't suppose that the man would survive the anger of the Bwana, but he should have thought of that before.

Sure as hell, a young warrior saw what he thought to be a crouching lion near his hut and fitted an *akocanthera* poisoned arrow to his bow and planted the shaft in the butt of the "lion." It turned out to be the chief and he was dead within three minutes.

Another troublemaker was also a victim of a poisoned arrow in a baboon drive a short while later. It was widely known that Ionides was hugely displeased with him. Ionides was getting his doctorate in wizardry.

The Greek's final show of magic was when he volunteered for the British Army earlyish in World War II. Crossing the ridge of mountains that separated his domain from Dar es Salaam, he passed a village that had planted crops slap across the border and promptly had his men pull them up as the villagers knew better.

Ionides had some problems with the district commissioner of the area and also with a petty chief by the name of Abdulla Mkaro, according to Ionides a professional backstabber; he professed warm, oily friendship until the Greek turned his back. Abdulla made trouble while Ionides was away in Somaliland, but Iodine was told what happened when he returned in 1943.

When Ionides was discharged and made the return trip by foot over the mountains and through the village, he learned that a very frightened Abdulla Mkaro had died of an undetermined African disease. Ionides was made as a sorcerer, and even his personal belongings took on a magical aura. His old hat, possibly the rattiest in Africa, was held in awe by his servants. Even his personal box was thought to contain something that made man-eaters fall asleep when Ionides was stalking them.

To return to World War II, Ionides was trying to get many hundreds of rifles away from cattle-thieving Somalis, who were stealing their Galla neighbors blind.

Whenever Ionides sent a detachment of his men to collect rifles, the young warriors would disappear leaving their only women, who did not know where the men were or what the story was. Constantine was quick to turn the tables. . . .

After the second time this happened, Ionides ordered that the women be taken captive and transported on trucks to his headquarters where they were, in fact, well looked after. He left a message that he would do his best to look after the pulchritudinous ladies, but after all, he was only a feeble old man and could not prevent his sex-starved troops from doing what came naturally. The longest the "old man" could guarantee the chastity of the women was three days, but if the rifles were to come in, then they would be returned. The rifles were turned in.

But Ionides's problems were not over yet. There was a tough group of Somalis under the command of one Sheik Hassan, a leader whose men shot up some Galla tribesmen after Ionides had returned their stolen cattle. Of course, Ionides knew the source of the slaughter—Italian rifles in the hands of Somalis. He sent in expedition to capture Hassan and bring him to headquarters.

Ionides asked the sheik when he could expect the rifles to be turned in and when the Galla would not have to worry anymore.

"I can do nothing," said the sheik. "I have no control over them."

"That is a great pity," Ionides intoned. "I believe you are a religious man?"

"Yes," affirmed the sheik.

"Well, you had better say some prayers."

The Somali brought forth his prayer rug and had some final words with Allah. As he was praying, a hangman's noose was put over his head and he was asked again if he would influence his men. The sheik said no and he was hoisted to kick for a while, then lowered, his neck definitely elongated.

Ionides said that he had decided to give the Sheik one more chance, and the Somali, after a long pause before he could find his strangled voice, allowed that perhaps he could help with the surrender of the rifles.

Ionides was a hard man, but he was thought of as a fair "Father." In his opinion there was no room for the white man's soft ways in Africa, a hard land. Ionides's thinking is illustrated by the example of a Major Measures, a believer in reasonable treatment. Ionides would not go on patrol with less than half a company, but Measures, who had a more gentle opinion of Africans than the Greek, went out one day with only eight *askaris* or native African troops. Worse, when he met up with what he thought was a counterpatrol of "reasonable" Somalis, he fraternized with them at once. The Somalis attacked the patrol that night and Measures had his head taken off by his own Bren gun.

As great a big game hunter as Constantine Ionides was, he will always be best remembered as the "Snake Man" of Africa, a title he earned the hard way after he left British service in March 1943. Returning to his game warden duties in Tanganyika, he passed through Nairobi, Kenya, the capital of the country to the north. Paying a courtesy call on the famous L. S. B. Leakey, the paleontologist and curator widely known for his humanoid fossil finds in the Olduvai Gorge, Ionides called in at the Coryndon Museum. Leakey had just started a new snake park that was attached to the Coryndon and asked Ionides if he could be of help in catching species such as cobras, mambas, and boomslangs. Iodine asked how, if he was successful, these should be sent. Leakey said in his offhand way that the post would be fine.

Before this goes any further, I should mention that I have had the most kind cooperation of the National Museums and Monuments of Bulawayo, Zimbabwe, and especially of the Senior Curator of Herpetology (snakes), Dr. Donald G. Broadley, who was a personal friend of Ionides and has been most helpful to me in the collation of the Greek's career. Ionides speaks not to some of the problems with the postal services, but Dr. Broadley himself and C. R. S. Pitman, Game Warden of Uganda, mention a few episodes that Ionides does not touch upon in his own writings for obvious reasons.

Ionides was once nearly prosecuted for sending poisonous snakes through the mail, although his boxes always bore the rather foreboding warning LIVE SNAKES. Pitman, also a close personal friend of Ionides and author himself of a book on snakes, notes that there was one instance when a thoroughly irritated cobra escaped in a mail-sorting office. Nobody was bitten but I am sure I don't know why. That Ionides was off the wall is also born out by the fact that he once sent a live black mamba to an enemy at the British Museum of Natural History. Happily, the mamba died from the rigors of transatlantic travel before the box was opened. Considering these escapades and his stature as a wizard, Ionides would have made a very fine enemy, indeed!

Ionides, in his early days, sent two spitting cobras (*Naga nigricollis*) in a canvas bag in the trunk of a friend's automobile to a pal from coastal Kilifi. Upon their arrival in Nairobi, the friend to whom the deadly hypodermic-fanged, spraying snakes had been sent—they can also bite as if on vacation as well as spray a very dangerous mist of venom at the face—found a very fine empty bag, and he wrote telling Iodine that it was, incidentally, a very nice bag. Where the spitting cobras went has fortunately never been solved. Iodine was therefore most interested to know that a night adder and a garter snake (poisonous) that he had posted to Leakey had finally arrived in Nairobi.

Ionides started at the bottom rung of the herpetology ladder with the time-tested and sometimes inadequate forked stick. As might be expected, some of his greatest adventures were with mambas. . . .

The largest by length and without doubt the most savage and speedy of the poisonous snakes of Africa is the black mamba, *Dendroaspis polylepis,* which can attain fifteen feet in southern Africa. This is a couple of feet longer than the supposed "record" of about twelve and a half feet. I know because I measured the skin of one at this exact length, minus the head, which came from a Namibian ranch owned by my old friend, Gerhard Liedtke. The skin was not stretched—easy to tell as the space between the scales was normal. It is now in America with another taken home by my good friend Stan Warren, the outdoor writer. The biggest ever taken by Iodine was ten and a half feet from Voi, in Kenya, but I suspect that the southern subspecies grows much bigger than the east African.

Ionides called mambas—especially black ones—"fabulous," as they lend themselves so perfectly to pulp fiction, which the Greek found out. Usually, the "black" mamba is not really black at all, but a dark olive to a pale slate color. The black comes from the lining of the mouth, which is indeed as black as a brigand's heart, flanked by a *canthus* or face that is slender and, appropriately, coffin-shaped. It has never been determined just how fast a mamba is, so just take my word that it can navigate even through heavy cover much faster than a man can run, even one in top form. Black mambas you do not need, nor do you especially require the Jameson's or even the green mamba, which are not remotely as aggressive as the black species.

Mambas are really a tree-dwelling variety of cobra or *Elapidae*, but they have developed, according to the late Mr. Darwin's theorem, to the point that even injections of antivenin effective against the bite of the hatful of African cobras do little good against mambas. Mambas even have prehensile tails.

That mambas are aggressive is axiomatic. That they are the world's most difficult and dangerous snake to capture alive is open to very slight argument, but Iodine, who also caught a number of King cobras in Asia in his later years, still gives the laurels to the mambas, especially the black variety. Iodine's first encounter with a black mamba well illustrates how he formed this opinion. . . .

The Greek found a black mamba lying across a bush path in heavy grass and, not realizing that perhaps the snake was a good deal longer than he supposed, pinned it down in the middle with his forked stick. Ionides was almost fatally struck as four feet of the provoked animal lashed out at his hand, which he pulled away a nanosecond before it was hit. Fortunately, there was just that little bit of snake length that prevented Ionides from being bitten and he was able to hold off the mamba. The white man was riding a serpentine tiger that he could not let go of, and Ionides responded with a string of his legendary curses. As he points out, he had no antivenin, he was on a private safari well out of range of any hospital, and, when he told his men to search for something heavy in the forked stick department, they kept returning empty-handed. I never knew Ionides personally, but his reputation suggests that by this point his invective was sufficient to peel old paint off hard wood. Finally, a chunk of rotting log was produced by his somewhat less-than-imaginative crew, which, coupled with Iodine's magic hat, enabled him to grab the black mamba by the neck and the head.

The snake was unbelievably strong and finally seemed to collapse from the pressure that Ionides put upon its neck.

Snakes have to breathe, too. Slowly, the slinky steel coils came off Iodine's forearms and the mamba was boxed. Ionides thought that there had to be an easier way to earn a living, if not a more fascinating one.

Space limitations do not permit inclusion of the complete history of Iodine's snake-catching, but there are certain highlights that I would not want you to go to bed without hearing. Possibly the tale of Mahomedi Ngelelo is worth a few minutes' sleep? I think that perhaps it is. . . .

Mahomedi Ngelelo was some sort of mystic who claimed that he had complete—or nearly so—immunity from snake bite of any kind. Africa is not full of these men, but there are enough of them to make the odd hair stand on end. Mahomedi was just a casual laborer who had worked for Ionides on and off—until the day when Iodine had the job of capturing *three* black mambas out of their condominium lair beneath a rotted tree stump. Mahomedi was one of his men.

Suffice it to say that Iodine was having a tough time snaring or noosing the three. He had recently gone to his new "catcher" stick, which used a cord through a hollow boring that ran up the shaft, but he had only put one mamba in the box. Mahomedi was trying to grab another one when he handed his noose to a porter. If you live in Africa, you don't need me to tell you what happened next. The porter created enough slack that Mahomedi called to Ionides, "Bwana, I've been bitten!" producing a four-letter-word response from Ionides, who had his own hands full with the first mamba.

Mahomedi didn't get a full bite but a slice across the hand from the enraged mamba. This was still quite sufficient to turn a man into an obituary, had there been bush Tanganyikan newspapers at the time. It only takes two drops of mamba venom to attain heaven, hell, or somewhere in between in quite a hurry.

Ionides yelled back from the other side of the termite heap

113

where he had been struggling with his own mamba that if Mahomedi thought he would lose control of the snake, he must kill it at once to prevent it from biting somebody else. When the three were safely boxed, Iodine asked casually, so as not to excite the man, how he felt.

Mahomedi answered that there was no problem at all, and that he was fine.

When all three mambas were boxed, Ionides called off the day's work and posted a careful watch over Mahomedi in case his central nervous system shut down, as is the normal effect of the neurotoxic venom of the mamba.

Ionides realized that Mahomedi Ngelelo had taken a course of *dawa,* magic, to become immune to snake bite, but even with his years in Africa he didn't fully credit such magic. Yet, the next morning when he inquired about the black man, he was told that he was out looking for more mambas!

For a man who had had a considerable amount written about him (two books and quite a few articles), Ionides disliked the purple prose and exaggerations of his exploits. He certainly did not believe in poetic license, as I have realized the hard way through my own experiences. Stuff such as mambas and cobras do not need the embellishments of pulp literature. He was especially irritated that he was portrayed as the hero of an incident that happened before he was born.

A black mamba, reliably reported, had fallen from the grass roof of a hut in South Africa and killed five of six family members before it escaped out the door. When some misinformation on Ionides was published, the place had become his home in Newala, the Tanganyikan highlands, and the number of people killed had been changed to eight. It had become a green mamba rather than a black and Ionides was the hero who'd captured it. No wonder he was disgruntled. . . .

To return to Mahomedi. This African's claim to fame of

being snake-proof intrigued Iodine. Perhaps the mamba slash had no effect because the venom had been depleted on the catch sticks? The Greek knew that Mahomedi had often provoked other snakes to bite him and had suffered no worse symptoms than a slight swelling from such venomous snakes as night adders. Was he really immune? Ionides prevailed on him to work his magic on the Bwana.

Ngelelo agreed with pleasure, and went off to the forest to collect an armful of different roots. Shavings of these were pulped and mixed with castor oil and rubbed into cuts made in Ionides's wrists, elbows, knees, and ankles every two weeks until Mahomedi pronounced eight weeks later that Ionides was now immune from snakebite.

Ever the small boy at heart, Iodine could not wait to test the *dawa* and managed to get himself bitten by a nine-inch night adder, about two-thirds of the adult size. In fact, he persuaded the snake, sometimes deadly, to bite him twice.

Ionides, to his astonishment, felt no pain whatever but for the actual bite! He also had no symptoms of snakebite. But, ever practical, Ionides wondered if the snake had somehow depleted its venom. He waited overnight until at least a certain amount of venom would be regenerated and then coerced the snake into biting him twice again. Nope. Hardly anything even though he had picked up the snake with its fangs embedded in his hand. On the second day after the bites, a small pimple formed at the site of the fang wounds.

A few weeks later Ionides was bitten by another night adder and experienced no more pain than a bee sting. He was also bitten by a burrowing adder twice, which had proved fatal to men before, but experienced few problems.

Ionides may not have been totally immune but he got off surprisingly well when he was bitten by a pet puff adder after a dinner party. His arm swelled up above the elbow for about ten days but he showed nowhere near the horrible symptoms of gangrene that Alan Root displayed on receiving a puff adder bite in the finger. Alan, who has a rather depressing way of showing up in these pages (see *Death in the Long Grass*, St. Martin's Press, New York, 1977) almost lost his hand. It is *his* paw that is featured on the cover of *Snakes and Snake Bite* (Visser and Chapman, Struik, Cape Town, 1978) and he was lucky to lose only an index finger.

The puff adder kills more people in Africa than any other snake because it is common and has a habit of taking its saunas on native footpaths. The mambas and cobras may be the favorites of armchair adventures, but the puff adder gets the job done.

What can go wrong with the snakes of Africa and their collectors was demonstrated very amply by the case of Iodine's friend and fellow in the game of game ranging, Eric Locke. It was 1953 in Tanganyika, at a place called Mbeya— the same place where George Rushby fought some twenty man-eating lions during World War II.

Locke took Ionides's lead when it came to capturing snakes and he had in his serpentarium a hissing sand snake, a young puff adder, and a vine snake, which he had had for some time. The latter was quite tame and until Locke abused it sufficiently, it would not bite. However, it finally acquiesced and grabbed him by the ball of the thumb.

It was Eric Locke's wedding anniversary. His last one.

Eric Locke was debilitated anyway, having a bleeding ulcer as well as bacillary dysentery and relapsing fever, both powerful components of the bushveld's revenge. After the bite, he first got a screaming headache that he put down to his anniversary celebrations and went to bed early. In the morning he was vomiting and by that night he had brought up blood, including stale blood that had obviously lain in his stomach. The next day he continued vomiting blood and went into convulsions. He was dead before fifty hours had passed from the bite of the vine snake.

That it was the vine snake was corroborated by one of

Young Fred on his first trip home in 1875. The photo was obviously taken in a Victorian studio with a Matabele assegai and a fairly thick tusk as props. He probably brought these home with him as he did the Hollis 4-bore elephant gun.

Below: Selous's almost fatal brush with a Cape buffalo on May 20, 1874. For his shooting pony it *was* fatal.

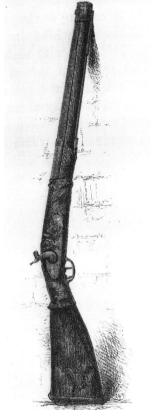

One of Fred's Hollis 4-bore elephant guns. The recoil was so ferocious that the grip and part of the forestock had to be bound with wet elephant ear skin to prevent the wood splitting. The gun was loaded with a *handful* of black powder and fired a .91 caliber, quarter-pound ball.

Selous under a wounded cow elephant in September 1878. Not many hunters survived this situation. Fred did.

Below: Selous in British East Africa (Kenya) about 1908.

Frederick Courteney Selous in his early fifties.

"Iodine" Ionides wearing his famous magic hat which probably had enough dried snake venom in it to kill a battalion.

The black mamba (*Dendroaspis polylepis*) clearly showing the classic *canthus* or coffin shape of the head. When it's looking for trouble, it's Africa's fastest and most dangerous snake. Only the lining of the open mouth is black; the snake is usually a dull olive to brownish.

Ionides with a big Gaboon viper in Tanzania. Their expressions show well the attitude of Africans to snakes.

The fifth-generation Anglo-Greek with a young green mamba.

John Boyes about the time he was King of the Wakikuyu. His bandolier shows that his rifle was likely a .303 British caliber. John later was made a Lt. Colonel in Kenya.

A typical reception by the Kikuyu of a party of explorers or traders in their country. This assault is upon the safari of Count Samuel Teleki on his way to the discovery of Lakes Rudolph and Stephanie in East Africa.

A Kikuyu warrior ready for his favorite pastime: ambush. His headdress is of black feathers and note the *simi* or short sword at the right side for easy drawing while pretending to shake hands.

Boyes with ivory he shot as a
professional elephant
hunter in his middle years.

Above: A lone Masai about 1900.
This single-handed lion kill wasn't as
unusual as it might seem. The Masai
and Kikuyu were mostly enemies but
sometimes teamed up, as in one case
to wipe out John Boyes. The Masai
lived largely on blood and milk.

Two Wandorobo hunters. Their
bows are much stronger than those
of the Kikuyu and they live entirely
on meat. John Boyes hunted
extensively with them as King of the
Wakikuyu.

A thoughtful Jim Sutherland with his dog Brandy in his trading days before he took up professional elephant hunting. The double terai hat was typical of the times, intended to prevent exposure to the "poisonous" rays of the East African sun. From the look of him, Jim must not have been long out of prize fighting.

Jim Sutherland's fox terrier Whisky atop a big bull elephant.

Jim Sutherland at the height of his career before he was poisoned by natives. Jim continued to hunt at a loss when the price of ivory fell tremendously during the Depression.

Right: Part of Jim Sutherland's staff at one of his camps—hardly the silk tents that he was reputed to use, although when poisoned and partly paralyzed, he was carried on parts of hunts in a *machilla* or hammock. An elephant never got him, despite his wish to die on the track of a big tusker.

Jim Sutherland and some of his followers with a huge bull elephant.

Locks's head scouts, a fine man named Musa Hawa, a Distinguished Conduct Medal winner in the war.

I should mention here that the vine snake is of the type exemplified by the boomslang or tree snake. It was not until the 1930s that the boomslang was even considered poisonous. Being back-fanged rather than front-fanged, the boomslang clan have fixed teeth at the rear of the mouth and have highly toxic saliva, gram for gram far more poisonous than cobra venom. Eric Locke, to his regret, believed that the vine snake was not poisonous. . . .

By the time the war ended, Ionides, had almost two years of accumulated leave due him from the Game Department. He also had the cash, even from such a low-paying job, to indulge in his fantasies, which were to collect the rarest game on earth for the Coryndon Museum in Nairobi, Kenya.

In his years of hunting, Ionides procured species of rare animals—now in the Coryndon—including the mountain gorilla, Lord Derby's eland, addax, addra, sitatunga, black lechwe, yellow-backed duiker, Hunter's antelope, giant forest hog, bongo, scimitar-horned oryx, Nubian ibex, Abbott's duiker, northern white rhino, and okapi. That he did the entire group with an iron-sighted .470 Nitro Express is incredible!

Constantine Ionides made more than a reputation, he made a *name*. He *was* Africa's Snake Man, but he was oh, so much more. He discovered many forms that were never before recognized. As I have access to some unique material about the man, let me tell it as he deserves it.

I am deeply indebted to Dr. Broadley of the Bulawayo Museum of Zimbabwe for his insight and his courtesy in sending some of these incidents to me. . . .

One that I feel necessary to include is the story of Ionides's capture of some water cobras (excerpted from Ionides and Pitman, 1965).

*Ionides commenced visual operations from a jetty (at the
southern extremity of the lake)* [Lake Malawi] *about 7 A.M. to
ascertain whether any water cobras were lying half-submerged,
or just above the water line, on the rocks, as was sometimes the
case. Then he and his assistants spread out and watched the
water around the rocks. When a snake was seen leaving or
entering a crevice, or cruising about, he was called. If it was
still visible he caught it with a grab-stick and lifted it out of the
water. Should it have disappeared into a crevice, Ionides waited
patiently for it to emerge, or until another one was seen.*

*This went on till sundown. Some big specimens required a
long "tug-of-war" before they could be hauled out of a crevice,
especially if held near the tail. His two assistants also had grab-
sticks with which they would seize and hold a snake in the water
when Ionides was otherwise occupied, until he was ready to deal
with it. The majority were taken in shallow water. The big
examples were the most easily grabbed, the smaller ones being
the more elusive. Sixty-seven water cobras were taken in the
course of twenty-two collecting days during two expeditions
between 16th and 27th August, 1958, and 22nd July to 3rd
August 1960.*

It should be pointed out that there is no known antivenin for
the water cobra. . . .

Ionides went far afield from Tanzania in his collecting and,
as has been mentioned earlier, this included India. There is
a copy of a letter that I have, again courtesy of Dr. Broadley,
from Ionides in which he says that he is off to the Baringo
region of Kenya to collect southern black mambas.

But Ionides proved himself to be only flesh and blood. In
1956, the Father had a very severe thrombosis of his leg and
then had to do most of his collecting in a *machilla*, the portable hammock of southern Africa, only getting out when a
snake was spotted and then potted.

The Greek died—thank Heaven—in the hospital in 1968
when both his legs had to be taken off. But let C. R. S. Pitman, game warden of Uganda and author of, among other
works, *Snakes of Uganda*, tell you succinctly of Iodine's life. . . .

C. J. P. Ionides

Constantine J. P. Ionides, known affectionately to his friends as "Iodine," died in hospital at Nairobi on 22nd September, 1968 after both his legs had been amputated, the final stage of incapacitating thrombosis from which he had courageously suffered during the past twelve years. So at the relatively early age of 68 African herpetology has lost a field worker of world-wide repute, indeed a legendary figure, unrivalled in his trade and unsurpassed in experience. He had developed a snake-catching technique of remarkable efficiency and above all never exposed others to the dangers of snake-bite, the actual capture of the large venomous species which were his principal quarry was his sole responsibility. Over a long period of years he supplied poisonous snakes in quantity to various organisations for the preparation of antivenom serum, as well as to snake parks and zoos. His personal bag of green mambas must have totalled at least ten thousand; black mambas some hundreds as well as many thousands of Gaboon vipers.

At one time he indulged in the highly risky and reprehensible practice of using the East African postal service for distributing large live poisonous species until one day a very angry cobra escaped in a sorting office and he was told in no uncertain terms of the enormity of his offence! He even posted to a senior official at the British Museum (Natural History) who he disliked, a mamba which luckily died in transit! An enthusiastic, indefatigable collector, he discovered many new reptile species and races, and he was particularly generous with his contributions to many scientific institutions. Knowing when and where to look he was able to find and collect novelties such as the vividly marked tiny burrowing Chilorhinophis carpenteri liwalwensis in hundreds, when other would have obtained but few.

Much could be written about this eccentric character, which would not be relevant to this testimony, but it was his desire to savor the wide, open spaces of Africa which led him to transfer from a British regiment to the King's African Rifles from which he resigned to enjoy life as a big game hunter and ivory poacher, eventually joining the Tanganyikan Game Department to become an enthusiastic wild life conservationist.

His main sphere of herpetological operation was in the

southern region of Tanganyika [now Tanzania]. *Though snakes, with which he had a definite affinity, always fascinated him, it was not until he retired from the Tanganyika Game Department that he became a dedicated, almost fanatical, herpetologist. Besides, he was a keen, all-round naturalist, an expert hunter particularly skilled in dealing with marauding elephants and a most successful collector of rare mammals for scientific institutions.*

Rebellious by nature, an unhappy childhood worsened by authority's unremitting brutality at preparatory and public school left him with a permanently soured outlook on life and in particular towards authority, which not without reason he regarded as utterly contemptible and despised; he was a self-avowed rebel and it was not his wont to suffer fools gladly. Intolerant of those who did not share his passion for snakes, his like is a refreshing rarity in an over-orthodox world from which he will be greatly missed.

His periods of leave from the Game Department he devoted to expeditions to the Sudan, Ethiopia and the Congo Rain Forest, mainly on behalf of what is now the National Museum in Nairobi, in quest of rare animals, which he invariably brought to a satisfactory, successful conclusion.

In his declining years, despite his acutely painful, crippling disability, he visited Southern Arabia to collect reptiles and had proposed other visits to Morocco and the Lebanon.

In 1966 he organized and financed an expedition to Thailand to fulfil one of his long-cherished dreams—to catch with his own hands the huge King Cobra or Hamadryad of ill repute. On this venture the bag consisted of sixteen King Cobras, all captured without untoward incident—one a male, the others all females guarding their eggs.

His African staff, who included expert snake-handlers, revered and respected him, besides regarding him with considerable awe, and his filthy, soft hat once described as only fit for the garbage heap—so frequently used as a last resource to quieten a refractory poisonous head and much permeated with all manner of venom, had became legendary. Much has been written about him—Snake Man, Life with Ionides, A Hunter's

Tale [sic]; *much more that could have been written will be lost with his passing.*

The writer of this tribute has for many years been privileged to enjoy the closest friendship with "Iodine," who to his friends was a friend indeed.

It's a shame that God didn't help his enemies. . . .

Part Three

John
Boyes

frica is full of improbable legends, but there are few men who had the impact on the early British settlements in East Africa as did an adventurer named John Boyes, born in Hull, in the East Riding of Yorkshire in 1874. That a runaway to sea would eventually be the uncrowned king of the most savage black tribe of the times as well as a successful trader, ivory hunter, and author is, indeed, improbable. That it is a historical fact merely points up that early East Africa was truly the land of opportunity for a man with guts and a good eye with a rifle.

John Boyes was educated in Germany from the age of six, when he was sent by his parents to stay with relatives in the small town of Engelfingen. By the time he went home at thirteen, he spoke German better than English, despite his renowned broad Yorkshire accent. In 1887, when he returned, his parents wanted him to continue his education in Hull, but John resisted further schooling out of a desperate desire to join the navy. He spent all his time at the docks watching ships come in and out and finally was able to run away as a cabin boy and cook on a North Sea fishing vessel under sail that planned to be gone for three months. That he was thrown overboard during a storm and very fortunately rescued by one of his shipmates putting a boathook through his belt with a wild thrust dulled his enthusiasm not a bit. Once, off Heligoland, he was the only man left aboard, set to make supper and keep the capstan anchor donkey boiler stoked, but he got sidetracked when a couple of German-speaking boys rowed out. John entertained them while the donkey boiler he was supposed to watch got so hot it set fire to its mountings. When he returned after six months with the fishing fleet, he was fifteen.

After this time with the fishermen he decided that he wanted some proper blue-water experience and thought that he could get a berth at Liverpool. Having almost no money, he walked the whole distance from Hull, pawning his spare clothes for food along the way via Leeds and Manchester, the width of England, about 150 miles. Finally, he got service on a tugboat bound for Rotterdam and was marooned by high tide but rescued by his ship, which, incidentally, lost the barque it was supposed to be towing back to England. John was keen to become an officer, but first he had to get an able-seaman rating. To become an officer, he needed four years experience at sea, one of which had to be on a sailing ship to foreign ports. He signed on with a barque bound for trade in South America and found himself up the Amazon stricken with yellow fever. This was his second brush with death. There would be many more.

When he was sent to the hospital in Brazil, in a frontier town called Laguna, he found that yellow fever and malaria leading to blackwater fever were so common and the rate of mortality so high that the hospital—which also doubled as a jail and lunatic asylum—had a coffin with a sliding bottom. When a funeral, of which there were several a day, was completed, the coffin was returned to the ward!

There was another curious thing: when a patient became very bad he was given a spoonful of a substance that, from the smell, John later decided was some sort of opium. What really got the attention of the sixteen-year-old was that invariably, after getting this mixture, the patient died! One evening, the spoon was brought to John Boyes by one of the harmless lunatics who also did duty as an attendant. The boy asked the attendant to just leave the spoonful of stuff on his table, but a Brazilian soldier, who was in the next bed and in terrible pain, asked John if he could have the mixture. He took it and was dead the next morning. John knew he must somehow escape.

The following Sunday, he recognized voices outside as those of some of his shipmates on the *Lake Simcoe* and screamed to get their attention. Begging to be released, he got the men to overpower the guard at the entrance and rescue him. He recovered at sea. After a severe outbreak of scurvy, the ship finally made it home to Falmouth Harbour in England.

When he had done his requisite year on sailing ships, he joined the Royal Naval Reserve in the hope of making it to lieutenant and signed on with various steamships. His adventures included a year on a boat trading between the various ports on the coast of India and another that took Arabs and Turks from Port Said to Jedda, where they continued their pilgrimage to Mecca. His first exposure to Africa was when he joined the Royal Niger Company and went up the west coast trading flintlocks and powder to the natives. Boyes was enthralled with the scenery and mystery of the country. The boy made up his mind that someday he would enter the interior, but at that time he had no idea of how far he would penetrate or the fame he would earn the hard way.

While on this trip up the West African rivers, he got into a tangle with malaria and, unable to slip it, he had to go into the hospital in Rotterdam on his return. When he recovered, he had another of his strange sea experiences when he joined a coastal vessel that traveled to the Channel Island, Guernsey. One night his ship was rammed by another that had paid no attention to warnings. Seemingly, the crew of both ships lost their heads at the same time and entangled the masts, which Boyes thought would crush the lifeboat. In the complete confusion, he found himself in a small boat with one other man and noticed the other vessel drifting away. He and the other man managed to crawl aboard and found the ship completely deserted as the crew had all jumped to his own ship on impact. Everything was in perfect order, even down to the navigation lamp being lit. John was able to steer it clear of another impact with a steamer and dropped anchor.

He was thrilled to realize that, as it had been abandoned, it was fair game for a salvage claim! His own ship had to be towed to London and, a few days later, he was asked by the captain of the second ship—also the owner—to join him in a trip to Guernsey to see about his share of the salvage money. As it turned out, he couldn't go and the ship sank along with the owner. The salvage claim came to nothing so John lost what might have been a substantial windfall. Yet he was not too upset at his loss when he realized that if he had gone with the captain he, too, would have been killed.

Since his last voyage, John had been working toward his lieutenancy by attending a navigation school at Hull, but his dreams of becoming a naval officer were doused with cold brine by the results of his medical exam. The yellow fever he had had in Brazil had affected his eyesight and he couldn't qualify. But the navy's loss would be Africa's gain and John decided to work his way before the mast to Durban, South Africa, arriving just after the Jameson Raid on the Transvaal in late 1895.

The Second Matabele war in Southern Rhodesia—as the conflict between the Matabele and settlers came to be called—had also just broken out and it is not clear whether John jumped ship to fight in it or whether the captain knew that he was only going as far as Durban. One thing was for sure: he had to get to the action in Bulawayo. He tried to sign on as a soldier, but as he had had no experience he was turned down and had to take a job in a steam bakery. With his slim wages, he made it to the Transvaal (then a republic) and finally took work as a fireman on the railway, the mail train to Standerton. He had originally planned to hop off the train at Standerton, which was 200 miles closer to Bulawayo, but his clothes were so greasy that he decided to do a couple more runs to earn enough to buy some new ones. Having conned a free pass to Johannesburg, he soon met a man named Adcock who befriended him and was headed toward Bulawayo himself. John went along with the fifty or so Cape Coloureds and Hottentots who accompanied Adcock, but on reaching a place called Maklutsi, Adcock decided that his livestock had had it and elected to head for Salisbury.

John had the choice of either returning or heading toward Bulawayo on foot, 150 miles on semibush roads. As he went along, John met an old soldier named Grant, who was out of chow. The two decided to travel together and share what supplies Boyes had tied in the trouser legs of his spare pants. After a few days, resting near a bush waterhole, they were completely out of food. Fortunately, when John stripped down to have a wash, he discovered that the water was full of mud fish (probably barbel, maybe lungfish), and what they didn't cook and eat on the spot they dried for the trip ahead. Later, they were overtaken by an Afrikaans farmer driving a mule wagon to Bulawayo and traded some of the dried fish for tea and flour as well as getting a lift with him. But John was so anxious to get to Bulawayo that he jogged the last few miles on foot and presented himself to the officer in charge of the Matabeleland Mounted Police. He was hired at the heady rate of 10 shillings a day and was provided with food, arms, and a suit of khaki clothes. He was in heaven.

As it didn't take long to join up, he ran back to meet the mule wagon, carrying his newly issued .500/.450 Martini-Henry rifle and fifty rounds of ammunition. He was such a dazzling sight that Grant decided to enlist instantly!

After three rather dull months with the Mounted Police, Boyes decided to transfer to the Africander Corps, an irregular outfit composed of experienced frontiersmen, in the hope that he would see some action. His commander was Captain van Niekerk, not F. C. Selous as some accounts fancifully imagine. What made the campaign difficult was that the Matabele were in the hills and shooting down on the whites, killing some but not as many as malaria took west. Giving the Africander Corp particular trouble was an *induna* named Umwini, who, despite his low opinion of the whites, was finally shot through the shoulder and captured. He faced a firing squad with great presence, refusing a blindfold as he "wished to see death coming."

During the campaign, John met the famous R. S. S. Baden-Powell, who would make quite a noise in the Boer War and subsequently founded the Boy Scouts. Baden-Powell dressed as an ordinary trooper and it was only later that Boyes realized that he had been speaking with the man who was in charge of the entire expedition.

John Boyes remained for a while at a new fort built in Umvunga Drift, suffering from severe dysentery, which he managed to cure with a diet of flour and water mixed. As the war simmered down, he returned to Bulawayo, where he guarded some murderers who were in the local jail, all of whom were eventually hanged. Finally, he entered into a partnership with a man named Frielich, founding the Colonial Fruit and Produce Stores of Bulawayo. It was in Bulawayo that he met an old pioneer, mentioned by Selous, called Elstop. Elstop changed Boyes's life when he told him tales of the old Mashonaland and advised the boy that such adventure and hunting still were available to the north. Although Frielich eventually made at least 100,000 pounds from the business, selling fodder he had laid in before the Boer War, Boyes dissolved the partnership and decided to head north. But first he needed a holiday and went to the Cape Colony city of East London where he lived on the beach with some pals from the Matabele war. Taking ship, he worked his way to Durban and, as he was broke as usual, signed on with a Shakespearian theater company. This lasted a month and John reckoned he was no worse than the other actors.

Again before the mast, he worked his way to Zanzibar and

gathered all the information he could about the east African interior. The sum total of this was that nobody knew very much except that it was wild as hell. That suited Boyes perfectly.

There were no ships running to his last coastal stop in those days, so he made a deal with an Arab plying his crab-claw–sail dhow to Mombasa. As per usual, there was no accommodation for passengers except on deck and the natives as well as Boyes had to "camp out" in all weather. The distance between Zanzibar and Mombasa was only about 250 miles and the fare was astonishingly cheap, two rupees or two shillings and eightpence for the entire voyage. Naturally, the fifty passengers on the miniscule ship couldn't make fires on deck so their food had to be ready to eat. The Arab captain remarked that what was good enough in the days of his father was good enough for him and his passengers. Boyes said that this was said in Arabic but there was a passenger who spoke a "leettel Engleesh." The boat had no compass or lights and hugged the shore, but it hadn't gone very far before there was trouble: the dhow hit some fishermen's pound nets. The fishermen raised simmering blue blazes and demanded to be compensated for their nets, which were destroyed. The captain didn't see it that way and refused, at which point the fishermen made a try for the small boat being towed behind the dhow. John realized that if there were any further problems, his and the other passengers' only safety lay with the smaller boat as the water was stiff with sharks. John grabbed a handy ax and jumped into the boat, promising any comer—in English—that he would meet Allah a bit ahead of schedule if he tried to board. If his language was not understood his intent was, and the fishermen backed off as the dhow proceeded on its way.

All went fairly well and at a good speed for a couple of days, when the dhow again came to a screeching halt in the water. The passengers panicked. Boyes noted that the captain was shouting as loudly as the rest and figured he was giving orders that the passengers refused to heed. Grabbing the man who spoke some English, John asked why none of the orders was being obeyed.

"He is not giving orders, he is praying," said the man. "He is calling on Allah to help him."

So, Boyes took charge. He was able to calm the passengers and crew a bit and then he began to make soundings with a jury-rigged lead line, finding much deeper water on starboard than on port. Obviously, they had hit a sunken reef.

John, as soon as he realized the problem, lashed some spare rope to the anchor and had it hauled out and dropped from the small boat about thirty yards away toward the open sea. All the while, he kept his ax handy in case of any trouble. After six hours of hauling, possibly helped by the tide, the dhow was free. Boyes continued to captain the boat until he saw a large white building on shore and asked what it was. On being told that it was the house of a white man, he took the dhow close, anchored her, and rowed the small boat to shore. It was the home of a British official who put up his countryman for the night, but when he returned in the morning, the dhow had already sailed. John walked the thirty miles to Mombasa.

It was certainly 1898 when John arrived in Mombasa—the Isle of War—and likely very early in the year at that. The Mombasa–Uganda Railway, "the lunatic line," had just been started and was encountering unbelievable problems such as hostile natives, man-eating lions, terrible heat, wild animals (a rhino derailed a locomotive), and shortages of food. Only a small bunch of buildings used by the British Government, a Greek-run hotel, and a sub-commissioner represented all of Blighty. Above the sweltering city, connected to the mainland by a bridge, loomed the Portuguese-built ancient Fort Jesus, constructed in the time of Henry the Navigator. Thinking that the sub-commissioner would be of help to him, John went to see him and was fairly astonished when he was told that white men were not at all welcome in the interior. They were not wanted under any circumstances and John was advised to leave the country as soon as possible.

On leaving the sub-commissioner's office, John happened to bump into one of the very few traders from the interior, a man named Gibbons. John knew of the recent mutiny of troops in Uganda—to the west of what would become Kenya—and of the subsequent problems of lack of food and the cost of importing it. At that time, in 1898, all goods had to be brought in in sixty-pound loads on the heads of native porters at a cost of from sixty to one hundred rupees, which often far exceeded the cost of the actual goods. He talked Gibbons into a partnership that would use donkey wagons for transport rather than porters. John evidently borrowed the money from Gibbons or elsewhere, as the partners assembled thirty donkeys at a price of a hundred rupees each and hired a hundred coastal-dwelling Swahili porters. There were no harnesses available in Mombasa for the donkeys but John was able to make up thirty rigs using rope and sackcloth. They were in business.

In addition to the hundred Swahilis, for each ten there was one *askari* or native soldier whose duty it was to patrol the camp at night, to act as police, and to capture any deserters from his "stick" of ten porters. Their effectiveness was enhanced by the fact that if they failed to catch a deserter, they had to carry his load themselves. As John wrote, "Apart from the unpleasantness of having to carry a sixty-pound load in the ranks of the porters instead of swaggering along with no burden other than his rifle, ammunition and blanket, the blow to his self-importance involved from the degradation from askari to porter is one that would be severely felt by any nigger [sic], who is probably blessed with more self-esteem than even a circus ring-master or a newly appointed Sub-Commissioner, and the fear of such degradation is a wonderful spur on the askaris' watchfulness." A cook and a private servant completed the outfit.

One thing I have always wondered about: how did the *askaris* keep watch all night and march with the safari all day without sleep? When did they rest? The answer is they must have worked in shifts.

When Boyes and Gibbons finally pushed off for the interior, they had 1200 pounds of government contract goods and a hundred loads of their own of trade goods that they proposed to use in the area of Lake Rudolph to buy more donkeys, which were cheap in that area. By March 1898, the railway had only penetrated to the area of Tsavo, where man-eating lions killed scores of imported Indian construction coolies until they had their collective hash settled by Lt. Col. John Henry Patterson, an engineer, who later for a short time became the first game warden of British East Africa. (See the Peter Capstick Library, *The Man-Eaters of Tsavo*, St. Martin's Press.) John actually met Messrs. Parenti and Heubner, who were the survivors of a classic attack by one lion inside a railway car that resulted in the death of a third man, Ryall, who was killed by the lion as it stood on Parenti. The lion then leaped clear through a window with the body, which was discovered half-eaten the next morning.

The railway carried Boyes and Gibbons, all the donkeys, wagons, and porters to the end of the line. But before they were done with the railway, John had a narrow escape himself. He was very nearly shot when he returned from dinner with a railway official two miles through the dark, unarmed and carrying only a campfire brand. The coolies and supervisors thought he was one of the lions and barely missed him with a fusilade of shots.

At the end of the railhead, Gibbons and Boyes tried to hire a massive group of porters from the Kamba tribe, 500, in fact. It was the right move as the donkeys didn't work out very well, never having been in harness before. There was a severe financial penalty in their contract for late delivery of the government stuff, which got more severe the later the goods arrived. So bad were the donkeys that they would not keep to the road and often turned over wagons. Many of the rivers had no bridges and it was a half-day's work to push the wagons through the soft sand of the riverbeds. They decided to leave some of the loads behind in the care of two of their men while Boyes pushed on with twenty porters and the wagons. As if he had not been shot at enough during the past year, John was nearly killed by accident by Gibbons. Gibbons was showing Boyes how the *askaris'* Snider rifles worked and how safe they were. He chambered a cartridge and, to show that the breech would not permit a cartridge to go off at half-cock, pointed the rifle at Boyes. "You see," said Gibbons to the horrified Boyes, "it won't go off now." John had just pushed the muzzle away when the rifle fired with a vicious whiplash, the bullet just missing John's head! His comments were not preserved. . . .

For days, the safari crossed the Athi Plains and then reached the swamp called in Masai, *Nairobi*, the Place of Cold Water. In later years John always shook his head in disbelief that it would shortly be the capital of British East Africa. Nairobi was completely empty in 1898. The Nairobi River and Swamp formed the border between the Masai and the Wakikuyu countries.

Some of the blood-drinking, lion-hunting Masai visited John's and Gibbons's camp and Boyes was very impressed with them. He was surprised to find them quite friendly despite much that had been written about them. The Kikuyu were quite a different matter, being at the time much more feared than the Masai. Sir Gerald Portal's book on that area in 1893 gives a fair account of the relations between the Kikuyus and the whites.

"The Kikuyu tribes [clans of the Kikuyu; they were only one tribe] were practically holding the company's station [Fort Smith, near where modern Nairobi now stands] in a state of seige." A bit later Portal describes a march through Kikuyu country:

We left the open plain and plunged into the darkness of a dense belt of forest, which forms the natural boundary of the regions inhabited by the treacherous, cunning, and usually hostile people of Kikuyu. Warned by the state of affairs which we had heard was prevailing at the Company's fort in this district, we were careful to keep all our people close together, every man within a couple of paces of his neighbor. One European marched in the front, one in the rear, and one in the middle of the long line. The Wa-Kikuyu, as we knew, seldom or never show themselves, or run the risk of a fight in the open, but lie like snakes in the long grass, or in some dense bush within a few yards of the line of march, watching for a gap in the ranks, or for some incautious porter to stray away, or loiter a few yards behind; even then a sound is not heard; a scarcely perceptible "twang" of a small bow, the almost inaudible "whizz" of a little poisoned arrow for a dozen yards through the air, a slight puncture in the arm, throat, or chest, followed, almost inevitably, by the death of a man. Another favourite trick of the Wa-Kikuyu is to plant poisoned skewers in the path, set at an angle of about forty-five degrees, pointing towards the direction from which the stranger is expected. If the path is much overgrown or hidden by the luxuriant growth of long grass, these stakes are of much greater length and so pointed that they would pierce the stomach of anyone advancing towards them. . . .

Outside the Fort itself the state of affairs was not so pleasant to contemplate. We were surrounded day and night by a complete ring of hostile Wa-Kikuyu, hidden in the long grass and bushes, and for anyone to wander alone for more than two hundred yards from the stockade was almost certain death. On the morning of our arrival, a porter of Martin's caravan, who had strayed down to the long grass at the foot of the little hill on which the station is built, was speared through the back and killed within 250 paces of our tents. A short time before eight soldiers [presumably heavily armed] *in the Company's service who were foraging for food—probably in an illicit manner—were all massacred in a neighboring village; and a day or two before our arrival the natives had even had the temerity to try and set fire to the fort itself at night. . . .*

Long before I went to their country myself I remember being

*told by an African traveller of great renown that the only way in
which to deal with the Kikuyu people, whether singly or in
masses, was to "shoot on sight."*

The Wakikuyu—the prefix "Wa" means the plural or "the
sons of"—are one of the largest tribal affinities in Africa.
Even in the late nineteenth century when John Boyes met
them, he reckoned them to be half a million strong. Today,
they are much increased, their homeland of Kenya for quite
a while having the highest birthrate of any country on earth.
I don't know the figures but I am sure that there are as many
Wakikuyu as there are Zulus in South Africa, and there are
more than seven million of them.

The Kikuyu at the turn of the last century were almost
indistinguishable in dress from the Masai, wearing ostrich
feather bonnets and carrying the same spears, even if their
poisoned arrows and small bows were not used by the Masai.
They worshiped the same single god—N'gai—and shared
many other traits. Yet, they tended to live in the forests while
the pastoral Masai, who lived on only a mixture of blood,
sometimes blended with ashes and cow's urine, stayed on the
plains. The Kikuyu were almost completely vegetarians,
growing what they needed in small garden plots called *shambas*. There gardens often yielded a surplus, which greatly interested John Boyes.

It was the Kikuyu who were ninety-nine percent behind
the terrorist Mau Mau movement against the white "settlers"
in the early 1950s. It is my understanding that Mau Mau has
no translation; nor does it have a meaning—the founders
chose the title because it would fit nicely into the large type-
face of a headline.

Gibbons and Boyes got through on the caravan road
through Kikuyuland without incident, but this route merely
brushed the borders of Kikuyu country. They took it because
every earlier caravan or safari mentioned had lost men and
goods to the tribe.

When they got through, Gibbons went on ahead with the

porters while John Boyes stayed for a few days to allow the donkeys to graze in the lush countryside. After a few day's rest, John then had to figure out how to get down the escarpment to the Kedong Valley. The mentality of his porters almost cost him the entire safari. On the steep decline, he told them to put rocks ahead of the wheels to slow the wagons' descent, but they were only used to placing stones *behind* the wheels on climbing hills and kept to their habits. Boyes was almost killed when they then released the braking ropes and the whole outfit ended up in the valley below, a tangled mess that took a day to sort out. Fortunately, nobody was badly hurt, although Boyes was dragged half-flying a long way.

The Masai lived in the Kedong Valley and John stayed there for a little while. While there, he was shown the place where a white named Dick was slaughtered along with more than 500 of his caravan. The ground was so covered with skulls and bones that John thought that even the usual native exaggeration didn't apply in this case. In fact, he asked one of his own porters what had happened to his missing eye and the man told him that it had been gouged out by the Masai some time ago—the usual penalty for any Arab or Swahili traders, or their porters, caught passing through Masai country some years back, that is, if they escaped death itself. After a few days, Boyes's safari was able to push on to the lakes without any trouble.

A few days later, at Lake Elementeita, he had an experience with a lion that showed his greenness. Short of food for the safari, he was stalking a lone zebra when he came around the edge of a termite heap and almost ran into a lion, about six feet away, also stalking the zebra. Short of ammo, he had already missed two animals and had his last cartridge in his left hand. When he saw the lion he forgot where it was and madly searched for it in his pockets. Fortunately, the lion pushed off before he found it as he would have been in a somewhat difficult spot if he had merely wounded it with his only cartridge. He went home meatless but was able to collect some game the next day.

John proceeded to Lake Nakuru and from there to the so-called Equator Camp, its location being exactly astride the equator. Two days later, he reached Ravine Fort, the only one that had not been taken over by mutineers during a recent uprising. Here he delivered his contract goods and, as Gibbons had gone ahead to Uganda and the season of the "long rains" was upon them, he decided to return to the railhead, about 300 miles away, to see about the loads he had been forced to leave behind.

John must have been ready to leave near the date of his twenty-fourth birthday, May 10th, 1898. He was not only young, but a quite slight figure in a savage world that must have seemed bigger than life. There is a surviving picture of Boyes in company with Frederick Courteney Selous, taken just before the First World War, and Selous towers over John. We know that Fred was five feet nine inches tall, and an interpolation would make John about five-five or five-six, weighing no more than about 130 pounds. Yet, in light of his later adventures, most of this must have been heart.

He had been having trouble with his Swahili porters—they weren't happy with the donkey wagons and were running short of food. The night before John planned to return to the railhead, he slept fitfully, being quite ill with malaria, but when he awoke, this was not his only problem. The porters had all deserted.

The feeling of being absolutely alone in the deserted Equator Camp was far from pleasant. He was a lone white man in the black heart of Africa. John thought he might be able to catch up to some of his men on the trail, but before following them he turned loose all the donkeys. When he was unable to find any of his porters, he regathered his stock and spent the next night building a series of large fires around them to keep off lions. Incidentally, this usually doesn't work as predators are not afraid of fires, despite the popular belief to the contrary. The bush is full of fire in the dry season and lions and such are used to this. Yet, John and his donkeys were not disturbed during the night. In the morning, not willing to abandon the valuable wagons, he tied them in tandem and put all of his mules into harness at the head of the column, hitched to the first wagon. It was a nightmare arrangement as the wagons kept capsizing at each turn in the caravan road and by the time that John had righted them, the donkeys were in a tangled mess. He had left at first light and struggled along until he reached the Njora River at about three in the afternoon. He had the luck to shoot an antelope and had a good dinner, his first food that day. Tethering the donkeys, he turned in and had a good rest despite his nagging malarial fever.

Inspanning the donkeys the next morning, he had only gone a short distance when he met a solitary black, a stray porter from another caravan, who was almost starving. John gave him some of the antelope meat, which the man wolfed down, and they went on together, trying to cover the thirty miles to the next water. Due to his usual problems with the wagons, it was ten at night when they arrived, half-dead of thirst as John's water bucket had upset in the lead wagon. The black had slipped off into the velvet darkness, leaving John alone once more. He walked more than a mile through the blackness to find the waterhole, drank his fill and put some into his bucket. He also surprised a lion at the water, but was too thirsty to make much of it. As he curled up to sleep, he noticed a distant fire and put it down to natives. At least he would have a chance of hiring some more men, he thought. The next morning, he walked to the place where the fire had been and found a camp of Indians who were transporting food to a party of railway surveyors well ahead of the tracks under construction. From them he was able to get some rice and a few porters and, after a long time on the trail, finally reached the railhead.

John remained only a few days before he was off on his next safari. The longer he was in East Africa, the more he began to realize that the key to commercial success was food—food for the black porters in the form of rice and rations for the Indians, which had quelled the Uganda mutiny, as well as for the Indian coolies on the railway. The Indian troops in Uganda had to have imported food for religious reasons, and John figured that the cost of carrying this was an incredibly expensive two rupees per *pound* by porter from the coast. Thus, it cost the British government at least ten shillings a day to keep an Indian trooper in the field, whereas their officers' rations cost almost nothing as they could live off the land most handsomely, not being bound by religious culinary regulations. So, John said to himself, who has food? Who has flour and other stuff? Aha! The Kikuyu do, that's who! What Boyes seemed to discount was that everyone who entered the Kikuyu country to buy this food had been murdered, sometimes in rather spectacular fashion, as shown by the case of a white settler in 1902. . . .

Although the Kikuyu clans were mostly vegetarians, they did keep sheep and goats as a form of wealth and for use in their frequent ceremonies or oathings. One white settler who tried to buy some sheep from the Kihimbuini clan was dragged to a nearby village where he was pegged down as every man, woman, and child in the village urinated into his wedged-open mouth. He drowned. When he was dead, the women then defecated on him until his head was covered with a stinking pile of human manure.

In charge of part of the punitive expedition against the Kihimbuini Kikuyu was Captain Richard Meinertzhagen of the King's African Rifles, white officers with black *askari* troops and Masai levies. The Kikuyu had also wiped out a mail-carrying party and Meinertzhagen was obliged to teach them a lesson. The killing of the settler in such horrible fashion so infuriated and revolted the captain that he decided to give the natives a whipping they would never forget. He recalled his actions (*Kenya Diary 1902–1906*, Oliver and Boyd, London, 1957) of September 8, 1902, as follows:

> *I have performed a most unpleasant duty today. I made a night*

*march to the village at the edge of the forest where the white
settler had been so brutally murdered the day before yesterday.
The war drums were sounding throughout the night we reached
the village without incident and surrounded it. By the light of
fires we could see savages dancing in the village, and our
guides assured me that they were dancing round the mutilated
body of the white man.*

*I gave orders that every living thing except children should be
killed without mercy. I hated the work and was anxious to get
through with it. As soon as we could see to shoot we closed in.
Several of the men tried to break out but were immediately shot.
I then assaulted the place before any defence could be prepared.
Every soul was either shot or bayoneted, and I am happy to say
that no children were in the village. They, with the younger
women, had already been removed by the villagers to the forest.
We burned all the huts and razed the banana plantations to the
ground.*

*In the open space in the center of the village was a sight
which horrified me—a naked white man pegged out on his back,
mutilated and disembowelled, his body used as a latrine by all
and sundry who passed by. We washed his corpse in a stream
and buried him just outside the village. The whole of this affair
took so short a time that the sun was barely up before we beat a
retreat to our main camp.*

Meinertzhagen had qualms of conscience for his actions:

*My drastic action on this occasion haunted me for many years,
and even now I am not sure whether I was right. My reason for
killing all adults, including women, was that the latter had been
the main instigators of not only the murder but the method of
death, and it was the women who had befouled the corpse after
death. McClean, who was with me as Political Officer, was
naturally consulted; though he refused to give his consent to my
action, he told me that he would not interfere if I thought it was
a just punishment, so the responsibility is entirely mine.*

Bear in mind that this action by the King's African Rifles took
place a full three years after John Boyes made first contact

with the Kikuyu, when they were even less pacified than they were in 1899, which wasn't very. . . .

By the end of 1898, John had lost all his mules save one (the Masai drank too much of their blood), all his porters but three had deserted, and he had abandoned his wagons, leaving the lid of a food box on the scene. He wrote in axle grease on the box top "DEAD DONKEY CAMP" and trekked back to Lake Naivasha.

When he got there, the thought of all that food and potential profit from the Kikuyu ate at him and he decided to try to penetrate their country, come what may. He reckoned on forming a small safari with trade goods and going north, across the Kinangop Plain, through the Masai country and over the forbidding Aberdare Range of mountains, about 12,000 feet high. This route would place him closest to Lake Naivasha, which, if his trading was successful, was the easiest point to distribute his collected Kikuyu food. I'll say this for John Boyes: he had a sense of humor.

John started off with a ridiculously small party compared to the large caravans and safaris that had been wiped out by the Kikuyu—only seven porters who could speak the native language. They were loaded with trade goods of copper and iron wire, mirrors, and such geegaws as John thought would please the natives. He also bought a rifle with fifty rounds of ammunition. It appears to be a .303 caliber by the bandolier that he wore in an early photo of him at about this time, 1899.

When John actually left for the unknown, the news reached a Captain Gorges, in charge of the station at Naivasha, and he immediately sent a Sergeant Miles to bring the little expedition back. When he arrived at Naivasha, Gorges asked him if he planned on committing suicide, and if so, he was not authorized to do it in Gorges's district. John offered to give him a written statement exonerating him of all responsibility should he be killed and affirming that he was going on his own responsibility, but the captain refused as higher orders prevented him from letting any white leave for the interior from his district. Of course, John had had the same reaction when he first landed at Mombasa, and he now set out to circumvent this policy. He was very hot about the fact that the administration did not even permit whites (theoretically) to have so much as guns and ammunition "while the Arabs and Swahili traders were allowed to overrun the country, carrying and purchasing arms and ammunition as freely as they liked." John observed that this Downing Street policy prevailed throughout Britain's African dependencies, that any three white men didn't have the consideration given to a single native.

John decided, on asking Gorges how far and in what directions his district ran, to pull a flanking movement: he went back to the Kedong Valley and crossed the Great Rift that perpendiculates most of Africa, this depression or fault beginning in Turkey. Shortly thereafter, John rounded the end of the captain's territory and set out for Kikuyuland in December of 1898.

John fought his way over the Aberdare Mountains, through almost impenetrable giant bamboo growing on the steep slopes. He had managed to pass through the Masai without any problems as two of his men were of that tribe. On the third day, he came face to face with the dreaded Kikuyu.

The encounter started with the sound of an iron ax ringing through the deep forest, and then the first village came into sight as war cries were taken up from hill to hill by the Kikuyu. At first, they ran away from Boyes's little party but then gathered in a force of about 500 warriors at the village, savage fighters smeared with grease, clay, and whitewash in outlandish and frightening designs. They carried spears and sheilds much like those of the Masai and wore iron rattles on their legs that clanked like the engine of a railway locomotive. On their heads were tossing manes of lion, ostrich, and colobus monkey. John, setting his jaw, told one of his interpreters to say that they had come in peace and that he wanted to see the chief of the district. Sort of a take-me-to-your-leader situation. So far at least, there had not been a sleet of spears thrown out of hand. . . .

The bravado and bluff shown by the small safari paid off, the Kikuyu not knowing what to do. They had never seen a white man before and were nonplussed by John's surprise appearance. So far, so good, he thought. After a few minutes, a guide came forward to lead them to the chief's *kraal*. Accompanying the native, John met Karuri, the chief of the clan, who demanded to know what was going on and what John wanted.

Boyes explained to Karuri his mission to trade with him and to buy food with goods. Immediately, Karuri asked what force John had brought with him and was told that as his visit was peaceful, he had left most of his guns in the forest to avoid a bad first impression. However, he further explained, that if his party was harmed, the whites would make war on the Kikuyu in revenge. Even Boyes, the little master of bluff, had to chuckle at this lie, but he brought it off okay. Karuri allowed Boyes to present him with a length of "Mericani" cloth, the chief's pleasure in it probably indicating that it was the first such cloth he had seen, as the Kikuyu dressed entirely in skins. So well did the initial meeting go that when John ventured to say that he planned to spend quite a while in Kikuyuland, Karuri insisted that a hut be built for him! The ice was broken.

The tribespeople were still very suspicious, but obeyed John's orders when he told them to bring wood and start construction as per his specifications. Shortly, a sheep was dragged in and gifts were made of sweet potatoes and some flour. John wasted no time slaughtering the sheep and getting a good meal on the go for himself and his men. Boyes's hut was constructed like all the others in the village—the walls were made of wooden slabs and the door was very low to prevent an enemy from entering standing up. The little party was goggled at all the time. The people fingered the cloth of John's clothes to see if it was part of his body and they were especially fascinated by his boots, which they were sure were part of his feet. Some became curious about his rifle, but he drew the line at this and kept it with him at all times.

When an interpreter told Boyes that the Kikuyu said he was a fool to come into their midst with only one rifle, John saw his first chance to make an impression. Taking his Martini-Metford .303, he slipped in a solid or full-jacket nonexpanding cartridge and had his interpreter explain that his rifle was unlike any ever seen before and could easily kill six men with one shot. It was, he said, completely different from those muzzle-loaders carried by Arabs and Swahilis. Choosing a soft-wood tree—probably a medium baobab, which has a pulpy wood—he fired the bullet right through it and out the other side. When the Kikuyu examined both the entrance and exit holes, they were mighty impressed, but John said that this was nothing. The bullet, he said, had gone right through a nearby mountain as well as the tree! Of course, this was sheer bluff and bravado, but John pulled it off.

That night Boyes went to lie down in his new hut, but kept awake most of the night, fearing treachery. He had just dozed off near dawn when the air was raped by the sounds of war horns and yelling Kikuyu. Crawling out of his hut, he saw a crowd of armed warriors running toward his hut and he determined to sell his life dearly. But, instead of attacking him, the blacks begged him for help! They themselves were under attack by another clan who had heard about Boyes's arrival in the village and objected violently to any white entering their country. They had once been part of Karuri's crowd but he had lost influence as he had aged and they had broken off from his rule. They had come to kill Boyes and a huge battle raged a short distance off. The early-morning light was clouded by the smoke of burning huts and the screams of the dying reverberated through the forest. Immediately, John decided to join in the fight. He realized that he *had* to since, if the village lost, he would be killed by the opposing clan, and even if he somehow survived, he would have to leave the land immediately.

As John joined the bloody battle, he saw hand-to-hand combat in all quarters, but as he opened up with his rifle and the enemy saw that reinforcements were coming, they ran for the woods. After scattering them, the returning warriors made something of a hero of John, convinced that his participation with his magic rifle had turned the tide. There is little doubt that in fact it had.

Obviously, John Boyes's stature as a friend of this Kikuyu clan was of immense value to his plans. He had instantly become an irreplaceable member of the community by defeating the enemy clan that had warred incessantly on their neighbors, killing their warriors, carrying away their stock and even their women. Karuri came to him and formally asked him to stay on in the village. John answered that although he had other work to do, he would return if Karuri's people would trade with him and sell him flour and other food. He said that the flour was for friends of his who were coming along the caravan road, to which Karuri replied that he did not want any more strangers in the country. John assured him that his "friends" had no wish to enter Kikuyu territory but would skirt it as the road ran along the border. This seemed to satisfy Karuri and his advisers and John said that when he had taken the first foodstuffs to his friends, he would come back and discuss the matter more fully.

Karuri asked John what he had to trade for the flour he wanted, and Boyes was able to stretch much of his goods by using small amounts of the then-new iodoform disinfectant, which he bartered for the flour. Until this time, spear and other wounds among the Kikuyu inevitably turned septic and many limbs were lost as well as warriors, who died of their wounds some time after battle. The standard white African disinfectant for everything from snakebite to lion maulings was potassium permanganate or permanganate of potash, which often caused as much tissue damage as the wound itself! After the fight, John had used some iodoform on wounded warriors and they had recovered in a way that they thought impossible. Boyes was able to trade a paper packet of iodoform powder that would cover a man's thumbnail for as much as twenty pounds of flour!

Boyes stayed for two weeks among Karuri's people, collecting food as it came in. When he had 200 loads of sixty pounds each he decided to head back, but he was stuck for porters until he managed to convince 200 Kikuyu to work for him. He headed down toward Kedong instead of Lake Naivasha, because of his experience with Captain Gorges. The Kikuyu would not go into Masailand so John decided to build a large hut along the caravan route to store his food and in a few days sold the entire shipment to railway surveyors and caravans for the most princely sum of thirty rupees per load. On the return journey, he sent to Karuri for more porters to carry back the trade goods he was able to buy from Arab caravans on their way to Uganda.

One of the first things John did on his return to Karuri's village was to have a proper European bungalo built for himself. He was now ensconced solidly in Kikuyuland, and that he paid his porters in cloth solidified his position as the Kikuyu had no use for money. He mentions timber being cut by native axs, which were more like the tomahawks that I found used in the Luangwa Valley of Zambia; use was also made of the native sword, the *simi*. The Kikuyu always carried this on the right hip and it was often drawn treacherously, on a pretense of shaking hands.

As John stayed longer among the Kikuyu, he realized that the country was in a constant state of feudal civil war. In fact, many of Karuri's men had been killed by the same bunch he had originally defeated, being marked by the cloth with which John had paid them. Eventually, he changed from a defensive turn of mind to an offensive one. He was getting tired of death threats every day. Some of Karuri's other villages had been burned and many people killed simply because they'd permitted the hated white to stay. First, John sent a messenger to the aggressive chief demanding him to return stolen property and to pay blood money. A dead warrior was worth a hundred sheep; a dead woman thirty. The Kikuyu were decidedly sexist. Boyes got an answer to the effect that he was afraid of the other clan and that the next time they raided, they would kill him, too.

He had a talk with Karuri and they both concluded that they would have to fight the matter out, even though John was most reluctant to become involved in native quarrels. Early one morning, as the cooking fire smoke writhed through the still forest, a force of 500 enemy clansmen came screaming and cavorting into the main village, the blaze of smaller hamlets punctuating their advance. John had had spies out and knew they were coming, but he was only able to muster 300 spearmen against a force almost double in size. But he had been working with the Kikuyu on tactics and finally had trained them to fight together rather than piecemeal as was their custom. When the enemy was almost on them, a storm of spears and a sleet of poisoned arrows poured into the enemy ranks. John worked his rifle as fast as he could, his bullets smashing down befeathered, screaming warriors into writhing masses on the dark ground. Hand-to-hand fighting followed as they closed and the Kikuyu fought until midday, when the enemy finally broke and ran. Fortunately, the enemy chief was captured.

The next day a *shauri* (a talk, council or sometimes interpreted as a business meeting) was held to determine the fate of the chief and John asked Karuri what would have been done with him if he had been captured before the white man came. Karuri answered that he would either be killed or very heavily fined. John pointed out that such treatment would only aggravate the enmity of the other clan and cause more trouble later on. Instead, he proposed that they merely demand that all property taken in raids from the time that he had entered the country—not before—be returned and that the chief be set free. After an impressive speech through his interpreter, the council agreed.

John oversaw the return of the property and the people of Karuri's camp were delighted as they had never expected to see any of it again. When this was completed, he invited both the enemy headmen and Karuri's people to his house and was amazed to see them eating and drinking *pombe*—native beer—together like a bunch of reconciled teenagers. He noted that the Africans were very changeable and that their tempers were not to be relied upon, being both fickle and treacherous. In fact, before he had a chance to trust them too much, he had nearly been killed by subterfuge on several occasions. However, after staying with the Kikuyu for several weeks, he learned of the custom of *pigasani*.

Pigasani is best described as group blood brotherhood, as opposed to the ceremony that binds two individuals together. It is a community or group agreement linking together two clans or tribes represented at the ceremony. A few days after the *shauri*, the former enemy chief agreed to this and the ceremony was prepared at his village. The proceedings are interesting, to say the least.

First, all the 2000 participants of this particular *pigasani* ceremony got motherless on beer, and then they followed this with dancing. Oratory was next, each speaker holding several sticks in his hand, which represented each topic he would cover, throwing them down one at a time when the subject was finished. A black goat was tied and dragged in, the oratory sticks being placed between the animal's legs in a bundle. The chief orator, who carried more of a club than a stick, repeated the tenets of the agreement—that both clans would henceforth be pals and, John inserted, would not molest any white men who came to the country. At the end of each clause of the contract, the chief speaker would fetch the goat one hell of a thump with his club, carefully breaking nonvital bones. An oathing was then given after each thwack to the effect that anybody breaking the oath would die like this goat. (This was very much in keeping with the oaths of the Mau Mau some fifty years later, although those oaths involved considerably more freethinking.) When all the clauses were repeated and sworn to, the goat was done in by a particularly savage whack. It then became sacred and nobody would touch it. In fact, Boyes learned, he could obtain any confession from a Kikuyu in the future by making him swear by that goat. But, Boyes also discovered that although his trading area had now increased to the banks of the Tana River, other clans were even more angry at the ceremony that had permitted a white to stay in Kikuyuland.

Boyes now found himself to be the most important personage of the local clans. He usually drank his water after infusing bubbling fruit salts into it and was surrounded by tribesmen come to see him drink "boiling" water. Soon, he developed the reputation of being immortal—that he could not be killed.

He was more than a trader—he was a politician and a psychologist as well as the most famous witch doctor in the country. He was smart enough, however, to invite the local witch doctors to live near him as he could do very nicely without their jealousy. On learning that there was a privileged class of troubadours who went with impunity into any clan's territory, he soon bribed them to become his spies throughout the width and breadth of Kikuyuland. They were most effective, bringing news of impending raids by other clans as well as dark tidings of some Arab and Swahili caravans that had been wiped out, particularly as they came down from the north from the Turkana country to the west of Lake Rudolph. John also became involved in training a first-class fighting force of warriors but noted a curious trait of the Kikuyu and natives in general: even though they expected imminent attack, they had no idea of keeping on the alert and posting guards! This sounds weird, but it was a fact.

This attitude was shown by John's own personal servant, a Swahili who had been the sole survivor of a caravan, whom John had found herding Kikuyu sheep. Yet even that harrowing experience did not influence the man's subsequent behavior:

> *I put him among my askaris, and one night when he was on guard, on making my usual round to see that all was right, I found him lying on the ground fast asleep at his post. I took his rifle away, and as that did not wake him I poured a bucket of water over his head. Even that did not disturb him much, the only effect being to make him shiver and pull his coat over his head—possibly thinking it was raining—and then go on sleeping as peacefully as ever. So I called the other men and pointed him out to them, and they slipped a noose round his legs and pulled him by his feet, while I fired a shot in the air over his head. I thought that this would give him such a fright that he would never go to sleep on guard again, but it did not work and I had to find him another job. It might have been thought that his experience of having all his companions murdered through not keeping a proper guard would have been sufficient to make him keep awake, but this carelessness of such dangers is a native pecularity which is very hard to overcome.*

With John's picked corps of elite warriors, things went better. He taught the spearmen the maneuver used by the ancient Romans, the *testudo* or tortoise, by having them link shields together when they advanced in formation. At the rear of the formation, he put ranks of bowmen taught to shoot all together as at the early English battle of Agincourt. The spearmen knelt while volleys of arrows winged over their heads, the idea having come to John from the volley fire he had seen in the Matabele war.

About this time, John had heard from his troubadour spies that there had been an Arab caravan massacred and some hundred rifles captured by the Kikuyu. Short of guns, he realized that they would be invaluable but when he took them by a night march, only about thirty were still in firing condition. This was nonetheless a help. Curiously, he trained his men to obey commands in English, although they understood not a word. He reckoned that they learned to associate the sounds of his orders with his own actions and learned to obey. He even appointed a native sergeant and a corporal, complete with stripes on their arms.

At this time, John received almost nightly warnings of major raids against his position—sometimes that the warriors of Wagombi, a paramount chief who could put 3000 men in the field, were coming or that the Tato clan was planning an attack with as many as 2000 warriors. John had tried to send messengers of friendship to Wagombi several times, but they were always murdered. He was anxious to expand his trading influence in Kikuyuland, but he dared not leave Karuri's village as he knew that the moment he did, the place would be razed and the people slaughtered without his protection. He established a series of outposts to give early warning of attacks, expecting any raids to come in the early morning when vitality was at a low ebb and confusion would usually result among the defenders. There was little he could do but wait. He didn't have to wait long. . . .

He had one minor skirmish in the interim, thoroughly beating a force of young warriors come to prove their bravery, who left several dead behind before being run off. Then, word came in that the Tato had made a treaty with the Masai and that they planned an attack together. The Tato lived across the Tana River, the boundary between hostile and friendly country. John thought there was something in this as the rumor was more or less confirmed. He decided on a preemptive strike.

It was a two-day march to the Tana, and John took his trained force a short distance from it to another river that was bridged by fallen trees, with a deep ravine, which the enemy had to use in their advance. He had had another house and trading store built on top of the mountain above the ravine and moved his headquarters to this spot, where he could keep watch. The first thing he did was to have all the tree bridges removed but one, his plan being to cut this one also when the enemy had crossed. There was only one way up the mountain from the ravine—a tortured, narrow path that would make the enemy come in single file. Boyes would have a deadly surprise waiting for them.

It was early in the morning—as Boyes had figured—when two men from the bridge guard burst into his camp with the news that the enemy were in sight, Masai and Kikuyu together. The enemy force came on without subterfuge, shouting war songs and flashing their gleaming iron weapons. They had raided the area each year after the circumcision ceremonies, which initiated new, young warriors, and had had little trouble in the past. They clearly expected an easy victory as before. John massed his men at the top of the ravine path, warning them on pain of death not to move until he had fired his rifle.

They were almost at the top when John squeezed his trigger and one of the enemy leaders collapsed in a squawking tangle of legs, arms, and warpaint. The rest of John's riflemen opened up and were immediately answered by a massed whizzing flight of poisoned arrows. Stunned, the enemy stalled as they were slaughtered one by one on the narrow path, and then Boyes's men charged them with spears and *simis* as sharp as anything Gillette has ever made. Panicking, they were killed in heaps in their flight down the mountain only to arrive back at the river to find that the only bridge was gone! They jumped into the stream and some got across but many were drowned. Completely routed, the survivors were captured; fifty lay dead on the battlefield. Boyes's losses were very minor. At last he had won a complete victory and could leave Karuri's precincts without fear of more raids. He decided to take the immense amount of food he had collected to the government station at Naivasha, Captain Gorges or no. When he got there, he found the garrison nearly starving and had no trouble getting rid of his flour. Things were as bad at Ravine Camp, too—so serious, in fact, that the government signed a contract with John to supply these two outposts of Empire with food. As he reflected, "I heard no more about my going into the Kikuyu country without permission!"

John's net profit for each of his trading forays was about 500 pounds, which might not sound like much today, considering that he risked his life for each venture, but let's put it in modern perspective. I recently received a new catalogue from John Rigby & Co., gunmakers of London, one of the oldest and finest firms in England. The catalogue mentions that on December 4, 1902, a .577 Nitro Express cordite sidelock double-barreled rifle was delivered for the price of sixty-four pounds and nine shillings, including a best-quality leg-of-mutton case. The same-caliber rifle was delivered in 1989 for a price of 25,000 pounds (without the case), and as I write this in August 1991, the tab is now 35,000 pounds! That's about $55,000—and that doesn't include a case, either. And, it also doesn't include British value added tax (VAT). The case alone is 1500 pounds extra! So, it comes as no surprise that John was practically beside himself with glee at his profit.

But Boyes had by no means subdued even a small fraction of the Wakikuyu, as his ex-partner, Gibbons, found out. Upon his return from Uganda, Gibbons had mounted an ivory-trading expedition with a fellow named Findlay into the Kikuyu country. They had with them fifty men armed with rifles and thought they would be pretty secure against arrows and spears. The method of trading ivory with the Kikuyu was rather strange as they never brought a tusk along for inspection but only the measurements from which the trader was supposed to figure out how much the tusk weighed. When it was paid for, the seller was supposed to bring it in. Gibbons had gone through this and had sent ten armed men back with the seller—a Kikuyu chief—to pick it up. The escorts were Swahilis, scared green of the Kikuyu, but they took delivery of the tusk and were bringing it back to camp when they were ambushed by the seller's men and all murdered. I suppose this pointed up the high cost of ivory. . . . The safari itself was thoroughly shaken and when they themselves were attacked, they were in such a funk that they hardly could defend themselves. Gibbons quickly saw that the only way any of them would walk away alive would be if they built a *boma*, a defensive wall of thorns and branches, and were behind this when the actual attack began. Gibbons, Findlay, and their men fought off the Kikuyu all night long through a storm of spears and arrows. At dawn, things looked even worse as the natives had received reinforcements and now had the safari completely surrounded. It was obvious that they couldn't hold the *boma* much longer against the hundreds of attackers and decided to fight their way through the enemy line and escape the country. Wishful thinking, indeed.

When Gibbons, Findlay, and their remaining men broke out, a ferocious close-quarter fight began, spear and sword against the hemmed-in rifles. Findlay was speared twice and would have been killed on the spot had not one of his Swahilis come to his rescue. He was so close to the man spearing Findlay that when he fired, he blew the Kikuyu's arm completely off! Must have been using a shotgun!

Realizing that they couldn't escape, Gibbons dragged Findlay back into the *boma* along with the few members of the safari still alive. Somehow, probably because the trapped men had given as good as they got, they were able to reinforce their defenses and hold out while a messenger slipped out and ran for help to a nearby government post. A relief force of King's African Rifles was dispatched but they took a week getting there. At last, after a terrible fight and scant food and water, Gibbons and the few survivors were rescued. Findlay was long dead of his wounds.

As his time among the Kikuyu lengthened, John's stature among them also grew. Under his leadership they had beaten the dreaded Masai and peace from petty squabbling had come to the land. As if to bolster the idea of his immortality, John took to taking solid poisons given to him by witch doctors, proving his immunity. He never showed the slightest reaction to these—he later decided that they were more psychological poisons than actual deadly concoctions—but he never took a liquid form and kept a sharp eye on his food.

As time went by John decided to expand his operations, starting with a bunch who had given him a great deal of trouble, the Kalyera clan. They lived across the border along the caravan road and on John's route to Naivasha. They had cut up several of his safaris in the past and had even savaged a force of armed men Boyes had stationed at the juncture of the two routes, several men having been killed. John's force traveled for a few days through friendly country, although he never let down his guard. At last he came to the edge of the Kalyera country, but the messages he sent were answered by threats to wipe him out. Thinking that more bloodshed wasn't worth it at the moment, John turned back and found that the usual clan warfare had broken out among his own people during his absence. He finally got it smoothed over and property, women, and cattle returned. But word had gotten around the Kikuyu that the Kalyera had bluffed John down. When he sent for a fractious chief who had been causing mischief in a nearby area, the chief replied with an insolent message and jeered that the white man was afraid of him. Boyes's prestige sagged. This headman was renowned as a great warrior who had killed several lions with a spear and had quite a reputation among Karuri's people.

After the chief had snubbed John several more times, it became a standing joke that he had defied the white man with only a hundred spearmen behind him. Unless Boyes did something, and soon, all his work in the country would come to naught.

One morning a fighting force of 500 of John's most loyal warriors gathered and asked him what he proposed to do about the matter. John said to hell with it and that he would bring in the man himself. His men wanted to go with him, but John thought that a do-or-die bluff might be the trick.

John announced (probably in Kikuyu as he had learned the language, although he usually used an interpreter to give him more time to consider his replies to questions) that he would go only with a small party of ten men, and that he would meet the chief alone to show that he wasn't scared of him. A murmur of apprehension went through the 500 warriors. Although John would not even take a rifle, he did take a war club and he slipped his revolver into his belt at the small of his back, it being covered by his shirt.

After a considerable march, John and his ten men came to within a hundred yards of the clearing where the chief and fifty heavily armed men were waiting for him. He had little doubt that there were many more warriors in ambush near the clearing.

He was impressed by the chief, a big man with regal bearing, and John knew that he was at one of the crossroads of his life. Perhaps he wouldn't be alive in a few minutes. Six revolver shots were of small consequence against fifty spearmen at close quarters, even if he was able to empty his chambers. Relying on his usual bluff, this cock-sparrow of a man walked up to the chief amid grunts of amazement from the enemy's men that he would make so bold.

In a flash, John skulled the chief with one blow of his knobkerrie (round-headed club) and the Kikuyu fell senseless to the ground. The warriors' grunts of approbation changed to surprise and uncertainty as John whipped out his revolver and shouted for the men to drop their weapons or they would all be shot down by John's nonexistent hidden force. Standing over the chief, he was astonished when they complied, the pile of weapons growing with every second. Perhaps John's reputation for magic powers helped, but it was his sheer bluff and bravery that cowed the enemy. Bravery is something that all primitive people respect. If John's small body was half heart, for sure the other half was *cojones*! Had he been with a regular British army unit at the time, he almost surely would have been recommended for the Victoria Cross.

Ordering the warriors to bring in some stolen sheep and goats, John had the still-unconscious chief carried to Karuri's village, the whole of the "captured" force marching ahead of him and his few men. When they arrived, John gave them a good meal and a stiff talking-to. He dressed the wound of the chief with sticking plaster and, to show there were no hard feelings, invited the force to spend the night at Karuri's.

After John had gone to sleep on his native mats, he was awakened by one hell of a row. The two parties of natives had been drinking *njoi,* a fermented beverage like mead, much stronger than the *pombe* beer, and had started their quarrels all over again. The brained chief was defending himself against the village elders with the flat of his *simi,* and doing quite a good job of it. John quickly squelched the fighting and took the chief into his own quarters for the rest of the night. The following morning the "enemy" force returned home and Boyes had made an awe-struck friend of the chief for his entire time in Kikuyuland.

Now that John had reestablished his position of respect, or more accurately, of semidivinity, he decided to make his long-desired expansion in trading, especially with people such as the Tato in the area of Mt. Kenia, as it was called at the time. He still had his problems with the witch doctors and sorcerers, though, as they were yellow with jealousy of his so-called powers. One of these was especially slick and thought to be able to disappear at night, when he would go to see N'gai—God—on a personal basis. There were no flies on this man, and he took advantage of a thunderstorm one night to bolster his position. He was drinking *njoi* with some tribal elders in a hut and when a violent storm came up, he managed to slip away from the circle of drinkers without being noticed.

At a savage flash of lightning and nearby thunder, he dropped through the roof of the hut and into the circle of carousers. Obviously, they were most impressed when the witch doctor announced that he had been to see God as usual and had hitched a ride home on a thunderbolt!

Boyes was determined to see the chief or king of the Tato—whom he had beaten so badly at the ravine and river—and convince him to open trade in, among other things, ivory. One witch doctor, who did not hold the poor opinion of John his colleagues did, prophesied death for the white if such a venture were undertaken and Boyes had a tough time convincing his army to go with him. As the clans near Mt. Kenya were supposed to have a lot of guns, John made another trip to Naivasha and then took his men to Mombasa, where he bought different trade goods more suitable for trading for ivory, mostly the iron and brass wire so dear to the sweethearts of the Kikuyu men. While in Mombasa, his men were completely flabbergasted by such items as the sea and boats, of which few of them had even heard. (When I was in both Zambia and the old Rhodesia, it was not at all unusual to be asked what train a local should take to get to America.) They thought that a locomotive was an animal with a fever and its roar meant that it wanted a drink—not a bad description.

While at Mombasa, John called again on the same sub-commissioner who had told him to hie off a year ago and asked for some rifles and ammunition for self-protection. The twit reiterated that whites were not welcome in the country and armed ones even less so. John pointed out that Arabs and Swahilis all had rifles, to which the martinet replied that they had not gotten them with official sanction. As John observed, "Such was the class of administrator approved by Downing Street for the opening of a new country!"

It was quite a hard and adventurous trip back to Karuri's territory. Arriving at his old food depot, called Menzini, where the Kalyera path met the caravan route, there was an attack and several of John's men who were herding cattle were speared to death. John was lying down in his tent when he learned of the attack, and immediately called for a mule he had bought to be saddled. Well ahead of his armed men on foot, he charged off alone and caught the raiders just as they were about to enter the forest. As he fired his revolver from the saddle, the enemy panicked and ran away, much more terrified of the strange mule than the white man. His warriors drove the cattle back and the rest of the trip "home" was without incident. When Karuri heard that Boyes was en route, he sent an advance guard and on his return, there was dancing, drinking, and rejoicing in general. Karuri's people had never seen a mule either and thought that it was some sort of big lion. One of the Kikuyus' most frequent questions of John was whether the mule ate people!

Within a week, John had prepared for his expedition north to Mt. Kenya. On his last trip to Nairobi—which had mushroomed from the spot where he had once camped in the wilderness—he had his thirty riflemen, elite *askaris*, dressed in identical military khaki uniforms, of which they were immensely proud. John decided to take a force of seventy more armed men and a hundred porters lightly loaded so that he could move fast. He had also managed to pick up a Union Jack that he flew at the head of this and all subsequent safaris. What with the khaki uniforms, his other warriors, and a hundred porters and assorted hangers-on—all led by the flag—it was quite an uptown procession that left Karuri's early one morning. They spent the first night at the site of the ravine fight, proceeding without any trouble through Chinga country the next day. The Chinga kept well out of the way of the impressive force, but a few old men did come in. John noticed with a chuckle that whenever he intimated that a Kikuyu was not a savage—*shenzi*—they immediately began to refer to other Kikuyu by this less-than-flattering term, which actually means "wild man." He got a good laugh one day when one of his own men informed him that some *wa-*

shenzi wanted to see him. When he went to see what was wanted of him, he found that the man had been speaking of his own father and relatives.

On making some gifts to the district chiefs of the Chinga, Bartier and Henga, he got on quite friendly terms with them, for the moment. He was warned by both these chiefs about Karkerrie of the Tato and John asked them if any whites had ever been to their country before. They answered no, not at this place, but long ago some had passed through another part. John suggested the possibility of a *pigasani* ceremony with Bartier's and Henga's people, but he was put off as this was very much a group affair. They admitted that it might be possible on his return through their area. John was at least able to trade for some ivory, which he would pick up at the same time.

This same day, he had a visit from the chief rainmaker of all the Kikuyus, who obviously had not been doing John's cause any good. He had told all who would listen that to allow a white into the country would cause the rain to cease falling as well as other not especially friendly things. The next day Boyes pushed on and met a very big chief–witch doctor named Muga wa Diga, which is an example of the Kikuyu patronymic, meaning Muga, son of Diga, rather like the Russian -vitch or the Scandanavian -sen. As he was deadly jealous of the chief rainmaker, Muga became quite friendly to Boyes and declared that he would go to the Tato country with him to trade ivory. Also, Muga said, there was more ivory in the Tato area than in Wagombi's country, nearer Mt. Kenya. John decided to visit Chief Karkerrie after first sending presents.

Over the several days that the white man stayed with Muga, he met another chief named Katuni—"The Lion"—a big, strapping man who also decided to go to Tato. Muga's people were, as to be expected, fascinated with the white man's trappings. John was himself amazed when he used one of his binocular lenses as a burning glass. The warriors would only look on in interest as the backs of their hands smoked and scorched. Tough guys . . .

Despite the chief's reputation, all went surprisingly well with Karkerrie at Tato and Boyes bought quite a bit of ivory at good prices, although about twice the price he was later to find in Wagombi's chieftainship at the base of Mt. Kenya. Perhaps I should say that things went well until, of all things, a musical clock almost cost John his life. . . .

One day Karkerrie and his elders, curious as always about the white man's mysterious paraphernalia, dropped by John's tent. He had, among his things, a clock that instead of striking the hour would play a merry tune instead. Obviously, the natives thought that this was magic of the blackest order. John secretly moved the hour-hand lever and said that he would command the clock to sing again, which it did. At this moment, as the clock was playing, it began to rain and the Kikuyu drew the obvious inference that the clock was making it rain. They asked John if this was true and, in an offhand remark, he said, "Certainly, it makes it rain all right." Thinking nothing more, he then showed them a few sleight-of-hand tricks and forgot all about it.

The following day, Karkerrie showed up again and told John that as rain was badly needed, he must instruct the clock to make some, quite a lot while he was about it. John answered that the best thing Karkerrie could do was to bring in plenty of ivory, go on trading, and the rain would take care of itself as it was impossible for any man—black or white—to make it rain. However, Karkerrie was not satisfied. He had *seen* with his own eyes that the clock could cause it to rain. Every day he came to Boyes begging for rain but the white had to put him off, saying that the rain would begin shortly. But when it didn't come, the next bit of Kikuyu logic was that John was using the clock to *prevent* rain. Things got threatening.

The Kikuyu refused to bring in any more ivory to trade and Boyes heard rumors that they were planning to kill him and wipe out his safari. John gave considerable credence to this rumor as there was a heavy, expectant air in camp. Every night the natives would sing, shout, and carry on and he knew that something imminent was up. One black, moonless night at about eight o'clock the crisis came. It had been as silent as a tomb in camp when suddenly there erupted a ferocious uproar of shouts, war cries, and screams. John remembered that even the hyenas joined in with their eerie whoops and cackles, recognizing that Kikuyu war cries meant meat. They were as conditioned as Pavlov's dogs to a fight and nice, fresh food as the Kikuyu had the charming habit of leaving their dead where they lay in the bush rather than burying them. By now, Boyes could make out individual yells of *"Kill the White Man!"* which left little doubt of the meaning of the disturbance. He didn't feel too hopeful there in the inkiness, with thousands of armed savages howling for his blood, but he reasoned that his best course would be to build a makeshift fort or *boma* out of the boxes of his trade goods and whatever else he could lay his hands upon. If he showed fear now, he knew that the Kikuyu would slaughter him and even if he managed to get away, all his goods would be lost, including the ivory he had bought. Nor would he be able to go farther north even if he survived. When the barricades of the *boma* were completed to the best of their ability in the dark, he moved his entire force into the enclosure and had all the spare ammunition made handy. He wandered among his men telling them that all would be fine, and I suppose they had little choice but to believe him. Still, it must have been hard to inspire confidence with a couple of thousand professional throat-cleavers close by in the blackness.

The demonstration stopped. Almost like a flowing, oily stream, silence oozed in where there had been chaos. As they listened, the only noise was the slither of half-naked bodies in the bush outside, a chilling sound that meant that warriors were moving around the *boma*. At any moment they could expect the swishing hum of scalpel-bladed spears and the flutter of poisoned arrows. The silence was worse than the noise had been.

Time crawled by like a sleepy earthworm, and the men added touches to the barricades by feel. Then John got the break that he had been praying for. Word was brought that Karkerrie had been seen, heavily armed, going to join a body of his warriors a little distance away. Impulsively, John grabbed a couple of his best men and eased out of the fort to cut him off. By the purest luck they were able to intercept him, make him a prisoner, and drag him back inside their defenses. John and his men knew that they now had a fighting chance with the chief as a prisoner, trussed like a chicken ready for the oven.

Waiting for the attack, John kept moving among his men and whispering encouragement to them. Suddenly he noticed that one of his *askaris* was missing from his post. Boyes remembered him especially as that very morning he had been on guard over John's tent and he had noticed that the man's demeanor was decidedly careless and lax. John had given him a severe dressing down at which the man only smiled queerly. Thoroughly irritated, John had snatched the man's rifle away from him, saying that from now on he was a porter as he was not fit to be a soldier. But at the moment, realizing that the man had deserted to the enemy, John thought it was only because of that incident. What he did not know at the time was that the man had originally come from this part of the country and had been carried away by raiders as a boy. He was to be the assassin in a plot to shoot Boyes—a plot that was only averted when John took his rifle away.

The night whimpered on with slight sounds of movement, the white being sure that his barricade was now completely surrounded. But he had not yet played his hole card of the prisoner. As the first false dawn was blushing in the east, John knew that he must act before the natives' favorite time to attack came. He whipped out his revolver, placed the cold muzzle against the wool of Karkerrie's temple, and spoke to the chief. He would be the first to die with the first spear or arrow. There was an ominous double click as he cocked the revolver. At the first sign of an attack the hammer would fall. Karkerrie swallowed and began to sweat.

Karkerrie, placing great value on his own skin, immediately shouted to the encircling attack force and they instantly lapsed into stunned silence when they realized that he was in the fort. Fortunately for both Karkerrie and Boyes, he had sufficient influence to make his people give up the assault and retire. As Boyes's men came out of their makeshift fort, they saw that the vegetation was completely beaten down around the barricades, signifying that they had indeed been surrounded by thousands of warriors. If they hadn't grabbed Karkerrie when they did, they would never have seen the sun rise.

But for this one almost-fatal incident, things went fairly well with Karkerrie's people. Boyes must have made the chief swear an awful oath to keep his people under control because there was no further enmity, save for one rather baffling turn of events.

John had previously sent cattle to be exchanged for sheep—the local Kikuyu exchange rate was twenty sheep for one cow—and he had sent three more cows in different directions without guards. But the sheep did not come in and the cattle were not returned. John knew he must do something, but he had so much ivory in camp that he was reluctant to put it at risk. However, he decided to leave ten riflemen and fifty warriors in camp and chase down the cows. Yet, as he was leaving camp, Karkerrie's own son and some other men who were in charge of the cattle returned with serious wounds and said that they had lost the cattle, obviously after a fight to keep them.

John saddled up his mule and as the wounded men were not able to show him the place of their fight, another of Karkerrie's men offered to do so. John took off on the mule ahead of his main war party and found the place of the battle absolutely deserted, but there were some men shouting taunts and insults from a hillock some distance away but who made no attempt to come any closer. Mad as a wet snake, John rode quite close to them and, as they did not break, waited until his main force came up, stopping about a hundred yards away. When it was apparent that the group of warriors on the hill intended charging, Boyes directed a volley of rifle fire at them and several fell dead and many must have been wounded. The enemy force then ran away shouting to their friends to help come and kill the white man. John thought that the recovery of three cows wasn't worth the trouble and, becoming worried about his ivory, headed back to his camp.

Again, he went ahead on the mule, firing his revolver every several yards into the bush in case of ambush. When he got to the camp, he found it surrounded by howling Kikuyu, not Karkerrie's men but a strange clan. As he got closer, the enemy broke off on hearing him shout to his men and retired. Several of his own force were wounded, but the ground was littered with dead enemy warriors. Later, John learned that these men had attacked when they heard he was away chasing cattle; they thought it would be a good time to loot. These Kikuyu very nearly won the assault, being barely held off, but John's quick return had thrown them off their stride. Obviously, the taking of the cows had been a diversion to get Boyes and his forces out of camp and his remaining force had had a hard time holding the enemy off.

Finally, it rained. As if by magic, the people's attitude toward the white changed as they thought that he had finally given in and forced the musical clock to make rain. Before he left, even Karkerrie was anxious to make blood brotherhood as well as *pigasani,* and John thought it was well to exit on a high note. He had been wanting to complete his trading safari to a chief Wagombi at Mt. Kenya. Rather than tote his heavy ivory all the way when he would have to return via Karkerrie, he secretly buried the whole lot at the edge of the forest and left. Later, he found that he and all his men were reported killed by the Kikuyu.

At the time Boyes was ready to move on, there were three paramount chiefs in Kikuyuland—Karuri, Karkerrie, and Wagombi. He knew that if he could get them to be friendly and perhaps blood brothers with each other and with him, the whole of Kikuyuland would fall into his hands. Wagombi was by far the most powerful of the three and as Boyes was on very friendly terms with the first two, he was sure that all the petty chiefs would fall into line if he could win over Wagombi. Yet, John knew that his success thus far had been due to his traveling with Kikuyus and their presence had permitted him stature that he would never have achieved alone. Yet, the first night on the trail, along the banks of the Tana River, there was bloodshed and death.

Some of John's men, unguarded, had gone down to the river to fetch some water. They were ambushed and three of them were speared to death. They had been attacked while passing through a *shamba* or area of native cultivation, but when John investigated, although there were signs of a considerable force, the murderers were not to be found. He directed that the bodies be buried—quite against Kikuyu custom as the hyenas knew—and retired for the night. In the morning, when camp had been struck for the final trek into Wagombi's country, he saw a throng of the chief's warriors doing a war dance. Going up, John found that they had dug up the three bodies and were reveling around them. Disgusted, he marched on.

He had sent messages to Wagombi to let him know that he was coming, and the chief actually came out ten miles to meet Boyes's force. He was also a big man, every inch a chief in his magnificent bearing, carrying a huge spear. He had only brought old men to meet Boyes with the exception of his young son, who would become his successor. He spat in his hand when he shook hands with Boyes, the reason for this custom being to show that the spitter did not fear witch craft from the other, as possession of a man's spit as well as his more personal juices were believed essential to casting a proper, iron-clad spell.

Wagombi, resplendent in silky, black-and-white colobus monkey robes, said he was very anxious to make friends with Boyes, of whom he had heard much. Wagombi was aware that he had a notorious reputation for murdering anybody who came into his country, but he claimed that he would like to be pals with Boyes because he had not brought any Arabs, Swahilis, or Wakambas with him. These sort of men were not wanted in Kikuyuland and would be slaughtered out of hand, said the chief. When John told the chief that three of his men had been murdered the night before, Wagombi made no bones about the killers being his people, but said they had acted on their own as he had sent messages that the white man's party was not to be molested. He planned to punish the murderers, probably with a fine of sheep.

As the procession approached the chief's capital, a huge crowd of curious Kikuyu came with them. One who joined them was apparently the head witch doctor, as he killed a sheep and scattered bits of blood, flesh, and intestinal dung in the path of the party, a very Kikuyuesque ritual of welcome. The old man also cut out two circles of sheepskin from the slaughtered ram and placed them on the chief's and John's upper arms as a sign of friendship. So far, so good . . .

The country was beautiful, thought John, hilly and with a magnificent view of small villages and streams running off the 17,040 feet of Kerinyagga, the ancient volcano of Mount Kenya, the second-highest peak in Africa after Kilimanjaro, or, as it was called at the time, Kilima N'jaro, the apostrophe varying according to different sources.

Wagombi's men had a considerable number of guns and rifles, almost all looted from wiped-out safaris and caravans of Swahilis and Arabs. The chief described them as a foolish lot who would take no precautions, trying to cross his country like idiots. He said that he had absolutely no scruples about killing such stupid people, who often were slavers to boot. John was most impressed with Wagombi's demeanor for the tribal leader pulled no punches and spoke frankly, which Boyes had found to be quite the opposite of most Africans, although he did not use the term "African."

John was chilled when he found out that he had no way, with his relatively small force, of keeping the thousands of Kikuyu warriors out of his camp. Before he always had had them disarmed but this time there were just too many of them to handle. Knowing Wagombi's reputation, he thought that the chief might be using confidence tactics to wipe them out and wasted no time in arranging with Wagombi that a "white man's house" be built, asking for the loan of some labor to construct it. Anyway, he told Wagombi, it was rather cold near the mountain.

Wagombi consented to the house with possibly real pleasure and John began to build the next day. The Kikuyu was told that it was the whites' custom to have a fence around a house and as Wagombi didn't object, John had a stockade built that was just high enough to fire over, which couldn't have been too high considering his own height. Of course he was building a defensive fort, but Wagombi had no reason to believe that all such "European houses" were not made like this. When his work was finished, he told Wagombi that he had not made the first fence quite high enough and, encountering no objections, proceeded to erect a strong second stockade inside the first, some eight feet high. The entrance to the first fence was opposite that of the second, and John knew that if there was ever an attack, he would be able to perform considerable execution between the baffled walls of the two fences before an enemy force could get into the fort proper.

The literally crowning glory of the place was a thirty-foot tower made of four strong corner posts with diagonal crosspieces lashed between them with bark fiber. On top was a protected platform that was super for observation and defense with rifles. Oddly, even this caused no suspicion. When it finally dawned on a thoughtful Wagombi that the place was perfect for a defensive fight, he commented to John: "What a good thing it would be to keep a rush of the savages out!" As John had found, by "savages," he meant his own people. . . .

Boyes's party spent considerable time at Wagombi's village and traded for a good amount of ivory, which, as previously mentioned, was half-price or less than that bought at Karkerrie's. John thought it was almost given away. As time went on, he became more and more friendly with Wagombi, teaching him to drink tea—which became a favorite beverage of the Kikuyu, but well displaced later by stronger stuff—and finally the chief said that he would like to have blood brotherhood with John, although he was most reluctant to make the ceremony with such as Muga, Karuri, or Karkerrie. Blood brotherhood being mainly between ruling individuals, let me turn to (then) Captain D. F. Lugard's 1893 classic, *The Rise of Our East African Empire,* a two-volume work that gives much insight from the eventual governor of Uganda on native customs, to see how this ceremony was conducted.

> *The method of making blood-brotherhood varies slightly among various tribes, but is the same in all essentials. We sit down cross-legged on mats and skins, and each of us cuts our forearm until the blood flows; the arms are then rubbed together to mix the blood* [with the recent emergence of AIDS I imagine that African blood brotherhood has somewhat fallen off], *and two small pieces of meat are supposed to be touched with the blood: he eats the piece which has my blood on it off the palm of my right hand, and I eat the piece which has his blood on it from his palm.* [Lugard mentions that at least one Kikuyu tried to cheat by cunningly substituting his finger to avoid the blood touching the meat, thus negating the bond only to the knowledge of one party to the ceremony, which would permit future treachery.]
> *. . . The headmen of the chief take his weapons of war—his*

spear and sword and bow—and holding them over his head, make a long speech, praising the warrior's valour and exploits, and swearing that henceforth we are brothers. His lands and food and house are mine by day or night, and he will forever be my friend. To make the speech more effective, the arms held over his head are struck continually to emphasize the point of each sentence with a spear or sword.

In like manner, when the chief's oath is done, my interpreter holds my rifle over my head and repeats what I tell him to say, of which the following was here the substance: "That he bound himself to supply us with food (on payment), to demand no hongo [tribute or bribe], *to do no harm or damage to our station, to be our friend and ally, and we promise not to harm or molest him and his people; and, if the Masai raid close to our station, to help him to drive them back."*

Boyes managed *pigasani* with Wagombi as well as blood brotherhood, but some time later. The chief did eventually also pledge blood brotherhood with Karkerrie and Muga wa Diga, but only at the price of expensive presents from Boyes.

This mass blood brotherhood ceremony was probably the largest gathering that the Kikuyu had ever had to that time. It was held on neutral ground, the incisions in this case being made above the heart by a sharp arrow wielded by Olmondo, the chief of a hunting tribe, the Wanderobo. John had nearly pulled the drawstrings of his bag shut on Kikuyuland.

As Boyes had heard that there was ivory to be traded nearer the coast with tribes other than the Kikuyu, and having iron and brass wire left from his dealings with Wagombi's people, he decided to go. The trip was a fiasco. At the cost of the lives of several of his own men and of many strange tribesmen, he returned to Wagombi, who promptly offered to wipe up the country with those who had interfered with his "brother." John declined with thanks and spent some time with Olmondo and his Wandorobo as they had quite a bit of big bull-elephant ivory.

Boyes loved living with the Wandorobo, strict carnivores,

and hunted with them extensively. When he first started trading, he had brought ten big bullocks with him, each of which he traded for a tusk in the eighty-or ninety-pound category. He was astonished and sickened when immediately the Wandorobo killed all of the animals and refused to budge until the ten carcasses were just piles of shining bones! Although he opined that the Wandorobo were the filthiest, laziest people on earth, he got on well with them and his reputation had gone before him. When there was a substantial shower of rain one day, he was visited by the tribal dignitaries and thanked for it. Although he denied any complicity with God, the Wandorobo would have none of his modesty.

So relaxed was he with the 'Derobo, that he even turned poet! One day Olmondo came to his tent and said that he would give ivory in exchange for "medicine" (a charm, in this case) that would enable him to kill more elephants while keeping him safe from death. John asked him what he wanted, and the chief said that he wished the same sort of medicine that Boyes had sent to two reported white men near the Uaso Nyiro River. Puzzled at first, Boyes finally realized that Olmondo wanted a piece of paper with writing on it. Not knowing what to write and having plenty of time, he decided to wax lyrical:

> *I am chief of the Wanderobo hunters.*
> *Olmondo is my name,*
> *Elephants I kill by the hundreds,*
> *And thousands of smaller game.*
> *I am up in the morning so early,*
> *With my bow and arrows so sharp;*
> *Over rivers I glide like a fairy,*
> *Over mountains I fly like a lark.*

John went on for several stanzas, and gave the paper to Olmondo, who carefully wrapped it up and hung it from his neck in a skin pouch. Curiously, perhaps because of the power of positive thinking, Olmondo's hunting was far more successful. It later happened that Olmondo, asking another white for additional fresh "medicine," showed the poem to a British official. At this time, John had again been reported killed and had not been heard of for almost a year. But when his countrymen read his work, the joke was on John. Instead of being dead, he was reported as living somewhere around Mt. Kenya, writing poetry for the bloody savages!

John finally had to leave Olmondo and his wild men and traveled back to Wagombi's and dug up his ivory. On his return trip to Karuri he noted with some satisfaction that he was received in great friendship by the Tato. The chiefs had been sending small gifts of sheep and goats to each other to reinforce the blood brotherhood and the *pigasani*. But trouble again reared its head just as John left Tato.

Three men from Portuguese Goa (in India) had safaried through Karuri's area and had had such a friendly time with their forty Kikuyu from near Nairobi that they were not prepared for problems when they reached the Chinga country. The Chinga will be remembered as the only major clan that John had not dealt with as they had been unfriendly when he passed through their territory, although there had been no bloodshed. The Goanese, not realizing that other members of the Kikuyu tribe might be quite different from the pacified clan under Karuri, were completely wiped out, murdered by the Chinga, despite the fact that fifteen of their men were armed with rifles.

When John first heard of this, he didn't quite believe the reports as he had himself been reported dead many times. But thinking that the Goanese might need some help, he decided to investigate and headed for Bartier's village for fresh news. That he lived to get there was due entirely to man's best friend, which Boyes would later argue was not the dog but the mule. . . .

He had foolishly gone ahead of his main body of *askaris* and warriors, starting out with his gunbearer, one *askari*, his interpreter, and the mule's syce, all of whom he quickly out-stripped. As he thought the country to be still friendly, he galloped ahead on the path, which ran between two hedges with *shambas* to both sides. But the mule was acting peculiarly. It finally decided with the stubbornness of untold generations that it would not stay on the path but wanted to go off into the cultivation. Irritated, Boyes finally let it have its head. It went along the cultivated ground for several hundred yards, then inexplicably returned to the proper path. John thought no more of it and arrived without incident at Bartier's at about five in the afternoon.

Boyes quickly learned that the killing of the Goanese whites was no rumor. Worse, John learned from Bartier, who was a neighbor to the Chinga clan, that while the natives had hitherto believed it impossible to kill a white man, they had mightily disproved this theory with the three Portuguese. Now, said Bartier, they were only looking for a chance to kill Boyes.

Bartier swore his loyalty to John and said that the cause of the uprising was that the head rainmaker, who John knew from previous experience, was dead jealous of him.

While Bartier was explaining all this to Boyes, two of the four men who had left the main body with John showed up. They blurted out that the other two had been killed in an ambush along the path and that they had barely escaped with their lives. In a flash, John realized that this ambush had taken place exactly where the mule had acted so strangely. It had obviously winded the lurking warriors and looped around them, unquestionably saving John's life. At least, the two survivors had been able to grab the speared men's rifles and had brought them to Bartier's.

Immediately, Boyes had Bartier send runners through the forest to warn his main force to take care. Shortly, the safari arrived, bringing in one of the men from the ambush, mortally wounded. The hostiles, and plenty of them, would not be far behind. He had sustained three spear thrusts right through the back and John could do nothing to help him. He died in about an hour. John sent his men, impossibly heavily laden with ivory from the year's trading, to make another *boma* as they had done when hard pressed by the Tato. John knew that he was in for the toughest fight of his life and if he lost, he was prepared to take a lot of passengers with him to hell. He knew that the Chinga were wild with enthusiasm for his death as killing his white Goanese "brothers"—as they saw it—had been so easy. Gone was the not-inconsiderable shield of being a pale-face. Of course, the Chinga were equally anxious to loot the rich safari of ivory and trade goods. Their enthusiasm was, in fact, contagious and several other tribes had joined them, swelling their fighting numbers to more than 5000, by far a larger army than John had ever fought before. To compound his problems, John was very low on ammunition after the year's trip as he had done a great deal of hunting in the Wandorobo country. Things looked pretty bleak, the enemy dancing and gesticulating as John had all the ivory buried in the floor of the little fort.

Soon, the whole country was alive with hostile warriors, screaming insults and threats as to what they would do when they caught him. John didn't think they were kidding, either. Some of the Kikuyu were disporting themselves in the bloody clothes of the butchered Goanese and then Boyes saw that they had cut off the heads of the murdered men and had impaled them on poles with which they were dancing.

Bartier promised to give all the help he could, but John realized that the chief's hands were somewhat tied; if Bartier sided with the white man and John lost, his people likely would be wiped out as well. The enemy demonstration was further enhanced by the firing of the eighteen captured rifles, but John wasn't too worried about these as most natives were terrible shots, usually closing their eyes and turning their heads away as they fired high. He had taught his own forces always to aim low and he reckoned they were pretty good out to a hundred yards or so.

There was little that Boyes could do while the Chinga were demonstrating and drinking *njoi* out of range, so he sent out a few scouts at first dark to try to discover the assault plans of the enemy. The evening dragged on, the distant shouts of the warriors muffled by the bush. He had learned enough about the Kikuyu to think that they wouldn't attack at night, instead preferring to wait until their favorite time of pre-dawn, but they were so het up that he wasn't sure. The way they were carrying on they could come at any moment, whacked on *njoi* and narcotic plants such as *bhang*, marijuana.

At midnight, some of his scouts returned and said that there was a massive gathering of the enemy about a mile away, in a clearing, having a *shauri* to decide how to attack the white. This news further upset his few men and especially those of Bartier's camp. Suddenly, everything went silent, as it had done before when he had waited for the Tato. John's brain whirled. What should he do? To wait for the Chinga and their allies was almost sure death. Slowly, an idea formed. It had worked before, he thought, and perhaps a preemptive strike might work again. It was his only chance and he began to give orders.

First, he instructed that big fires be built up to look as if the entire force were in the fort. Gathering his men about him, he left a few in camp and quietly stole out with his main force, edging silently toward the enemy gathering, ghosting through the black, moonless forest. It was literally a do-or-die move.

John was planning on the Kikuyu ineptitude of not being prepared—on their not even posting sentries before a main engagement was expected. He was right. The force managed to creep up to the very edge of the clearing, black with enemy warriors, to point-blank range. The surprise was complete. John smiled grimly in the damp, warm blackness—the tight smile of a predator about to strike.

Slowly, he drew a bead on an obvious leader and started to squeeze the trigger of the .303. As it whiplashed and the man's head disappeared in a mist of blood and brain matter, there was a roar of rifles at his sides, scything the electrified, stunned Kikuyu into crumpled, agonized piles of dead and wounded. Over his head came a deadly shower of hundreds of poisoned arrows from his allies, followed by the slicing sound of thrown spears and their *thug!* into human meat.

It was a pandemonium of howling, shocked Kikuyu, surprised to death at John's tactic. They rushed about in the dim light of their campfires, not knowing from where the onslaught came, so close was it, falling over bodies and not even able to see who had attacked them. While they milled about, John and his men reloaded and fired another scorching blast into their mass, killing many and putting the rest to a most undignified rout as the poisoned arrows continued to thump home. Of the thousands who had been in the clearing a moment before, only a broken and terrified mob ran away in the smothering, gunsmoke-filled dark.

Not a man of John's force was hurt.

John fell back on the fort grimly satisfied, knowing that it would be a while before the Chinga dared to try him again. Leaving his buried ivory with a small force as he didn't expect another attack on the camp, in the morning he proceeded into Chinga country with utmost caution, halting every few minutes to scan the green bush for an ambush. He knew that his blood brother, Karuri, must have heard of his peril and would be bound to send out a relief force. Yet John was worried that the slaughter of the night before couldn't have been more than a dent in the 5000 enemy warriors. They would have another try, he thought, and he was not wrong.

There was a ravine through which John's forces had to pass, a dangerous place perfect for an ambush with high seven-foot grass and rough terrain at the base of a hill. Reluctantly, Boyes and his men entered the grass knowing that if there was to be an ambush, this would be the likely place. . . .

A sweating black silhouette was seen for a second, and then

captured rifles were fired at close quarters and poisoned arrows began to wing overhead from the enemy. Instantly, the grass was alive on all sides with charging *washenzi,* and the ambush became a *mano a mano* affair, every man of Boyes's force fighting desperately against much heavier odds. So furious was the fight that John merely fired from the hip as fast as he could load and for a while it looked as if his men would be annihilated and become just another shady rumor of the Kikuyus' murderousness.

Then John got a real scare in the form of a huge warrior who suddenly appeared, towering over him with a drawn-back spear. His rifle was pressed against the black's body when he fired, the bullet somehow paralyzing the Kikuyu, but it took two more shots before he fell—without striking with his spear. All John's men were fighting for their lives when Boyes happened to look up—and almost gave up. The slope of the overhanging hill was swarming with enemy warriors, evidently just waiting to see how things went before they committed themselves to the massacre. The rush of the enemy force in the grass-filled valley had been blunted by John's desperate defense, and instantly he realized that if the second force poured off the hill there would be no way that they could weather the attack. Knowing that their only hope lay in the lull in the valley and immediate attack up the hill to scatter the small army, John shouted to his men to follow him and they went swarming upward. John knew his natives. As soon as they saw that the offense had shifted, the warriors ran away down the other side of the hill. It was a marvelous escape in the true sense of the word. Even losses to John's men were surprisingly light.

By the next day, reinforcements had arrived from both his blood brothers, Karkerrie and Wagombi, with more promised if they were needed. They came in hourly until Boyes now had several thousand men under his command at Bartier's.

As the friendly forces built up, things became more and more frantic, huge groups of warriors dancing themselves into a bloodlust, stabbing trees with their spears and slashing with their *simis*. In the meanwhile, the Chingas, too, had gotten reinforcements and John realized that at this level he was helpless to prevent a showdown. The final campaign went John's way and his allies absolutely wiped out any Chinga and their allies who showed any hostility. In a month, the Chinga ceased to exist as a force in the whole of Kikuyuland. John was now the uncrowned king of the tribe, every chief swearing allegiance to him. Even the Goaneses' goods were turned in and their murderers killed—John hints at torture being the method of their execution. Unfortunately, when this property was sent to two of their brothers in Nairobi, the recovered goods included a captured sack containing the heads of the murdered men.

Possibly the only remaining enemy that Boyes had was the Chief Rainmaker, who was also a tribal chief and had a small territory. John already knew that it had been this man who was responsible for the attack on the Goanese and that he continued to scheme for Boyes's death. Hearing that there was a disturbance in the country some twenty miles from Karuri's, John and Karuri marched at the head of about a thousand warriors to quell the uprising. The rainmaker met the column with feigned friendliness and John was willing to bury the hatchet and told the man to have his 300 warriors fall in with the main force and join him and Karuri, which he did.

When the invading force met resistance at the first few villages, a general attack developed. Both John and Karuri were coming up a hill somewhat to the rear of their main force, the rainmaker being with them. The order to attack had just been given and they were nearing the brow of the hill when John was startled by a shot just behind him. He turned around and immediately saw the rainmaker dying on the ground just a few steps away, a 480-grain .577 lead bullet from one of John's personal bodyguards having hit him in the hip, the Snider-Enfield slug passing completely through the man's sword and mangling his lower chest. Clearly he was beyond help.

Boyes asked what in hell had happened. Pointing, Karuri's and John's personal guard both indicated a spot a short way away where an ambush body of bowmen had been hiding. The rainmaker was in the act of signaling them to kill John when the *askari* fired.

The rainmaker knew that he had only a few moments to live. His last request was that his body be wrapped in several blankets that John himself had given him and that he be buried and not left to the ubiquitous hyenas of Kikuyuland. This was granted.

Meanwhile, it appeared that the rainmaker might succeed at last in causing Boyes's death. There was another ambush ahead that had permitted the main force to pass and concentrated on Karuri and John, who were hard put keeping their collective noses above water until the main force could return and rescue them, which it did.

During the main fight at the villages below, John noticed that Karuri's eldest son, a newly circumcised warrior called Cachukia, had not returned from the action. On inquiring, he was told that the young man had been killed. John decided that he owed it to Karuri to make sure that he had not merely been badly wounded and went down the hill, finding Cachukia with two bad spear wounds in his chest, both penetrating the lungs in what would be called a sucking chest wound. Although he considered the case hopeless, John did all that he could and after a time the man survived to become a strong and healthy heir-apparent to the chieftainship after Karuri's death. Obviously, this made John's and Karuri's relationship even stronger than their blood brotherhood had.

Incidentally, the bodyguard who had shot the rainmaker was so overcome with what he had done to such a powerful and magic man that he left immediately, fearing reprisal and revenge, and he never went home again. John met him years later near Naivasha.

As John settled down in Kikuyuland, there was soon more trading competition as things were quite quiet. Many of the traders were Swahilis and such, and their poor treatment of the Kikuyu won them little favor. Boyes cites one case in which three Swahilis, about a day behind John's own trading safari, rustled about sixty sheep and then proceeded to trade them to John in payment for ivory. When he found out what had happened, he had the men arrested by the Kikuyu and thrown out of the country, where they immediately began passing some less-than-flattering comments about John and his own treatment of the natives. Since the government was jealous of any whites in the area anyway, this did not do much for John's standing.

But perhaps there might have been something to their tales. There is an impression written by Richard Meinertzhagen, the same man who revenged the death by urine-drowning of the white settler in 1902, that does not put Boyes in a terribly good light. Writing on November 6, 1902, in Nairobi, Captain Meinertzhagen says:

> Met a man called John Boyes, a cheerful rogue who years ago impersonated the British Government at Karuri's in Kikuyu. The Government foolishly brought all sorts of charges against him, but Boyes was acquitted. But, I believe he got away with a lot of Karuri's ivory, which he sold at the coast, and never refunded Karuri. I sold Boyes a rifle, but he has never paid me for it; he says he cannot do so, as he is broke—a slippery customer.

In Boyes's defense, I would suggest that Meinertzhagen— although one of the most fascinating characters to haunt any African history book—was not known for his lack of opinions. Personally, I do not believe that John would have put all his work at risk by sleight-of-handing some of Karuri's ivory. Very possibly, Meinertzhagen was monumentally irritated that he had not been paid for that rifle, but one would think that if he did not expect to get paid, he would have

taken back the gun. He only mentions Boyes once in his jour-
nal and perhaps he was paid later. John was a tough nut of
a bantam rooster, but I somehow don't think he would have
soiled his own nest. Further, a great many people were jealous of what he had accomplished in Kikuyuland, by single-
handedly subduing the most savage tribe of the time in British East Africa. After all, nobody hates success like the unsuc-
cessful. . . .

But then the darkest of shadows fell over Kikuyuland—
smallpox.

One day, when John was in a crowd of Kikuyu, he saw
an old man, a stranger in those parts, who obviously had
the pustules of the disease. Horrified, he quickly explained
the problem to the Kikuyu, who suggested that the man
be shot immediately. John could not do this, but he reckoned later that if he had he would have saved thousands
of native lives.

He directed that a separate isolation hut, well removed
from the others, be built, and that the man be incarcerated
under guard. His food would be left at a respectful distance
from the hut where the man could collect it until he either
recovered or died. His final orders were that under no circumstances was the man to leave the isolation camp.

Some days later, thinking that he had been able to head
off disaster, he again saw the man in a crowd, his guards
obviously having lost interest in their duties. John immediately sent him back to the isolation camp, but it was too late.
Whole families died when they would not report the disease
and continued to live together. Boyes sent to Naivasha for
lymph serum and treated as many people as he could, probably saving thousands, but many thousands more died.

As John noted with almost primitive awe, Karuri had made
a preventive "medicine" by splitting sticks that then had some
blackish powder poured into the clefts. They were stuck into
the ground at every footpath approaching his village. Amaz-
ingly, not a single person caught the smallpox plague in his

area. Of course, Karuri took the credit for having saved his people.

To compound the disaster, a great drought descended on the Kikuyu country, almost no rain having fallen for two seasons. John's men told him that there were many cases of cannibalism and he himself saw starving natives boiling and eating their filthy skin garments. Of course, this shut down his trading activities for food, but there was still some at Karuri's village as he had again gotten lucky, this time with the weather. John led a safari of several thousands of starving tribesmen and became very depressed when he saw hundreds constantly dropping out of line to die by the roadside. On a trip to Naivasha, he practically waded through bodies along that path, too.

Those Kikuyu who tried on their own to reach relief near Mt. Kenya and the Aberdare Range were set upon by the Kalyera tribesmen and murdered for their possessions as they traveled with all their household goods. John was powerless to stop the Kalyera, so crippled were the Kikuyu forces in the countryside.

John had decided on the safari to commandeer the few sheep and cattle remaining and to kill just enough of them to sustain life in the worst cases. Of course, there was a great outcry from the owners—who later complained to the government—that Boyes was stealing their stock. John, in defending himself later for his life, explained that he had not eaten one bit of the meat nor had his men touched a morsel, but had used it to keep as many natives alive as possible. When he reached more prosperous country, he spread the survivors out among many villages with instructions to behave themselves. Typical of Kikuyu nature, when these people had recovered their strength, they started to bully and dominate those who had saved them and helped them in their misfortune. John tried to get the former refugees to leave the country, but they refused. Some of them were criminals, deserters from Swahili caravans who simply settled in among the Kikuyu for as much as a year, living off the village food at gunpoint, rather like Mexican bandits of yore. This all became Boyes's fault in the eyes of the government and he received an ominous letter from a Mr. Gilkison, an official in Nairobi. John immediately sent Karuri and some headmen into the frontier town to explain and clear up the mess, which they did.

Finally, rain came and life returned to as normal a phase as it ever was in Kikuyuland. Once more trading for food, Boyes was able to eject the hangers-on in the villages and settle into his routine. Two-and-a-half years had now passed since John Boyes, King of the Wakikuyu, had entered the country. But his troubles were just starting, and not with the Kikuyu. . . .

Boyes had received word that a party of whites had entered Kikuyuland, an unprecedented event in all his tenure there. Within a few days, he learned that they consisted of two whites and a large native *askari* force, and that they were building a fort at a place called Mberri, about thirty miles from John's headquarters. Assembling most of his thirty-six loyal chiefs and their followers, he had a force of more than a thousand men trooping after him for the purpose of introducing the chiefs to the whites. He had explained that the government had apparently come to take over the country and to see to the settlement of all the petty squabbles and quarrels that had formerly been his own lot to administer. Boyes traveled all one day and camped, heading on in the morning. As the framework of the new fort came into view, it struck him that as there had been no warning given as to his coming, let alone with such a big force, they might be mistaken for a war party. He ordered his men and the chiefs to wait about two miles from the fort (which became Fort Hall) and went on alone.

Reaching the fort, he found that he knew the two white officers, a Mr. Hall and a Captain Longfield, both of whom received him with a snakelike cordiality, inviting him to breakfast. John explained his mission over eggs—that he had come to introduce the chiefs, and with their permission, he would bring his men to the fort. On their arrival, John heard a lot of shouting and talking and went out to see what was the matter.

Asking what was up, he was brusquely told that his personal *askaris* were under arrest for being in uniform. John objected that they were *not* in uniform, especially not British uniform, and that they simply all had the same sets of khaki clothes. Regardless, the officers proceeded to have some buttons cut off and the sergeant's and corporal's stripes removed, all of which proceedings started to make John boil at their officiousness, seeing it as insulting and rude.

Yet, rather than start blood flowing into the dark ground, John ordered his men to disarm; this order was obeyed quietly. But John's greatest crime in the eyes of the British officers was his flying of the Union Jack, as he had done for some time. Boyes asked the whites if he should have rather flown the Russian flag or some other. Unless he was part of the official oligarchy that ruled—or thought it ruled—the country, an Englishman's most heinous offense was clearly to fly his own flag, under which he had been born and for which he had fought.

At the disarmament of his personal troops, the other Kikuyus went wild, scaring the ten commandments out of the British officers and the small garrison. They asked Boyes to order the warriors' disarmament, which he did, and, despite many grumbles and threats, the Kikuyu weapons were placed in a nearby hut under guard on the understanding that they would be returned. No sooner was this done than Boyes himself was placed under arrest. Realizing that there would be considerable bloodshed if he did not obey, he acquiesced, being permitted to keep his cook and a couple of personal servants. John knew that his real offense was to have brought a state of peace to a country so filled with blood that the British had not dared to cross its borders before it had been pacified by Boyes. They were actually jealous and felt that there was room for only one empire-building force in East Africa.

John asked the highly agitated Hall and Longfield just what the charges were and one of the men unfolded a piece of paper from his breast pocket.

"I charge you, John Boyes," the officer read, "that during your residence in the Kenya district, you waged war, set *shauris* [made treaties], [im]personated Government, went on six punitive expeditions and waged dacoity.

"I must warn you that conviction under any one of these charges is a capital offense," he added.

Boyes thought about each of the specifications and finally asked, "What's dacoity?"

"Banditry," he was told.

"That part's a lie!," exploded John. "I was never a bandit in my life!"

John retired to a tent where he spent the day listening to his gramophone. None of his men knew he was under arrest; if they had, John was sure that they would have wiped out the fort contingent. For four days, Hall and Longfield took depositions from the Kikuyu and Longfield himself went to John's camp to try to gather some more damning information.

John was arraigned by Hall and Longfield, but he refused to say anything before his formal trial. He was then sent with two hundred of his personal bodyguards, riding on his mule, under an escort of only ten men under a native sergeant! The escort was frightened to death each time a native village had to be passed, fearing that they would be wiped out. John thought the whole business was quite funny:

> Here I was, a (so-called) dangerous outlaw, being sent down to be tried for my life on a series of awful indictments, through a country in which I had only to lift a finger to call an army of savage warriors to my assistance. I was accompanied by a personal following twenty times as numerous as the guard of ten natives who kept me prisoner, and who trembled every time they

passed a native village lest the inhabitants should rush out and wipe them out of existence; while on the first day out the humor of the situation was considerably increased by the sergeant in charge of the escort handing me the large blue envelope containing the statement of the evidence against me, with a request that I would take charge of it for him, as he was afraid he might lose it! I must say that I thoroughly appreciated the humor of the whole affair. I was the only mounted man in the whole outfit, still having my mule, and it struck me as distinctly amusing that I should be practically taking myself down to Nairobi, to be tried for my life, with the whole of the evidence under my arm!

The trip to Nairobi took a full five days, although it was only sixty miles as the vulture flies, but there were no roads and several swamps had to be skirted. The escort soldiers tried to impress some of John's bodyguard into carrying their loads but he drew the line at this. When he arrived at Nairobi and presented himself to the Goanese clerk of the sub-commissioner at headquarters in Nairobi, the humor persisted and the clerk told John that the official was busy and couldn't be disturbed. He commented that it was amazing how "busy" these petty men always were when someone not of the official or missionary sects came to call. Boyes told the clerk that he would come back in an hour and spent the time freely wandering about the new town. On his return, the sub-commissioner asked what he wanted and John handed him the blue packet of charges and evidence. The man was horrified, telling John that he was a dangerous criminal, an opinion that was quickly reinforced when he stepped out of the office and found himself surrounded by a guard of six Indian troops with fixed bayonets!

It being decided to send Boyes down to Mombasa for the main trial, he was escorted by another covey of Indians under a white officer and clapped for several weeks in the massive, brooding Fort Jesus, that ancient landmark of the Isle of War. John was somewhat surprised to find that the accommodations in his jail were not too bad, a spacious apartment being alotted him while he waited for the paperwork to be sorted out. As usual, it was in a snarl. He was free to wander about the fort, but he was, of course, not permitted outside.

John had been jailed for about three weeks before any of his friends heard of his predicament. At last, a casual friend named Claude Smith, who was also a trader and ivory hunter, came the 400 miles from Nairobi to Mombasa and hired the only lawyer in the territory, an Indian Parsee. Smith took 10,000 shillings from his own pocket as bail for John, not a small service. As John wrote, Smith did so out of the feeling of camaraderie that traders shared against their common enemy, the official bureaucracy, who considered traders of any sort—especially white ones—as the *washenzi Uliya,* the savages of Europe. In fact, Smith had been ivory hunting at the time he heard of John's predicament and had probably incurred quite an additional loss. Smith stayed with Boyes until the case was ultimately won and John acquitted, earning for himself arrest and a trial under similar charges at which he, too, was proved innocent. This was Hall's probable doing; he was furious that Boyes had been bailed out. I am sure that traders generally were not all sweetness and light, but the government of the day hated them with a passion as they managed to rove with comparative freedom where officialdom could not. This was probably thought to be somehow unpatriotic. . . .

By the time the trial came due, the government realized that they had nothing on Boyes and all the charges except "dacoity" were dropped. The government had found that most of what it had heard about Boyes stealing sheep and cows, his innoculation of the Kikuyu with "hollow thorns" that hurt, and his treaties and "punitive expeditions" were not fractures of any laws on the books.

At the trial, which was by judge and jury, the judge heard the evidence and directed the jury to acquit him. As his worship said, there was no stain on John's character and he further stated that he did not understand why there had been a trial at all as it was a waste of valuable time and money.

After his trial, Boyes resumed trading for a while, but with the advent of British Government rule, Kikuyuland began to slip back to its old ways of gore and greed. Wagombi, in particular, went on one hell of a warpath with his thousands of men, which took the King's African Rifles (including Meinertzhagen, among many others) years and many punitive campaigns to settle. Gradually, Boyes fell out of trading, primarily because the strife throughout the land under British rule made such a living impossible. I do not mean to say that this was the fault entirely of the British; it's just the way the things worked out. John's last days among the Kikuyu were spent as a guide and interpreter, starting with an expedition headed by a Captain Wake with a Mr. McLellan as political officer.

The reign of John I, uncrowned King of the Kikuyu, was over.

John Boyes lived for many years to become a legend in British East Africa, which, after his death, became the Republic of Kenya following 1963's *Uhuru*. He had a way of making money disappear even faster than he could make it. He became a professional ivory hunter in the Lado Enclave of Sudan, and was very successful at this, avoiding death at many a turn, and also had a fascinating adventure bringing horses, mules, and camels, as well as government ivory, across the northern deserts to Nairobi from Abyssinia. He wrote a second book about these adventures called *The Company of Adventurers* (1928), which was, by my way of thinking, fully as fine as his *John Boyes—King of the Wakikuyu* (1912).

John began his last great adventure into the unknown when he died on July 21, 1951, in Nairobi, his casket followed by most of the prominent folk of Kenya Colony. They saw a rough-cut page of history turn that day.

For me, the little man from Yorkshire was really one of the

greats of his native England, especially considering that he accomlished his amazing deeds with virtually no money or help from other men, white or black. He seized Fortune by the scruff of its neck until it howled; what he could not accomplish with steel guts he managed to do by sheer bluff and raw courage. Perhaps there is something to the saying that they just don't make 'em like they used to.

Part Four

Captain
James H.
Sutherland

It is autumn of 1908, the season that is a flirtatious whore in what was German East Africa: the time before the rains. The grass is a pale, Viking-beard yellow, the wait-a-bit thorns scar and cut the elephant hunter's skin. At first, there are simply white lines, but with time they blossom into blood—the red, trickling blood that is the result of miles of tracking.

The five bull elephants have covered perhaps thirty miles from the appearance of the early golden veins of dawn, until they have come with their giant strides to what were the watery, pale blue fingers of the Luwegu's tributary streams, reduced by the sledgehammer heat into mere tendrils of white reflective sand. Now, the terrible sun starts to sink into the bush-snaggled plain of the horizon. Finally, there is a flat area of parched grass, a *dambo,* which has been leveled by the cutting, whip-edged winds and the hooves of thirsty game.

The setting is perfect for the professional ivory hunter and the dark man measures the five bull elephants. He lifts his .577 Nitro Express Westley Richards rifle and eases the foresight against a dusty bull for a deadly side-brain shot, just ahead of the ear hole. The smell of fresh elephant dung mixes with the aroma of crushed, dry grass in the parched nostrils of the man as he squeezes the trigger and 110 grains of stalky bullet propellant throws the 750-

grain solid slug into a burst of wallow mud against the bull's temple. His hind legs collapse first and he falls in a welter of trunk and ear blood, his brain scrambled and his huge body as limp and gray as a giant sack of cement.

One of the other bull elephants swings forward as the shot rocks the sere landscape, offering a frontal brain shot. With the practice of long years, the man touches off just above the animal's eyes and watches as the bull crumples with the surrender that shouts death. Even before the last bull hits the dry earth, another massive bullet is on its way to penetrate with a wet, yet sharp *thwock!* in another brain shot.

In an almost-liquid movement, the man ejects the two empty cartridges and chambers two more, gleaming brass-and-nickel panatellas that will soon smash into two more skulls. Four of the five are down, dead from hemorrhage and shock as the thick, short slugs punch home. But the fifth bull elephant is another story. . . .

The big male takes a near-miss from a heart shot, the bullet staggering him but not knocking him down as he ponderously crosses a clearing where the natives have burned the grass. As the slug slams home, he instantly rushes the hunter, his immense head and tusks sheltering his trunk, drawn up between his ivory, his ears wide as sails. With a savage, shrill scream he charges the hunter, straight as a six-ton javelin.

Jim Sutherland waits as the elephant eats up precious yards, a juggernaut of irresistible meat, bone, and mayhem. At twenty paces, the man triggers his remaining barrel of the double rifle and takes the bull straight through the left eye, the bullet bursting from the skull to rattle against a stunted tree in the line of fire. The bull continues on without any sign that he has been hit.

Jim Sutherland, possibly the best ivory hunter in the world, is astonished. The bull keeps coming, his big, sap-stained tusks parentheses of death as he bears down on the white man. So surprised is Sutherland that he does not even try to reload, though he probably could not have completed the operation, the bull is so close. A terrible blow interrupts his amazement as the elephant smashes him on the thigh and sends him flying into his gunbearer, Simba, a couple of steps to the hunter's right.

The white and the black end up in a tangled heap of arms and legs, and before Sutherland can sort himself out, he feels himself wrenched by the right shoulder and thrown bodily in a long, khaki arc high into the air.

Although conscious, Sutherland is thoroughly shaken by his spin through space and has a very solid conviction that he has seen the last of his hunting days. With a lung-smashing impact, he lands square on the elephant's back, where he rolls off for the eleven- or twelve-foot drop to the ground. Only one thought goes through his scrambled brain: keep still. Do not move. Play dead. Maybe you won't be mangled by the feet.

Jim Sutherland lands with a sickening thud on his face, lying with his legs below the bull's huge body and actually between the front and hind feet! In fact, he is touching the elephant's left hind foot with his own. Strangely unafraid, Sutherland wonders how he will be finished off by the jumbo. . . .

"In which way is he going to kill me?" wrote Sutherland four years later. "Will he kneel on and trample me horribly? Will he drive his tusk right through my body, or will he, by some heaven-sent chance, leave me alone? Whichever way it is, may it be swiftly over and done with!"

But the elephant finds him through his semilucidity and again throws him into a treetop some forty-two feet away! The impact knocks Sutherland senseless and he only recovers consciousness as Simba shakes him awake. The elephant stands some thirty yards away trying to find Sutherland with his trunk.

I made a desperate effort to rise to my feet, but found, to
my intense dismay, that owing to the injuries I had received,
this was an impossibility. My back, head, and legs felt as if

197

they had been thoroughly beaten, my left hip was terribly bruised, while my left eye was almost closed up, but, judge of my annoyance, when I discovered that my left thumb was dislocated and my left arm and shoulder so badly strained that I was quite unable to hold my rifle in position. In the melee, I had dropped my heavy .577 elephant rifle, so bidding Simba sit down beside me, I managed, with some difficulty, to place my .318 [a light rifle] across his shoulder and fire for the elephant's ear; but owing to the shaking I had received, I couldn't, try as I would, keep my rifle steady, and the bullet, instead of hitting him in the desired spot and penetrating his brain, went wide and struck him high up on the right side of his head. At once, he slewed around and advanced towards us as if utterly surprised to find that he had failed to annihilate his enemy. So, telling Simba to hold my rifle barrel firmly, I drove another cartridge into the breech and waited patiently for my bulky opponent. When he was within fourteen or fifteen yards of us, I took aim and making a supreme effort to control my breath and steady my hand, pressed the trigger. The bullet struck him between the eyes, bringing him to his knees as if poleaxed, and as he struggled gamely to rise, I finished him with another shot.

Sutherland found, on examining the carcass, that the tail of the elephant was the strangest he had ever seen. It was totally without the flowing, stiff black hair of the normal jumbo, being covered with a sort of peach fuzz.

Sutherland wrote well, not surprising of a man who made his living from his senses. His book, *The Adventures of an Elephant Hunter* (MacMillan, London, 1912), is today more than a classic, being one of the great elephant hunting books extant. Yet, the adventures encompassed in his book represent only a small portion, about one third, of his professional ivory-hunting career. An example is the day after he was thrown by the elephant bull:

Never was return more welcome, [the return to Sutherland's main camp by a portable hammock known as a machilla] *and the picture that met my gaze as we approached is still vivid in my mind's eye. The greenish canvas of my tent gave a curious illusion of faint luminescence in the dusk; above it, in the sky, hung the golden sickles of a young moon, and on the horizon, as if tangled in the branches of a tree, there flashed that glorious jewel of the tropical heavens—the Southern Cross. Here and there, around the dark shadows of the huts, burned fires, round which sat or reclined the shapes of men, women, and children, some in silhouette, some lit up by the ruddy flames.*

There are probably three great names in the short history of what John Boyes, the King of the WaKikuyu, called the "Company of Adventurers," the professional ivory hunters of East Africa. Of these three were Walter D. M. "Karamojo" Bell (see *Death in the Silent Places*, St. Martin's Press, New York, 1980), Arthur Neumann, and Jim Sutherland. All three wrote books that are treasured Africana today and their reputations are really equal, given their very different approaches to ivory hunting (for example, light versus heavy rifles) as well as their personalities and their individual hunting techniques.

James H. Sutherland was a Scot who left "the old country" in 1896 for Cape Town. He had no idea of what his career would be, but he always attributed his wanderlust to his father's blood, Jim's dad having been a gold prospector in both New Zealand and Australia. Somehow Jim had managed to accumulate 500 British pounds, a near-fortune for a twenty-four-year-old immigrant, but, true to the adage, that a fool and his money are soon separated, Jim and the money were soon separated by "bad investments," probably two-legged ones. An interesting point that Sutherland mentions is that, in his early days, he spent some time in hospital from a bullet wound. Many years later he told one of his best pals that this wound was due to his "cleaning a revolver," hardly a mistake that one of the leading elephant hunters in all of Africa

199

would make. The truth of the matter remains after many years still to be seen.

Sutherland never might have mentioned it in his book were the wound not honestly inflicted and not an attempt at suicide, as the term "cleaning a revolver" is usually a euphemism for ventilating one's skull.

Besides his own book, probably the best sources of material on Sutherland are his two close friends, G. H. "Andy" Anderson, M.C., and George Rushby, both professional elephant hunters of considerable repute. Anderson first met Sutherland on board ship on the way to England when Jim was delivering the manuscript of his book to London. Anderson describes his first impressions of Sutherland as being those of a missionary. As Andy said, Jim looked just like a hard-bitten parson who, through his years in the bush, tended to get his KiSwahili mixed up in an unintelligible mess with his English. Sutherland was about five-foot-eight, very compact and well built. He wore glasses due to his eyes weakening from a bad bout of spirillum fever and indeed looked every bit the missionary returning home on leave. Andy asked of a German officer he happened to know who the missionary was and the German answered that it was Bwana Sutherlandi, the elephant hunter. He and Jim hit it off almost immediately, and started a friendship that only ended with Sutherland's death in 1932.

Jim had been sixteen years in Africa, ivory hunting for fourteen of them, when he met Anderson in early 1912. Anderson himself was one of the lynchpins of African hunting adventure, hunting during leaves from his regiment, the 18th Royal Hussars (Queen Mary's own). Eventually, after meeting and liking Sutherland, Andy decided to make professional hunting his career, both as a later founder of the East African Professional Hunters' Association and as an ivory hunter with Sutherland. Handicapped by a severe mauling by a lion in Somalia and later by a battlefield wound, Major Anderson resigned his active commission until the Great War when he took it up again.

On shipboard and later in England, Andy began to learn quite a bit about Sutherland. Apparently, the mild-looking Scot was quite an amateur boxer, which later stood him in good stead. Anderson says that Sutherland told him that on his, Sutherland's, first trip on the way out to Africa, he met "Kid" McCoy, the middleweight champion of the world, in 1896. Jim was the only person who could stay in the ring with McCoy as a sparring partner; in fact, he was so good that later, after his mysterious bullet wound, McCoy offered to set him up as a professional in America. Sutherland realized that the fight game was one of shady dealings and less than wholesome personnel. He declined in favor of a somewhat fuzzy future in Africa.

Sutherland, according to Anderson, fought several times in Johannesburg, although he was very reticent to speak of those bouts.

The man who would become Bwana Sutherlandi made his next stop at Beira, the ancient port of what was then–Portuguese East Africa; Mozambique and Portuguese East Africa have always been the same place. Still living a hand-to-mouth existence, Jim was persuaded to fight the ex-heavyweight champion of India. The ex-champ was an old soldier and the stake was 200 pounds, 1000 dollars, an immense sum in those days when one was very fortunate to earn $40 a month at hard labor. Sutherland knocked the champ out in the ninth round. Sutherland, at this time, weighed about 154 pounds and his opponent around 180.

That Jim Sutherland knew how to use his fists is shown by a snarl he got into with the Portuguese police, who sent an officer to arrest him for a minor infraction and then take him to the local cop shop. With what was probably not more than a single punch, Jim put the policeman in the hospital. Knowing that his actions would not be thought of kindly, he came on board a British steamer bound for British Central Africa (later Nyasaland and now Malawi).

At this point, Jim had visited and spent time in Cape Town

and Johannesburg, and had also been to Mafeking as well as Matabeleland. He had been a labor recruiter for the Beira Railroad, an agent for trading companies, a prize fighter, and a store keeper. Not liking any of these occupations, he resolved to be a professional ivory hunter, which, in his case, wasn't a bad idea.

Jim Sutherland had a passion for dogs, not at all strange as he lived a lonely life for years in the bush, speaking KiSwahili nearly to the conversational loss of his own tongue. His first dog in Africa was a bull terrier named Brandy. The description of this dog's fate was typical of Sutherland's good prose. As Anderson wrote, it "was full of romance and sentiment," which may seem strange if you have never known any ivory hunters. . . .

Perhaps Sutherland told it best in his book, *The Adventures of an Elephant Hunter*, in 1912:

> One night, one of glorious tropical moonshine, I had Brandy chained up at the door of my tent, while close to the tent was a fire by which sat the watchman, who replenished it through the night as the fire burned low. I had also arranged cut thorn-bushes in such a way that any prowler of the night would have to pass close to the fire ere he could reach the door of the tent and, feeling everything was secure, had gone peacefully to sleep. I was awakened some hours later by the yell of a frightened human being and the snarling growls of a leopard. Instinctively seizing my magazine pistol, which I always keep under my pillow, I jumped out of bed to find a leopard and my bull-terrier in the throes of a fierce encounter, the faithful watchman having long since made himself scarce. Now Brandy was endowed with all the pluck and fighting instinct of his breed, besides being fully trained to take care of himself; and at the very outset of the combat had, with his usual instincts and extreme quickness, managed to fasten his teeth into the side of the leopard's neck. Here he hung on like grim death, his own neck fortunately being protected by a broad brass-studded collar.
>
> Afraid of wounding my dog, I fired two shots in quick succession into the leopard's hip and another into his shoulder;

> *But these failed to finish it and the conflict continued as fiercely*
> *as ever. As they writhed and fought, I could see every movement*
> *of the leopard in the bright tropical moonshine and, seizing the*
> *first favourable opportunity, sent a bullet through its head to kill*
> *the leopard instantly. Even then, Brandy clung to his opponent*
> *as if determined to avenge himself for the mauling he had*
> *received. It was some time before I could coax the plucky dog*
> *into loosening his hold. When I did so, I found that my bull-*
> *terrier's chest and left hip were terribly torn by the leopard's*
> *sharp claws. Very gently I cleansed, disinfected and stitched up*
> *the warrior's wounds and made him as comfortable as possible,*
> *but so badly had he been lacerated in the struggle that it took*
> *him two months to recover from the effects.*
>
> *Poor Brandy, he afterward succumbed to the bane of Africa,*
> *the tsetse fly. At that time I happened to have a store in the*
> *district for purchasing rubber, beeswax, etc. from the natives;*
> *and, wrapping up the remains of my poor old friend in a roll of*
> *cloth, I buried him in the earthen floor of the store. So upset was*
> *I at losing my old chum that some how or other that store became*
> *intensely obnoxious to me; so, putting a match to the place, I*
> *sent it with the stock of goods and chattels heavenwards in smoke*
> *and flame—a funeral pyre to as fine a dog as anyone could wish*
> *to meet. I left the district the same day, and have never returned.*

Sutherland also had another bull terrier that Anderson mentions, one by the name of Mosoko. I have checked five Ki-Swahili (KiSwahili, meaning the language of the Swahilis, coastal dwellers) dictionaries and cannot find an appropriate translation. The name is probably what Sutherland would have termed in *shenzi* language—that of wild people, those who were not "enlightened" by Arabic and the Arabs. However, we must keep in mind that KiSwahili (or, as it was known in less formal circles, Swahili) was still quite phonetic in Sutherland's day and for a long time afterward.

When Jim was hunting in the Belgian Congo, he came to stay with Anderson and his wife. While near Nairobi, Sutherland hired a cook to take back to the Congo, but the fellow got smashed one night, went into Jim's tent and took all of

Mosoko's worm tablets for reasons best known to himself. Of course, he nearly died. As Andy Anderson points out, Mosoko came to the same end that Brandy barely avoided: leopard.

While Sutherland was hunting elephants on one of his frequent forays in the Congo, Mosoko was left with an Englishman. The bull terrier was sleeping at the foot of the Englishman's bed, nearest the tent flap, when a leopard walked in and grabbed the dog. Naturally, there was one hell of a fight, which was interrupted when the leopard took off and Mosoko streaked after him. At dawn the next morning, both Mosoko and the leopard were found dead a few yards from each other.

Anderson mentions that Sutherland occasionally used to come out with offhand remarks, which had not been thought through, one of which was voiced when he was visiting Anderson and his wife, Lorna. Anderson says that it was after several "sundowners" in the hard-drinking area of Nairobi that Sutherland, sitting on his heels native fashion, suddenly turned to him and in a loud voice said: "Andy, Andy, if I had a home like this and a charming wife like yours, go hunting? No, no—old man! What's the good of your rifle? You can't go to bed with your rifle!"

This, of course, brought the house down with laughter and Sutherland became flustered. "Oh," he said continually, "forgive me, Mrs. Andy. I'm so uncivilized!"

There is at least one more dog story in Sutherland's repertoire, that told in his own book about a fox terrier he had named Whisky. In fact, the tale of the terrier and the tusker was chosen for the gold embossment on the cover of his book, which was the custom around the turn of the century.

It was the forenoon of September 15, 1909, near a stream called the Kitulika, which Sutherland describes as a tributary of the Mbarangundu, a river we will have to presume was either in the Congo or, more likely, in Portuguese East Africa. It is not well known and does not seem to appear on maps of the period.

Sutherland had shot two big tuskers and, as there were three together, he took off following the remaining one about a mile behind. Believe me, *that* is the longest mile in hunting. The bull ran into the wind of Sutherland's staff, left behind and supposedly out of danger. As the elephant caught the scent, he turned immediately and headed back toward Sutherland. As he drew closer, Jim caught his movement in a thicket a few hundred yards off. He was coming straight on, about a hundred yards away.

There were two men with Jim, his head tracker, Hyiah, and Ntawasie, his number two. There was also the fox terrier, Whisky, but Sutherland doesn't say why the pup was along.

Leaving Hyiah to take care of the dog, Sutherland started crawling forward, with Ntawasie behind him and the heavy .577 shoved ahead, and his lighter rifle handled by the second tracker. Jim crept nearer and nearer on his knees and elbows until he felt sure of a killing shot at about forty yards. The tusker had a fine pair of tusks, more than five feet out of the lip, but as Sutherland crept closer, to within about fifty yards, he was suddenly aware of the growling of Whisky behind him and saw the dog rush past, its leash trailing behind.

Sutherland thought the elephant would rush off into the bush at the appearance of the dog, but he didn't. He was fascinated, coming forward, without doubt wondering what on earth the fox terrier was.

The bull tusker was only forty paces away, offering a perfect shot to the man. Yet, the attention of the jumbo was centered on the dog, which was completely unimpressed, dancing around the elephant.

The elephant put out its trunk to smell the dog, but it was promptly snapped at. In a blurr, the elephant grabbed Whisky and threw him some sixty feet into the bush, then faded away into the yellow, sun-seared bush.

At this point, Sutherland decided to intervene, placing a shot at a rear angle to the tusker, which fell and then tried to get up. Jim smacked it again in the heart and it collapsed a few score yards away.

The dog was in fine fettle, considering his unauthorized air trip, and although Whisky resisted at first being placed on the dead elephant, he soon realized that the bull was dead and assumed the pose of the conqueror. I suppose he will live forever there.

Cross-referencing Jim Sutherland's career through several books is fascinating fare, especially when one tries to pin down such personal aspects of his life as why he started hunting ivory. One source, a modern hunter from Europe, says positively that Jim was influenced by Marcus Daly, an adventurer and elephant hunter who authored the book *Big Game Hunting and Adventure 1897–1936*. The story goes that he met Daly and saw the ivory Daly had taken, which persuaded Jim to become an elephant hunter. I don't know where this story comes from as I have all the books mentioned in the European's bibliography and none contains this information.

I am willing to go on record that this information is suspect for several reasons. For a start, in 1897–98, Daly was in Matabeleland; then, in 1899, he was in South Africa fighting in the Second Boer War. He was not ivory hunting and selling his tusks at Beira, Portuguese East Africa, where Sutherland is supposed to have met and been influenced by him.

For another thing, George Rushby, a great elephant and lion hunter of whom I have written, and who was one of Sutherland's closest friends, says in his book, *No More the Tusker* (1965), that Marcus Daly and Jim Sutherland didn't get along. Speaking of 1928, Rushby says: "For some reason he [Daly] took a great dislike to Sutherland but whether the reason was professional jealousy I do not know. He had, of course, heard much about Sutherland down the years, as all of us had, but he had *never previously met him*."

The italics are mine. Rushby goes on to say: "Although I had some respect for Daly as a hunter, and for his toughness, I would not have trusted him under any circumstances." This seems to be a common opinion of Daly.

Andy Anderson says that Sutherland told him he started professionally hunting elephant after the death of Brandy and the burning down of the store, beginning in Portuguese East Africa. Andy says that Sutherland had shot a few elephants before, but he only became a professional in 1899. He was continually in the field for thirty-three years except for three quick visits to England, one to the United States, and participation in "three wars." Here, there is a slip of the tongue as Sutherland was in one insurrection and WWI only—two, not three, wars.

The first of Jim's wartime experiences was in 1905–06, when he fought with the Germans to put down the Maji-Maji rebellion. This was at the same time that the Germans were trying to suppress the Hereros in German South-West Africa, and did so to the tune of 80,000 dead members of the Herero tribe in four years.

Writers are all but unanimous in saying that Sutherland spoke of obtaining an "unlimited" elephant hunting license from the Germans by means of his participation in the Maji-Maji affair, where he was wounded by a spear and was one of the few Britons awarded the Iron Cross! In fact, as Anderson protests, Jim was granted an unlimited license for German East Africa (next Tanganyika and now Tanzania) in about 1902, several years before the Maji-Maji rebellion. Anderson says—and I think his comments very germane to the history of Sutherland:

> *I do not know what year Jim started hunting in German East Africa, but I should say it was about 1902. After crossing the Ruvuma River he proceeded to Dar es Salaam* [Haven of Peace] *(the chief port and the capital) and obtained a license to shoot elephants ad lib. These elephant licenses were only granted as a special privilege and with the sanction of the Governor. I have heard, and seen made, many statements to the effect that Jim received this privileged license for his good work in the Maji-Maji rebellion. That is quite untrue. I do know, however, that when the new game laws were enforced in 1912, all licenses*

for shooting elephants were stopped by the German Government.
The German Governor, Baron von Rotenburg, told Jim
personally that, if he went to the north of the territory and
poached elephant in the Belgian Congo, the German
Government would take no notice of the ivory which he obtained
and would allow him to export it through German territory. As
it was not much of an elephant country, Jim decided not to do
so. He returned to England for a visit. It was then that I met
him at Tanga.

The Maji-Maji rebellion is worth mentioning. *Maji* meant water, and the concept was that the bullets of the Germans when fired at the insurrectionists would be turned to water. This is very similar to the idea of the Congolese in the 1960s, who believed enemy bullets would turn to water if certain magic regimens were followed. As many gut-shot, cane knife–wielding Simbas found out, it didn't quite work. . . .

During the Great War, because of his knowledge of German East Africa as well as his leadership qualities, Jim Sutherland was appointed captain and became chief intelligence officer of "Norforce," the main force under Brigadier General Edward Northey of the British Army. Jim actually was part of the Nyasaland (Malawi) Field Force and had been badly wounded when acting along the Portuguese East African border. His familiarity, with the southern part of German East Africa was immensely valuable and he was twice mentioned in dispatches and awarded the French Legion of Honour. I suspect he probably kept quiet about his Iron Cross!

Jim Sutherland usually hunted from a main base camp and made ten-day or two-week safaris from it, until he had as many tusks as his carriers could take back. In addition to Portuguese East Africa and German East Africa, Jim hunted extensively in the Belgian Congo, French Equatorial Africa (today the Central African Republic and areas of Chad), and, starting in 1919, in Uganda.

His favorite elephant gun was a .577 Nitro Express by Westley Richards of London—an ejector gun that snapped the empty cartridges away automatically when it was fired and the breech opened. Some elephant hunters favored the non-ejector type or had the ejector mechanism neutered when hunting elephant. The idea was that there was no *pinnnng!* when reloading and removing the empties by hand rather than by automatic ejector. Personally, I would rather be re-loaded immediately by the cartridges I hold between the fingers of my left hand than have to dig out two empties from previous shots before I stuff fresh rounds in. I bite my nails, anyway. Using the ejector system has twice saved my life by enabling me to reload quickly, so I am a genuine, no-kidding believer.

Although it is true that Sutherland used a .318 Axite (Axite being a new type of powder in those days), and he did very well with this light backup rifle, it was no more than the .30–06 with a 250-grain bullet. Precisely placed, it would kill the biggest elephant with a brain shot, but if the bullet was not accurate, the elephant hunter usually ended up as the pink stuff between an elephant's toes.

Most writers who touch upon Sutherland say that he always used the combination of .577 Nitro as his first rifle and the .318 as his second. This is not entirely correct as he frequently mentions using a 10.75 mm. Mauser rifle instead of the .318 and he also says he used a .303, the standard British service round.

Sutherland also mentions using a .500 Nitro cordite rifle, a caliber that nearly got me subdivided by a wounded lion (see Peter Capstick's Africa: *A Return to the Long Grass*, St. Martin's Press, New York, 1987), although I was not using the rifle personally.

Sutherland chose the .577 (also Axite, later cordite) Nitro probably by listening to the cognoscenti of the time and place who had found that the 750-grain bullet penetrated much better than the more powerful .600 Nitro Express with a 900-grain slug. Compared with the .577 Nitro, very few .600s—probably well under 200—were built by all makers.

As one might figure, Jim Sutherland had a lot of experience with our old friend, Death. Perhaps, though, he had it in balance with life a lot better than most of us. . . .

As he wrote in 1911, in his only book: "Give me the life of the *pori*! [the bush or wilderness]. I think it would be difficult to find another so full of wild, exhilarating excitement, hair-breath escapes, and devil-may-care risks, and though the end is usually swift, perhaps that is better than flickering out slowly on a bed of sickness. If anyone has a desire to live, where living is really full-blooded living, let him go and spend some of his time among wild animal life—far away from the insidious comforts and the petty restraints of life in a civilized community."

Sutherland was certainly correct about the "exhilarating excitement" and the "hair-breath" escapes, although he was not as fortunate in his way of dying, as we shall see. But his days were hardly crammed with boredom. . . .

At dawn one morning in eastern Africa, probably Portuguese territory, Sutherland and his bearers set off on the spoor of four bulls that had passed the night before. Sutherland had managed to kill three of the tuskers, two with brain shots that felled the jumbos where they stood and the other with a heart-and-neck shot combination that left the three almost in a single heap. The fourth was discovered, some half-hour before sunset, to have circled around his pursuers and come back to the three dead. Astonished to hear the tusker in bamboo behind him, Sutherland told Simba, his chief tracker at this time, to climb a tree to see if he could spot the bull.

As Simba almost reached the tree, rare in the flat cover, he gave a shriek of deadly surprise, running as fast as his legs would carry him from the elephant he had almost walked into. Jim answered Simba's scream telling him to run to the left to give him a clear shot, which the African did. Sutherland planted a 750-grain solid, nickel-jacketed slug in the side of the elephant's head. The tusker staggered, but did not fall.

Despite the terrific blow, the bull kept up his charge, to the horror of both Sutherland and Simba.

Jim watched the scene as if in a dream as the bull faltered and then came on at full speed after Simba, a race the native could not win. As Jim screamed at him to break off from his direct line of retreat, which prevented a shot, Simba did the unthinkable: he fell over a vine or a piece of bush and landed sprawling in the bull's path!

Yet, he somehow recovered from the blow in his face and started running again, terrified, directly toward his Bwana, obscuring further the chance of a shot for Sutherland. Jim was the only one who could break the straight line between the black, the elephant bull, and himself. He ran to his right, opening up the angle, and fired his second barrel. The big slug smashed the tusker too high but turned him, the bull heading back into the long grass from where he had charged Simba.

Jim Sutherland drew a deep breath and followed him into the long grass, more determined than ever to kill the bull that had given them such a scare. In any case, the elephant had beautiful, long tusks.

Jim grabbed his light rifle from Simba as he passed, giving him the empty .577 as he went by. He ran for a hundred yards through the thick cover and fired a shot that took the tusker somewhere near the heart. The bull immediately turned and, screaming like a lashed-down calliope, charged straight at Sutherland.

It was a long charge, about forty yards, giving Jim time to decide on his shot and take his time. Personally, I am rather surprised that Sutherland merely fired at the bull's face, as he says, but the light was growing very dim and perhaps he could not see for a direct brain shot.

The light slug was as effective as a piece of grass and Sutherland smacked the bull again with another .318, but he came on, blood blowing from his trunk, streaming down his face. He was within fifteen paces of Sutherland when Jim realized that he had an empty rifle!

As Jim Sutherland, dean of elephant hunters, drew back the bolt of his .318, he was astonished to realize that he had never reloaded after he had shot the last of the three bulls! Amateur mistake. Now, he had to die for it. Jim threw his rifle into the face of the tusker in a final gesture of frustration.

But, then, somehow, the elephant was pulling up, his head towering, his trunk gushing even more blood, his ear holes red with a gout of crimson. Slowly, as if he were sleepwalking, the sound reached him and shook Jim to the pit of his stomach. It was the .577 bellowing a few inches behind him, the power of its shot washing him in hot vapor. It was Simba. Good old Simba. Simba with the .577 in a final bid to save Sutherland, *Bwana Ngonganjaa.*

His ears ringing, Sutherland turned to find Simba with the .577 still in recoil. Realizing his Bwana's problem, he had gotten up, thrown a cartridge into the .577 Westley Richards, and loosed a bullet through the elephant's trunk and into his mouth. The bull collided with a tree, knocking it over, and sped on like a juggernaut for another fifty yards like a huge, gray, screaming bowling ball. Sutherland grabbed the rifle from Simba, dunked a pair of cartridges into the .577 and ran forward. When he was point-blank to the bull, he shot the tusker through the heart. The old boy toppled over and lay still at last. It was a very close thing.

But the effort of staying alive wore very heavily on both Jim and Simba. As the sky turned from gold to crimson to kingfisher-wing cobalt, Jim dragged himself over to where Simba stood, leaning against a tree in his exhaustion:

> *I gave his hand a hearty grip—it was by no means the first*
> *occasion on which we had faced a life and death encounter*
> *together—and being utterly exhausted, flung myself on the*
> *ground. My tracker followed suit and for a long while we lay,*
> *too tired to think or speak or move. During the tense excitement*
> *of the hunt, we had temporarily forgotten our bodily discomforts,*
> *but now a swift reaction set in, and we became the prey of a*

*burning, intolerable thirst! No words can depict the awful
suffering that the simple want of water can inflict, and poor
Simba, unable to bear the cruel pangs any longer, crawled over
on hands and knees to where the elephant lay and began to lap
up the half-congealed blood which had flowed from the animal's
head and gathered in a tiny, shining pool. I myself, half-crazy
with the agony, struggled to my feet, pulled a handful of leaves
from an adjacent tree, and hoping that the moisture contained
in the foliage would cool my parched mouth, was about to chew
them. All at once, Simba, having seen my action, rushed up and
caught my arm.*

*"Don't, Bwana, don't," he cried, "it is the poison tree! Wait a
little while and I'll try to get you some roots."*

*Somewhat refreshed by his awful draught, he staggered off
into the forest, while I again flung myself down and strove
calmly to bear the torturing pangs until my tracker returned. I
had only lain a few minutes when, to my joy, I heard yell after
yell of delight.*

*"Bwana, nemepona! Bwana, nemepona! (Master, we are
saved! Master, we are saved!). Getting up, I tottered in the
direction of the voice and ere long came upon Simba, busy with
his knife at the stems of a water-bearing creeper which the
natives call* ntamba. *After he had cut several lengths of about
two feet each from the rope-like stems, we applied the sections to
our baked lips and greedily sucked the deliciously cool, watery
juice. Again, we cut and drank; it seemed as if we should never
thoroughly slake our thirst! Our next move was to appease the
gnawings of our hunger. A glorious moon had now risen and
hung low and large, silvering each twig and spray with a
ghostly light, and making the jungle a web of vein-like shadows.
By its beams we could see to collect fuel, and coming across some
dry branches of the* mangu *tree, set to work to light a fire.
Cutting a hole in a flattened piece of the dry branch, Simba
inserted a rounded stick of the same wood and twirled it rapidly
round and round, the resulting friction causing sufficient heat
to smoulder a portion of my shirt which I had frayed for the
purpose. Gathering some dry leaves and twigs, we soon had a
roaring blaze, over which we quickly toasted choice bits of
elephant's heart.*

213

*A right hearty meal we made, and following up the repast
with another long draught of the* ntamba *creepers, we lazily
stretched ourselves beside our fire to dream of some privileged
hunt with Diana and her Nymphs.*

The next morning, Sutherland and Simba reached the
Nbemcuru River and found the rest of Sutherland's crew.
They had a hot bath and a full meal, which did wonders. Finishing their meal, they went back to where the elephants
lay. The best weighed 102 and 107 pounds, exceptional
ivory.

Sutherland's exertion on his hunt brought on a recurrence
of malaria, which was only alleviated by a multiple dose of
tea, quinine, and whiskey. Nothing like whiskey for what ails
you.

The field life of a professional ivory hunter is obviously
not just confined to elephants. Perhaps one of Jim's more
interesting adventures was with snakes. . . .

Jim Sutherland does not say in his book how many pairs
of shoes or boots he wore out over his career nor does he
attempt to suggest how far he walked in his career chasing
elephants. Yet, we know that he was a great walker and probably did every bit as much hiking as did Walter "Karamojo"
Bell during his career, which spanned about the same length
of time. Bell reckoned on at least 60,000 miles. In those days
the dictum that, on the average, a hundred miles had to be
walked to shoot a bull elephant, no matter what his tusk
weight. What must be remembered is that almost any path
in Africa is, if not studded with poisonous snakes as the pulp
writers would have us believe, at least a warm, likely place
to find the odd puff adder, mamba, or cobra. For sure Jim
Sutherland found them, too.

Jim recalls—and he was apparently not much of a herpetologist in his knowledge of snakes beyond the common species—an evening when a snake very much entered his life as
well as his bed.

He was somewhere between Beira and the Zambesi River,

214

which could be almost anywhere in the northern part of Portuguese East Africa. Jim says that his porters were a considerable distance behind him and that he had settled in some thick bush to avoid the terrible rain that swished and swirled above his oilskin shelter. He praised the god of ivory hunters as he had thought to bring his blankets along with him. Jim says he was at the point of falling asleep from fatigue when he felt a "chill, slimy contact with my skin and knew that a snake had crawled under my blanket and curled itself up between my legs."

(I must interject that snakes and "assault weapons," no matter what the Congress says, are smooth and cool to the touch and in no way slimy.)

It was a big puff adder, that viper that kills more people in Africa than any other serpentine species because of its habit of lying still in dusty paths and in mixed leaves, sluggish until it strikes with a massive injection of venom as amber as tobacco spit, as smooth as goat snot, a huge, tissue-destroying dose of poison that is one of the world's most destructive to man.

Jim Sutherland felt the snake slide against his leg skin, a slow, sinuous touch he would never forget. Finally, after many minutes, he felt it coil in the warmth of his groin, curled up between his legs.

Jim lay still, almost afraid to breath. His hushed call to his gunbearers sounded like the smooth *screeeek* of a sword being sheathed on the wet night air. But two of his men heard him. Jim spoke quietly—*very* quietly—with them and asked them to slip off the blanket covering him. With trembling fingers they did as he asked and revealed a massive puff adder. All or nothing. Double or quits. Jim Sutherland told his men to grab him under his armpits and make a concerted snatch of his body. The men counted to three and yanked Sutherland free as he spanned his legs to avoid the probable bite.

His men, seeing that Jim was not bitten, then killed the big snake with sticks.

Sutherland would have been drummed out of—his brass buttons cut off by—any local society of snake experts, because he used native names to describe most species besides the most common ones. Sutherland records an instance when a very black-skinned snake, the species chiefly found in trees and rocks, killed a brother of one of his men.

The man had been hunting rock rabbits. The rock rabbit, *dassie,* or rock hyrax, is most closely related to, of all things, the elephant by a quirk of foot structure. Upon breaking the leg of one by a thrown stick, the man reached into a dark hole where the *dassie* had run, under a big boulder.

The man stuck his arm into the hole to catch the rock rabbit and was bitten, at first certain it was by the *dassie.* However, he was to discover on jerking his hand back that a snake clung to the tip of his finger. As Sutherland says, the man was dead within a half hour. Jim describes it as only a very black snake found "chiefly in trees and among rocks." It was most likely a spitting cobra—which can also bite as if there were no next year—as he said it was a glossy black in color; the black mamba is dull. I don't think it was any form of mamba from the description, although the spitting cobra doesn't spend all that much time in trees. Still, the only ones I have found—plenty, to be sure in the rainy season—were in rocky country living on young hyraxes the way the prairie rattler lives on small prairie dogs.

It must be understood by the reader that native Africans often die from the reputation of a snake rather than from its venom. There are many cases of people in Africa turning toes-up from such things as a scorpion sting, which, although painful to a crescendo, is not fatal. It is a case of matter over mind. . . .

There are several more interesting incidents related by Sutherland of which I have some knowledge. Sutherland writes that "two years ago" (probably in 1909 as it took him until 1911 to write the manuscript of his book, printed in 1912) he had missed several chickens from his henhouse and, thinking they had been stolen by some of his men, accused them of the crime.

Jim says that they denied the charge about the same time as his cook brought him several onions from his stores that bore weird toothmarks. Strangely enough, the marks on the half-eaten onions were sworn by the blacks to have been made by a snake.

Well, I cannot say as to onions being gummed or otherwise by snakes, but I do know about chickens.

Some years ago, I was staying with a friend at a place called Zebediela, the largest citrus estate in the world, situated in the northern Transvaal of South Africa. Among the pleasures of the *plaas* were towering cliffs, verdant pastures (with resident flies), and a few fine trees as well as chicken coops and assorted runs.

One morning we got up and found six of the chickens dead. On inspection, it was clear they were bitten by a snake or possibly two. There were two adults and four chicks. It was not guesswork as the marks of the snake fangs were obvious on turning back the chickens' plumage.

While I was away with my wife Fifi for a few days, our host killed two *rinkhals* or spitting cobras, a black mamba that had chosen the main tree in the center of the kitchen area in which to roost, as well as a free-lance green mamba and a boomslang, a tree snake of back-fanged persuasion. That's quite enough snakes for anybody's bad dreams.

Curiously, even though I give as much credence to the onion-eating habits of Sutherland's snakes as you would expect, one was found inside the pulp-hollow of a tusk. It ran to seven feet of snake! I know even less than Sutherland what species it was from his description, but it was killed to a glossy pulp by his men with staves.

Africa is a land of sorrow because death is frequent, or at least was until modern antivenins and antibiotics came to the fore. A typical and almost certainly true tale told by Sutherland is of a woman who left Chimbunga's Village for a *kraal* some miles distant with a native basket and a small child tied to her back in the usual fashion.

Along the way, the child suddenly gave a sharp cry, but aside from briefly comforting the child, the woman continued upon her way. When she got to the far *kraal*, the child was dead, the top of the head swollen and the skin and flesh puffed beyond life. Near the center of the swelling were the obvious marks of a snake's fangs.

It turned out that this spot had yielded several deaths of tribesmen from the same village, surely by the same snake.

A few weeks later, Sutherland happened to be coming along the same path and a tracker saw overhanging the path a large snake which Jim blew to perdition with a shotgun. Sutherland reckoned it was a fine specimen, dullish green and called a *nakahungu* by the locals, one of the most dangerous snakes in Africa.

The *nakahungu* sounds like a typical color variant of the black mamba—*Dendroaspis polylepis*—which may range between olive green and a dull dun and any shade in between. As I've mentioned, "black" refers to the color of the mouth lining, not that of the snake itself. Certainly the choice of a specific territory is typical of the black mamba. A black mamba bite you do not need.

Sutherland speaks about the *songwe,* the semimythical snake popular in Mozambique as well as in today's Zambia. According to widespread belief, the *songwe* was a variation of deadly snake that had a red cock's comb on its head and crowed in the same way that the rooster did. Needless to say, and typical of most central and east African legends, this fabulous snake waited for men along paths frequented by humans and killed them deader than the penny postcard.

That Sutherland offered a reward, dead or alive, for this snake doesn't make it any more believable or fabulous than it is. Personally, I think that the *songwe* is real, a part of African legend but a part of reality also.

Certainly, the idea of a cock's comb and the cry of a rooster is invention, but I have seen two huge black mambas, both of which I killed, that had a "frill" of sloughed skin around their necks, which, because of the waist-shape of the head leading into the body, did not come free with the last shedding of skin. I believe that this was the origin of the *songwe*. These mambas were very thick for mambas and certainly long. Maybe they weren't as long as a black mamba is supposed to get (one was nine feet and the other a bit over ten feet), but they were obviously very old snakes and most cantankerous. The backlighted view of these snakes would have made them appear was if they had a ruffed collar; the fabrication of a comb and a cock's crow would almost naturally follow.

That Jim Sutherland had been a professional ivory hunter a bit over a decade when he published his book, leaves a great deal open to speculation as to what he experienced in his last twenty-plus years of ivory hunting. Although my own writings are very much centered on the horror of man-eating lions as well as other species, Sutherland's experiences themselves are superb:

> *People living in the perfect safety of their homes in a civilized country have no conception of the insecurity that is felt by natives in their kraals in the interior of Africa. The cause of this insecurity is chiefly the man-eating lion, and no other animal of the forest inspires such terror into the black man's heart. Naturally, there is a reason for this. In those villages, far in the heart of the pori, where the white man is never seen, not hundreds but thousands of natives are annually killed by these monsters.*

Sutherland goes on to explain that, nearly always, the man-eater is on in years and unable to hunt his normal prey and thus turns to man. But my own experience is that it is the *exception* to Sutherland's rule that applies today. It is the young, very fit, beautifully furred and muscled lion that is the guilty party. Perhaps this change from the moth-eaten and tired old chap is a sign of the times? Perhaps they are the new game park lions that have associated with and gained a new disrespect for man? Are these the reasons for the change? Of course, we still have old or disabled lions whose shift in their usual culinary practices make them man-eaters, but, generally speaking, it is those lions who choose man-eating as a vocation as well as an avocation that are "normal." They just know too much of humans. "Elsa" (the lioness heroine of *Born Free* by Joy Adamson) had to be put down after she killed humans. So did Norman Carr's "tame" lions. Lions have changed with the times. Let's face it: they *like* to eat people, despite the probable taste. . . .

As Jim Sutherland says, one of the biggest problems is that information as to the whereabouts of man-eating lions is often withheld, kept from the very man who wants to kill them. The reason is that every man-eater is believed to be a spirit of a reincarnated powerful person such as a witch doctor or chief who is taking his vengeance on people who wronged him during life. This revenge is in the form of a man-eating lion or lions. . . .

Jim Sutherland had much experience of man-eaters in his years hunting and mentioned several in *The Adventures of an Elephant Hunter*. In one case, a lion had broken into a native hut and killed a woman and her child. Afraid to lose the lion, five *askaris* or native police emptied their rifles into the hut. Then they fired it with thrown brands. When things cooled down, they found there a lion, shot through the heart, the much-eaten body of a woman that had been hit three times with bullets, and a child with a crushed head, probably a victim of a stroke of the lion's paw.

One of the more interesting of Sutherland's adventures with man-eating lions took place in the country of Sultan Leanduka, a spot that Jim hunted for many years. Jim noticed that the natives were always in groups of two or three and heavily armed with spears and such. Soon he learned that a man-eater had killed fifteen people when the grass was high during the rains, but the killer had learned never to hit the same village twice.

When Jim Sutherland was returning from hunting one day, he was met several miles from home by a very distraught native who stammered that the lion had killed his brother and two of the brother's wives in one attack as they passed between villages. Jim went back to his camp, changed his nickel-jacketed, lead solid bullets for expanding ones and followed the spoor for two days, sleeping on it rather than going home. Nothing. Jim found that there were several lions but they kept running ahead of him, not offering a shot.

The cold month of the Southern Hemisphere, July, came along and Jim found it necessary to send a couple of his old hands from the Rovuma (or Ruvuma) River to Songea, about eight days' walk. As they later said, they were about thirty miles away from the fine place where Jim had his camp, and spent the night at a village controlled by a headman named Gwia. It was 1905.

From this village alone, nine people had been taken by man-eaters. Sutherland's two men, Hyiah and Manjemba, were given a hut in which to sleep, and they kindled a large fire in the center of it and especially secured the doors with lashings and wedges. Manjemba was on one side of the fire, Hyiah on the other.

The night was quiet, the chant of fruit bats and frogs the only sounds that penetrated the soft screech of insects in the bush nearby. It was about three o'clock when the door was smashed into so much kindling and a lion grabbed Hyiah by the thigh!

Manjemba, shocked by the screams and growls, still managed to grab his rifle and put a slug near the lion's heart, which made it drop his friend as it tried to drag him out of the hut. The lion then ran off into the night. Its body was found some seventy yards away in the dense bush.

The locals washed Hyiah's leg wounds with hot water and made a *maschilla* (better known as a *machilla*) and carried the

221

injured man back to Sutherland's camp in the portable hammock. Jim immediately disinfected his wounds as best he could and Hyiah recovered within six weeks.

A later conversation, in 1907, between Sutherland and Gwia, the headman of the beseiged village, seemed to show that Manjemba had killed the only man-eater there was or at least scared away the others, if they existed.

When Jim Sutherland first started his career as a professional ivory hunter, he was for a time on the upper Shire River in then–British Central Africa, which became, subsequently, Nyasaland and Malawi. Jim was sitting in his tent when one of his men, whom he had paid off two days ago, came screaming beneath the canvas.

"Lion, my mother! Lion, my mother!" he screeched in dialect. Sutherland quieted him down a bit and asked what had happened.

Several lions had killed his mother, his wife, and two of his children—that was the matter. Further, they had taken over his hut. Actually, the lions had only killed his wife and one of his children, as later events proved, but this didn't cheer the man up a great deal. . . .

As "Sutherlandi" later said, "Though I found this to be an exaggerated account of the disaster, the matter turned out to be serious enough."

Jim grabbed his rifle and set out for the hut, about a mile away, and found, on his arrival, quite a few tribesmen in an advanced state of perturbation.

Sutherland found that the man's wife had had his youngest on her back, as was usual, and had been grinding corn for the evening meal when a lion charged up and killed the baby with a terrible bite. Possibly thinking that the child was part of the woman, the lion immediately dropped it when it realized that it was not. The lion then grabbed the mother, bit her through the back of the neck, and started to eat her in the alcove of the hut where the corn was kept.

In a few seconds, a second lion appeared and also began

to eat the man's wife. While this was going on, the husband was fishing a couple of hundred yards away.

There was not good news when he returned to the hut. The child, who had been executed by fangs through the skull, lay in the doorway. A pair of lions were already fighting over the man's wife's body. Where the man's mother had gotten to, along with another child, was not recorded.

Jim almost ran the mile between his camp and the scene of the deaths. As he said, "I went at once into the *shamba* [farm or area of cultivation] and discovered the horribly mangled remains of the unfortunate woman lying among the *matema* corn, but as nothing more could be done as far as she was concerned, accompanied by two of my men, I immediately set out in pursuit of the lions."

Sutherland and his men followed the tracks until the light abruptly faded in the few minutes that it only does take in Equatorial Africa. He saw no lions.

Jim tried his best. He used the body of the woman for bait for at least a night, himself snuggled in the dubious joy of a tree's branches. Although Jim waited until dawn, the lions were smarter. They never showed.

At least Sutherland appreciated the irony of Africa that still exists: "Strange to relate, the native who had thus lost wife and child in one afternoon was, a few days after his bereavement, himself seized and devoured by a crocodile."

Jim Sutherland knew: when Africa decides to kill you, it will. . . .

George Rushby speaks very well of the physical and mental fitness of Sutherland; probably as well of his hunting abilities and marksmanship. Sutherland, as we know, was a Scot of medium height and about 155 pounds. Yet, Sutherland always made the most of his body, as did men like C. Hugh Stigand (see *Death in the Silent Places*, St. Martin's Press, New York, 1981) who was considered by Sandow, the early body builder, to be one of his finest students. Likely used to exercise during his prize-fighting days, Jim was very tough and wiry and when he wasn't hunting ivory he spent a daily half-hour doing handsprings and exercising with dumbells. At least one of his staff was trained to massage him and did so every evening, probably even in the bush. Sutherland didn't smoke but took sparingly of snuff. He was a teetotaler in some accounts, but he was known to take at least some strong drink.

The proof of the regimen was easily seen in the Upper Ubangui region of central Africa where Sutherland hunted for many years. His pal, George Rushby, had this to say about Jim and his prowess despite his age:

> Although Sutherland was in his late fifties he stood up to the arduous life as well as any of the other hunters, most of whom were much younger. During the time I was in the Upper Ubangui he headed the yearly list three or four times in weight of ivory killed by each of the hunters. It may be vain boasting on my part to say that the year he came second in the weight of ivory shot, I topped the list. I was then twenty-seven, extremely fit and tireless, whereas Sutherland was more than twice my age. This gives a measure of his quality as an elephant hunter.

One of the more interesting and whistling-in-the-graveyard traits of Jim Sutherland, as well as ivory hunters in general, was exemplified by a bet made before the Great War between Charles Grey, the late Earl Grey of Fallodin's younger brother, and Jim.

Before telling the anecdote, let me say that Charles's brother, George, was killed by a lion. George was in Kenya in the company of the Hill cousins, Sir Alfred Pease, one of the Percival brothers, and Sir Alfred's son, who was also named George. That Charles's brother was chewed to shreds is confirmed by the fact that Sir Alfred mentioned that even if he had regained use of his mangled arms, he would still have been short quite a few fingers. . . .

Some time after his brother died, Charlie Grey was terribly shot up near Kisii when with the King's African Rifles and lost his left arm. This happened near the beginning of the war. When he recovered, he became an intelligence officer under Sutherland in Norforce and had a custom rifle made for one-armed use by Rigby of London. Grey became famous for his adroitness with the rifle. He was a great sportsman and hunter.

Anderson says that Jim and Charlie Grey were great friends—not only were they both hunters but Grey worked for Jim during the war. Charlie walked up one day when Jim was exercising outside his tent and said:

"Well, Jim, I suppose you're doing that to keep fit? Well, anyhow, I will bet you 100 pounds that I live longer than you."

"Right!" says Jim and both of them put it down in their wills.

Sutherland won the bet by about two years when Charles Grey was killed by a wounded buffalo that he had followed into heavy bush, despite his one arm. Charlie was killed around 1930, while Jim lasted until June 1932. Yet, Jim would have rather had his old pal than the money.

As a best friend, Andy Anderson also tells another tale on Sutherland that is only found in Anderson's small book. Jim, fairly early in the war, was about twenty-five miles north of Lake Nyasa, now called Lake Malawi, hog-tied to an army desk, which he hated. When his day was over, he used to go for a walk with Mosoko, the bull terrier that came to a bad end. One dusk, as Anderson says, Jim Sutherland was followed by two talkative natives who didn't realize that Sutherland spoke the KiSwahili language possibly better than his native English.

> One native said to his pal: "You see that mzungu *(white man)* in front. He must be a very old man. His hair is white and his dog is white." Jim's hair was very slightly grey; Natives always exaggerate everything.
> Much to the Native's astonishment, the "old man" suddenly about-turned, and hit him with the open palm of his hand,

*sending him flying. His pal, the second native, took to his heels
and fled, pursued by Mosoko, who kept jumping up and trying
to get the man's cap—a trick he would always do if told to do so,
never biting them, just pure devilment and play.*

For those who think that this is a "racist incident," be advised
that although Jim Sutherland was easygoing, he demanded
respect from *anybody* he met. I think he would even have
done this to a white man. For sure, he had earned it. . . .

There is another interesting story about Sutherland related
by Anderson. Jim was staying at a captured German barracks
in Njombe, 158 miles south of Iringa in German East Africa
(later Tanganyika and now Tanzania) while the war was rag-
ing. Jim had an upstairs room with a narrow staircase leading
down from it and he had a very fine personal servant named
Matola. Strangely, although Matola was of an age to have a
normal voice, his had never "broken" and was a curious,
childlike whine.

When Jim finished up his duties one evening, Matola, always a source of amusement to all who heard him, made
Jim's bath in a tin basin that looked like a modern laundry
tub, at least here in Africa. As it was the high point of his
evening, Sutherland was completely relaxed when he called
for the second bucket of hot water, in which he would stew
until he decided to get out. Only Matola made an error, one
that sent a shriek of frozen indignation through Sutherland.
He had somehow poured a bucket of icy water over Jim.

Of course it was a mistake, but one that Matola would long
remember. Sutherland threw the now-empty bathtub at Matola, and the man and the tin tub came to a tangled mess at
the bottom of the steps. What's interesting was that when Matola had finished with his scare he had a perfectly normal
voice! Obviously, as Sutherland and Anderson found out
from the doctor, the shock of the ruckus over the icy water
had been enough to jolt Matola's voice into normalcy.

Almost anyone who mentions Sutherland was impressed by

his extremely polite manner—especially in dealing with government officials.

As Sutherland's best friend, "Andy" Anderson observed, Jim was by no means the easiest person to live with. He was a curious blend of competence and shyness, always trying to turn a conversation from elephant hunting to "lovely ladies," as Sutherland always called them. Sutherland was, as Anderson maintains, less at ease with whites than blacks. At one time, his pal mentions, Jim always carried a pocket edition of FitzGerald's *Rubáiyát of Omar Khayyám* and constantly quoted from it. Anderson also says that Jim was a great reader and considered doing another book for MacMillan, which had published his first, in London. Although MacMillan was all for it and Jim kept up his diaries, he never did produce another manuscript.

Anderson says that he didn't know Sutherland's taste in literature, but that for a period in French Equatorial Africa Jim read the Bible a good deal. He wrote quite a bit to a few good friends (George Rushby among them) and had a rather simplistic view of the next world. Sutherland reckoned that the views and the deeds of a person in this life would be carried on to the next. Anderson tells of Sutherland once waking him up in the very small hours to discuss this.

It was about two in the morning and Anderson was not feeling his best. He asked Jim what the hell he meant awakening him at such an hour.

"Oh," he said, "Andy, old fellow, let's talk about when we go to the Back of Beyond." Anderson called for some tea and cigarettes—maybe Sutherland had begun to smoke?—and he and Jim discussed the Hereafter until near dawn.

As might be expected, Sutherland was almost a mythical character to settlers and other ivory hunters. Anderson does say that there was a very definite misconception that Jim let his trackers and gunbearers shoot ivory. This was not only untrue but put Sutherland in an evil temper when he heard the charge. At the time that he completed the manuscript of his book, he had killed 447 *bull* elephants; Jim did not count cows that sometimes had to be taken for safety's sake. Jim probably killed at least 1200 or 1300 bulls in his life. At his best, he made at least 2000 pounds per year—a princely stipend when the pound was worth five dollars and a dollar bought at least eight times what it does today!

Several false impressions about Jim Sutherland were written after his death, one misinformed source being Commander David E. Blunt, RN, himself a control officer and author of the excellent book *Elephant* (East Africa [newspaper], London, 1933). Blunt wrote:

> *Captain "Jim" Sutherland, who had shot over a thousand elephants, and whose death occurred last July* [wrong—June 1932] *when hunting in Africa, lived as an Ivory King. In the old per-War* [sic] *days he used to* safari *into the wilds with as many as eight hundred to one thousand porters, men women and children; his tents were made of silk, and from his main base to his different hunting areas he had organized relays of hammock boys who carried him at a run all the way. His native nickname was "Ngongonjaa." Most of his hunting was done in what is to-day Tanganyika Territory,* [wrong] *in which, as some recompense for the valuable services rendered during the Maji-Maji Rebellion of 1905–06, the Germans gave him* carte blanche *to shoot; of that he took the fullest advantage* [Wrong].

It is just as well that Sutherland was safely dead when Blunt decided to smear him as Blunt might well have been added to Jim's bag. . . .

Can you imagine trying to manage an ivory hunting operation with at least a thousand followers? Silk tents would have been impossible in the rains, sodden and unmanageable. Really, it is unworthy of such a fine personage as Commander Blunt to put such trash into writing, unless he thought it was true. Maybe he did. . . .

There is, of course, a defense of Commander Blunt, that

of the popular opinion of the time. As Anderson points out, many miconceptions concerning Sutherland surfaced. Sutherland *did* have a very large retinue of servants. That he is supposed to have had a thousand men, women, and children may have come from the fact that Sutherland did not suggest that his men remain celibate during the long ivory season and welcomed their wives and girl friends into camp. Jim's reasoning was that it kept his men contented as the women cooked for them and generally looked after them.

As far as Sutherland using *machillas,* or traveling hammocks, this was only partially true during the last few years or months of his life when he had been almost killed and left partially paralyzed. But, I get ahead of myself here. . . .

Jim Sutherland is the only person I know who included a chapter in his book on that most hoary of African arts, poisoning. It is curious that his own death, despite his popularity among the indigenous people, was directly related to this charming and delicate practice.

As George Rushby says, in 1930, when the Depression really found legs, the price of ivory fell below ten shillings a pound and at that price, the best a professional elephant hunter could do was to cover his basic expenses and leave nothing for profit. Yet, Jim Sutherland was hooked after his more than thirty years in what was to him far, far more than a business. Sutherland said several times, Rushby records, that "he would continue hunting elephants up to the end." Jim's greatest wish was that he have the luck to die on the spoor of a big tusker. He hoped that this would happen before he became too old or crippled by bad luck or killed by an elephant.

Probably in September of 1929, Jim wrote an answer to another close friend of his, W. Robert Foran, which is recorded in The Peter Capstick Library (*Kill: or Be Killed,* St. Martin's Press, New York, 1988). Foran, himself an ivory hunter until his gunbearer was killed, knew Sutherland from his days afield. Foran quotes the abridged letter as follows:

*"Only taken nine solid months for your altogether welcome
letter to reach me," he wrote. "Been following me around the
Belgian and French Congo. However, I'm damned glad to hear
of you, old man. I swear it seems like a thousand moons since I
saw you last. East Africa takes a lot of beating to live in, or
rather vegetate in, as you know full well. . . . As for my own
piffling self, I'm still after the tuskers, and always will be.
Financially, 'tis a wash-out now. Still, all in all, roaming about
the 'Blue' is not such a bad life. And I, for one, will roam into
the depths of the wilds until the very end of the chapter. Am just
off again, starting from Mengo, Port Natal, for the Belgian and
French Congo; and, barring accidents, will make a bee-line for
the Sudan and the Old Country about the autumn of this year.
If you are in London then, let's meet and discuss the glorious
past and the uncertain future. . . . Let's meet soon, old lad, and
fix up another hunting trip together. I'm yours to a cinder at
that joyous game."*

I think that George Rushby told best what happened to Jim
Sutherland. . . .

*Early in January of 1929 I left my base camp at Mutombo on
the first hunt of the year. On the morning of the third day we
picked up the fairly fresh spoor of a medium-sized solitary bull.
By mid-afternoon of the following day we caught up and I was
able to kill him without too much trouble. I decided to spend the
whole of the next day near the dead elephant, cut out the tusks at
leisure and replenish our stock of dried meat. Late that
afternoon two of my men, accompanied by a third man and my
dog, arrived from my base camp at Mutobo. The third man was
a runner from Sutherland carrying a message from him saying
he had been poisoned. Sutherland's runner had arrived at my
base camp on the afternoon of the day that I left.*

*On receiving Sutherland's message I left immediately with his
runner, one of my trackers and four porters carrying my bed-roll
and a few essentials. The rest of my men stayed behind with the
dead elephant to finish drying the meat and cutting out the
tusks. They were told to return direct to my base camp at Mutobo
when that work was finished.*

*We headed for Sutherland's camp and after travelling as
hard as we could reached there after three days. When I arrived
Sutherland was in a rather poor condition physically as a result
of the poison. Both his legs were partly paralyzed, he had a
facial twitch, his nerves were in a bad state and he was
obviously suffering from shock. Beyond keeping him company
and trying to cheer him up there was little I could do for him.*

*The poison he had been given is made from the tips of the
buds of a species of a flame tree common to that part of Africa. It
is tasteless and colorless and its effect is to paralyze the nervous
system. Starting at the extremities the paralysis eventually
reaches the nerve centres, causing death within four to six
hours. Sutherland had been given the poison in his tea, and
fortunately for him it was just after he had eaten his lunch. On
feeling his legs becoming paralyzed he sensed what had
happened and was able to vomit his lunch with most of the
poison.*

*I suggested that a "tepoi" be made out of one of his camp
chairs so that he could be carried to Yubo on the Sudan border
but he refused. Yubo was a sleeping sickness station established
for the treatment of that disease and two doctors were
permanently stationed there. After I had been at his camp for six
days he had recovered so well that we were able to travel
together to Obo. There a complaint was laid before the new
Adjoint, a Monsieur Pillet. The Adjoint investigated the case
and the result was that a sub-chief named Basibiri and three
other Africans received long terms of imprisonment. Sutherland
never really fully recovered from the effects of the poison and his
left leg remained partly paralyzed. In spite of this physical
handicap and general ill health he continued to hunt elephants.*

That Sutherland refused to stop hunting ivory probably was
the start of the legend that he was carried everywhere he
went by hammocks.

Jim continued to hunt elephants on muleback until around
June of 1932. He was then taken by a relapse and the residue
of the poison did its worst. He was mostly paralyzed and unable to bitch about finally being taken to Yubo, where he
breathed his last.

Jim had been the victim of a conspiracy by a tribe in the area who had tried to take revenge for real or imagined wrongs done by the French. The poison he was given was usually known as *banga* or *bhanga*.

A short time after his burial, Andy Anderson and one F. S. Joelson, a newspaper publisher, had a stone cairn made with a cross, and a bronze tablet adorning the lower reaches.

The plaque erected by Anderson, Joelson, and apparently several of Jim's friends (probably including Foran and Rushby) read:

> *To the Memory of*
> *That*
> *Great Elephant Hunter*
> *Jim Sutherland*
> *Who Died At Yuba On June 26, 1932*
> *Aged 60 Years*
> *Erected By A Few Friends And*
> *Fellow Hunters*

Above the inscription is a bas-relief of two elephants and what is probably a *Borassus* palm.

A Spanish friend of mine took the plaque off and had it built into his fireplace in Spain in 1961, twenty-nine years after Sutherland died; his reason for taking the plaque he said, was to prevent it from being stolen by locals who would probably have made weapon heads out of the bronze. This man, to be completely fair, was apparently the only one to find the grave after many years and after Jim's hunting friends had gone to their own rewards, if that is what they were. Also, my friend of Zambian days looked after the grave for several years. I think that Jim Sutherland would have preferred his plaque to be in the hands of one who has spent his life in the pursuit of elephants rather than to have it destroyed or lost. Others, quite understandably, put such actions down as sheer grave robbery. They may have a very good point. Take your choice.

Bibliography

FREDERICK COURTENEY SELOUS

Books

Abel: *The Gun At Home and Abroad* (London, 1914).

Barclay, Edgar N.: *Big Game Shooting Records* (1932).

British Museum (Natural History): *Catalogue of the Selous Collection of Big Game* (1921).

Catterick, Alan: *Spoor of Blood* (1959).

Farwell, Byron: *The Great War in Africa* (1987).

Von Lettow-Vorbeck, Paul: *My Reminiscences of East Africa* (1920).

Miller, Charles: *Battle for the Bundu* (1974).

Millais, John G.: *Life of Frederick Courtenay Selous* (1918).

Selous, Frederick Courteney: *A Hunter's Wanderings in Africa* (London, 1881).

——————: *Travel and Adventure in Southeast Africa* (London, 1893).

——————: *Sunshine and Storm in Rhodesia* (London, 1896).

——————: *Sport and Travel East and West* (London, 1900).

——————: *Recent Hunting Trips in British North America* (London, 1907).

————————: *African Nature Notes and Reminiscences* (London, 1908).

Selous, F. C., Millais, J. G., and Chapman, Stoneham, C. T.: *From Hobo to Hunter* (1956).

Taylor, Stephen: *The Mighty Nimrod* (1989).

Watson, J. N. P.: *Millais: Three Generations in Nature, Art and Sport* (1988).

Articles

Marsh, Brian: *F. C. Selous—Some Personal Glimpses* (*Man-Magnum*, May 1989).

Selous, F. C.: *Hunting in Central Africa: The Sportsman's Outfit* (*Travel and Exploration*, February 1909).

JOHN BOYES

Books

Boyes, John: *John Boyes, King of the Wakikuyu* (London, 1912).

————————: *The Company of Adventurers* (London, 1928).

Cranworth, Lord: *Kenya Chronicles* (1939).

Foran, W. Robert: *The Elephant Hunters of the Lado* (1981).

Hunter, J. A. and Mannix, Dan: *African Bush Adventures* (1954).

Lugard, Captain F. D.: *The Rise of Our East African Empire* (1893).

Portal, Sir Gerald: *The British Mission to Uganda* (1893).

Meinertzhagen, Richard: *Kenya Diary* (1957).

Rigby, John & Co.: *Catalogue* (1991).

CONSTANTINE J. P. IONIDES

Books

Ionides, C. J. P.: *A Hunter's Story* (published in the U.S. as *Mambas and Maneaters*) (London, 1965).

Lane, Margaret: *Life with Ionides* (1963).

Wykes, Alan: *Snake Man* (1960).

Articles and Miscellany

Broadley, Donald G. (Senior Curator of Herpetology, Director of the Natural History Museum of Zimbabwe): Letters (1991).

Index

INDEX